STIFF-NECKED
PEOPLE
BOTTLE-NECKED
SYSTEM

JEWISH POLITICAL AND SOCIAL STUDIES

*Daniel J. Elazar and
Steven M. Cohen, Editors*

STIFF-NECKED
PEOPLE,
BOTTLE-NECKED
SYSTEM

The Evolution and Roots of Israeli Public Protest, 1949-1986

Sam N. Lehman-Wilzig

INDIANA UNIVERSITY PRESS
Bloomington and Indianapolis

The paper used in this publication meets the minimum requirements
of American National Standard for Information Sciences--
Permanence of Paper for Printed Library Materials,
ANSI Z39.48-1984.

⊗ TM
Manufactured in the United States of America

Library of Congress Cataloging-in-Publication Data

Lehman-Wilzig, Sam N.
Stiff-necked people, bottle-necked system: the evolution
and roots of Israeli public protest, 1949 - 1986 /
Sam N. Lehman-Wilzig.
p. cm. -- (Jewish political and social studies)
Includes bibliographical references.
ISBN 0-253-33293-1 (alk. paper)
1. Israel - - Politics and government.   2. Political
participation - Israel.   3. Demonstrations -- Israel.
I. Title.   II. Title: Israeli public protest.   III. Series.
JQ1825. P359L44   1990
323'. 042'095694--dc20   89-45858
                                                         CIP
1 2 3 4 5   94 93 92 91 90

Dedicated to the two women in my life:

My mother,
who exhibited remarkable tolerance
for my perpetual childhood protests.

My wife,
whose constructive
protest
has pushed me throughout into producing
the best which I have in me.

Contents

	Page
Acknowledgments	ix
Introduction	1
Part I: Theory and Methodology	5
1 Theories of Protest: The Need for a Case-Study Approach	7
2 Source Problems and Methodology	13
Part II: The Typology of Israeli Protest	25
3 The Periodization of Israeli Protest, 1949-1986: Issues and Intensity	27
4 The Categorization of Israeli Protest: Variables and Demographics	46
Part III: The Environmental Bases of Israeli Protest	65
5 Economic, Social and Political Bases of Israeli Protest	67
6 A Stiff-Necked People: The Cultural Bases of Israeli Protest	77
Part IV: The Structural Bases of Israeli Protest	87
7 Bottle-Necked System: Israeli Political Blockage and Decay	89
8 Bypassing the Ossified System: The Protest Phenomena	100
Part V: Additional Aspects of Israeli Protest	111
9 Israeli Protest: Is It Successful?	113
10 Conclusions: Findings, Prescriptions, New Directions	120
Appendices	137
Notes	150
Bibliography	198
Index	210

Acknowledgments

No man is an island unto himself--especially in hothouse Israel. In the specific case of this book, a reverse simile is closer to the truth, as I have incurred a jungle of intellectual and research debts regarding my work over the previous decade. A number of them are acknowledged in the body of the book where specifically relevant. I would like to take the opportunity here to thank all the others not mentioned.

First, to the Israel Council of Research and Development which graciously granted a substantial research stipend enabling me to carry out the public opinion poll as well as to pursue other more specific research avenues. It is a measure of the Israeli establishment's openness that such a subject could be funded, whatever the ultimate conclusions (and in this case, they were not altogether complimentary to the established political system). Special thanks as well go to Dr. Mina Zemach under whose highly professional auspices the poll was conducted.

Second, to many of my departmental colleagues: Professors Stuart Cohen, Charles Liebman, Dan Elazar, Eliezer Don-Yehiya, Bernard Susser, and Drs. Ella Belfer and Gad Barzilai, all of whom read parts of the manuscript and offered comments that were extremely incisive and helpful. In the true "protest" spirit of this book they did not hold back their sharpest intellectual barbs--and I am the wiser for it.

Third, to Dr. Giora Goldberg and Dr. Meyer Unger who coauthored several articles with me on two of the central topics. Their methodological (and analytical) assistance was invaluable in pointing me toward the right quantitative directions. Regarding a significant portion of the actual statistical work appearing in this book, I am heavily indebted to Dr. Haim Shor without whose guidance, expertise, and work this study would have been far poorer. Among other things, he left his invisible mark by making sense of the large number of independent and dependent variables with which I had to contend. The results of chapters 7 and 8 are testimony to his methodological skills. In addition, many thanks also to Ms. Andrea Berger for the great time and effort expended by her in getting the myriad cross-tabulations plus other tables and indices out of my data bank into readable and usable form.

Fourth, to my students who have added finer detail to many points, and who have served as a much-needed sounding board for several of my (originally half-baked) ideas and theories: Craig Kugler, Muni Ben-Dor, Daniel Bianco, Naomi Gross, and numerous others who shared in my annual seminar on the general topic.

Fifth and finally, to Mrs. Menuha Kutner for her secretarial assistance in typing certain chapters, stepping into the breach when my own word processor decided (perhaps in the spirit of the book) to go on a prolonged sit-down strike.

My heartfelt thanks to all. Ultimate responsibility for the work, of course, is mine-- with all the criticism (and hopefully credit, as well) which will invariably ensue.

Introduction

This book is a work of construction, destruction, and reconstruction, along two parallel paths. From the perspective of Israeli politics it attempts to construct, almost *ex nihilo*, a descriptive and analytical edifice regarding the place and meaning of public protest within the Israeli milieu. In so doing, however, a number of methodologies had to be employed whose results (in several central areas) destroy or severely undercut the very foundation of most protest research conducted heretofore in hundreds of cross-national studies. Thus, the present work seeks as well to begin the task of theory reconstruction based on the Israeli case-study data.

Public protest is one of the most ubiquitous socio-political phenomena to be found in Israel--not merely today, but from virtually the inception of the State. It is, therefore, quite surprising to find that relatively little has been published on the issue in general. The number of students of Israeli protest who have addressed the subject from somewhat more than a specific protest-group perspective is less than a handful: Sprinzak, Etzioni-Halevy, Wolfsfeld, and I nearly exhaust the list.

Sprinzak was the first to notice that here lay a subject area worthy of scholarly attention. His first monograph surveyed a number of Israeli radical/protest groups in order to understand the process of their cooptation into the Establishment.[1] No attempt was made, however, to place these groups in a historical continuum, i.e., their relationship to, and representativeness of, other such groups from the two previous decades. Since then he has on occasion tackled the dynamics of other specific protest movements,[2] but aside from one general-interest essay on the phenomenon[3]--and that with an almost exclusive emphasis on organized *group* protest--there is little reference in his work to the broader context of public protest as an integral aspect of Israeli politics *per se*.

Such an attempt was made by Etzioni-Halevy.[4] Here one finds an effort to understand the factors underlying Israeli protest and what such a phenomenon has to say about the strengths and weaknesses of the political system. Unfortunately, the entire analysis rests upon the shoulders of only two (!) protest movements. Nevertheless, her central conclusion--albeit put in tentative and general terms--bears repeating: "What is the significance of the Israelis' high political involvement coupled with a widespread feeling of political futility? It is our contention that it both reflects and precipitates political discontent. We could not supply direct proof for this contention. . . . "[5] To that end the book before you is devoted in part, necessitating a more comprehensive methodology than that used in the past.

More recently, Wolfsfeld has significantly added to our understanding of the Israeli protest phenomenon through a micro-analysis of protester attitudes and behavior.[6] Through survey and on-the-spot research (polling, interviews, etc.), he has produced an interesting study of "what makes Shmulik protest"--as well as the dynamics involved in the media/protester and government/protester interrelationship. As a snapshot of the contemporary Israeli protest scene it is superb, but it does not tell us much about the historical development of such protest in Israel.[7]

Why the need for a more extensive data base? It is one of the central contentions of the present work that the comprehensiveness of the methodology is critical to any understanding of the public protest phenomenon in its totality. It means much more than "fleshing out" the general picture through added case studies of protest groups, movements, alliances. A major flaw of several of the aforementioned Israeli studies is their underlying assumption that interest-group protest is the *sine qua non* of Israeli protest, i.e., that by focusing on "professional" or dedicated protest groups one comes to a clear understanding of the Israeli protest phenomenon.

Sprinzak, for example, argued that "political history and political events are primarily understandable through the explanation of the behavior of political groups rather than individuals."[8] As we shall see later on in this book such an assumption is false, as approximately one-half of all protest events are carried out by individuals or groups who gather together temporarily against a specific policy or to resolve a discrete problem–and then "disband." In short, there is much more to Israeli public protest than organized protest groups such as the Black Panthers, Peace Now,[9] *Gush Emunim*,[10] et al. Wolfsfeld, of course, is well aware of this, and consequently his level of analysis tends down toward the individual. As a complementary balance to his colleagues' work it is excellent; but as just noted, it too presents only a partial picture (as it focuses on a limited time frame).

In short, this book is an initial attempt to systematically analyze Israeli public protest (through longitudinal aggregate protest data in addition to the more widely used survey data) from a comprehensive *historical* as well as *functional* perspective, i.e., the evolution of protest from the establishment of the State of Israel until the mid-eighties, the objective environmental factors underlying the phenomenon, the internal characteristics of protest events, and the place of protest within the body politic.

As noted above, another aspect is addressed which is important in understanding the general phenomenon of protest in Israel and abroad. It has to do with methodological issues and the substantive difficulties which they engender. This book attempts to come to grips with problems that have not been dealt with adequately in the general academic literature, and as a result may prove to be pioneering in its own way. It should be made clear from the outset that the central conclusion of the book is a direct outgrowth of some of the methodological questions under scrutiny. In any case, I have attempted as much as possible to steer clear of undue academic jargon for the benefit of all who might be interested in the problems and pitfalls of methodology in the area of protest. When discussion of some of the finer points was called for, I have tried as much as possible to place them in substantive footnotes at the bottom of the page so as not to unduly encumber the nonacademic reader.

Two further methodological notes are necessary at this point. First, my central methodological thesis is that most previous studies based on aggregate protest data are unreliable, and that great exactitude is a Holy Grail unattainable at this juncture in the relatively brief history of public protest work. Thus, I felt it only intellectually fair to play devil's advocate at times and point out where the available data could be interpreted in ways different from the one which I present. There is, of course, a dual danger in this. The "devil" in me might succeed too well in convincing the reader that the alternative interpretation is more persuasive! More likely, doubt will be cast upon my initial interpretation, thereby weakening the thrust of the argument. Nevertheless, as one brought up to view with some skepticism the definitive truth of statistical data ("there are lies, damn lies, and then statistics," a noted wag once put it, only somewhat unfairly), I feel it necessary to present both interpretive sides of the numbers (when more than one possibility is at least logically possible). For the reader weaned on Olympian scientific declarations this may be a bit disconcerting; Olympus, it may be well to remember, was only a mythical place.

Second (and a point to be reiterated throughout), every researcher who deals with empirical and/or statistical material eventually comes upon the problem of overload. Given that I discovered over 3,500 protest events, with each scored for ten different categories, the temptation to overwhelm the reader with a flood of (mostly interesting) statistical compilations, cross-tabulations, and correlations was great. Indeed, the possible combinations and permutations of slicing them up are virtually infinite. Not wishing to have this book look like a gigantic computer printout, I tried as much as humanly possible to resist the temptation of more and more. Nevertheless, I am sure that some readers will be disappointed that I did not present additional data on specific aspects which may interest them personally. My only consolation here is that at least I whetted their appetite (of course, I would be pleased to answer any requests for more information, as much as the data in my possession will allow). Others may find the relatively limited number of tables, graphs, and statistical lists to be more than enough. To at least partly satisfy both kinds of readers, I have placed additional information in the book's appendixes whenever I felt it was not critical to the understanding of the chapter at hand, but of significance nonetheless.

The book is divided into five major parts. As each part will be introduced by a short explanatory preface, the following schematic synopsis should suffice to indicate the overall thrust of the work as a whole.

Part I (chapters 1 and 2) addresses several important aspects regarding theorizing about "public protest" (mostly relating to the choice of concentrating on a single-nation case study), and discusses indepth my study's methodology: the different types of research methods employed and data sources utilized in previous work around the world; what types of public protest were surveyed for this book; the means by which my data were collected and their respective reliability; the remaining problems of incomplete information; and the implications of all these for the research field of protest in general and Israeli protest in particular.

Part II (chapters 3 and 4) presents a typology of Israeli extraparliamentarism through a broad historical survey of public protest in Israel, viewed chronologically from the standpoint of frequency as well as from a number of subsidiary variables (e.g., issues, intensity, size, organization, location, among others). In addition, based on survey data we shall analyze the demographics of such protest, i.e., what types of Israeli citizens tend to protest most/least, etc.

With Part III (chapters 5 and 6) we begin to move into the entire question of causal factors underlying Israeli extraparliamentarism. In chapter 5 the sundry economic, social, and political influences are tested statistically--through a regression analysis as well as other simpler but more in-depth statistical calculations. Many of these factors relate to the cross-comparative theories mentioned in Part I, affording us an opportunity to test them through our Israeli case study.

Of course, there is no Rosetta Stone of protest causality; no one factor can by itself explain the entire phenomenon. This is especially the case when one takes incommensurable factors into account. Thus, chapter 6 briefly surveys the culture of protest in the Jewish heritage, and then analyzes in some depth several contemporary features of such a politico-cultural proclivity.

Part IV (chapters 7 and 8) is devoted to an added factor underlying Israeli protest: systemic dysfunction within Israel's polity, especially from the standpoint of a political-communications breakdown between the citizenry and its leadership. The connection to extraparliamentary behavior is then developed from a number of perspectives, using in different ways some of the statistical data presented in previous sections.

Part V (chapters 9 and 10) rounds out the picture by addressing several questions of great importance. Chapter 9 asks: how successful is Israeli protest in achieving its goals? While this question is fraught with methodological difficulties (which are addressed), a novel attempt is made to come to some sort of precise understanding within the Israeli context.

The final chapter sums up the general findings of the study as a whole, and then proceeds to suggest several courses of action which would help mitigate the problematic aspects of Israeli protest. It concludes with a number of unasked and/or unanswered questions, which I leave to future researchers interested in further broadening our understanding of the entire protest phenomenon.

PART I:

Theory and Methodology

The scientific study of conflict in general and protest in particular has been going on unabated from the early 1950s, although a number of studies were carried out before World War II. Unfortunately, the more that has been done on the subject the greater the ensuing confusion. Many hypotheses and theories which seem highly logical have been found to have little support when tested in reality. Others, no less logical, have led to contradictory evidence both supporting and negating many suppositions. The overwhelming majority of all such studies, however, are based on cross-national research. Hardly anything has been attempted from a more intensive single-nation case-study perspective. The justification for such an approach is outlined in our first chapter.

Much of the reason for the aforementioned confusing results and conclusions may lie in the significant weaknesses of these studies' data bases, upon which their entire theoretical edifices are founded. Our second chapter not only will discuss the problems of previous data sources, but will suggest (and explain this book's use of) some new approaches to overcoming the shortcomings of previous studies. In addition, it will describe the several research methodologies (with emphasis on the plural) employed in this work-important not only for academic reasons, but also for an understanding of the strengths and shortcomings contained in this study of Israeli public protest in its variegated manifestations.

Chapter 1

Theories of Protest: The Need for a Case-Study Approach

Why do people protest? On the face of it, the question seems rather strange, especially to the protester. There are inevitable answers: "because I don't like the government's new policy"; "we have to stop the war"; "without a traffic light at the school corner my kids are in danger"; etc. In almost every case of peaceful demonstrations, and in most situations of violent riots, there is a specific reason for the protest--certainly obvious to the participant, and usually quite clear to anyone on the outside looking in.

Nevertheless, over the last thirty years or so a huge body of literature has arisen attempting to answer this "simple" question, for on closer inspection, it is not so straightforward at all. We know that most people, even in democracies, never participate in a protest event; that some nations with serious problems have far less public protest than others with a better situation; and that within each country the frequency of protest may change dramatically over time without obvious deterioration or improvement in the overall situation. In short, there seem to be many factors at work behind and beyond the consciousness of the individual protester specifically, and society in general.[1]

If we start out by asking "why do people protest?" our next question is a necessary corollary of the first: Why do *Israelis* protest? Such a question has two implicit, albeit countervailing, assumptions--that Israelis are intrinsically no different from other people (and thus we can learn some general things from the specific case); and that some aspects of the Israeli environment (political system, culture, etc.) are different enough that we cannot merely rely on more general cross-comparative studies for an adequate explanation of the Israeli protest phenomenon.

Indeed, as will be made clear, one of the major reasons that such empirically based single-country case studies are necessary (but heretofore almost nonexistent in the professional literature) is that too much of the "unique" or at least "different" is missed in more general cross-national works. Past theorizing has been impressive in its intellectual quality, but sorely lacking in its discrete applicability. In short, attractive theoretical blueprints abound, but the actual bricks are hard to come by. This book is an attempt to build a modest theoretical construct for the specific Israeli case, which could also serve as at least part of the foundation for a larger theoretical edifice in which more generalized protest phenomena explanations may come to be housed.

The use of a single nation as a case study, however, is not without its problems and critics. Lijphart divides all political (empirical) research into three levels: the "statistical method" which incorporates many cases (countries) albeit with relatively poorer data overall; the "comparative method" which includes a few cases each having much richer data; and the "case study method" where the data may be richest but which suffers from severe noncomparability.[2] Nevertheless, as Scarrow argues, a case study may still be labeled "comparative" if "the analysis is made within a comparative perspective [which] mandates that description of the particular be cast in terms of broadly applicable analytic constructs."[3] For his part, Campbell sees great utility in such a method, but only if it ensures enough "degrees of freedom" (in the nonstatistical sense of the term): several possibilities of explaining the phenomena, sufficient

7

amounts of data and phenomena independently arrived at, and a large number of theories considered in developing conclusions.[4] It will become obvious in the ensuing chapters that the present study has been written in the spirit of both Scarrow and Campbell.

However, there is no reason to be only defensive about the case study approach. Lijphart himself notes how several researchers view intranational studies as being more fruitful and scientific than international ones. As Eulau put it: "if 'control' is the *sine qua non* of all scientific procedure, it would certainly seem easier to obtain in a single culture . . . than across cultures."[5] Bueno de Mesquita highlights still another aspect of the problem. He argues that "since methodologies are tools for evaluating the empirical usefulness of a theory, their selection must be guided by the requirements and limitations of one's theory (and data). In that sense, nonstatistical case studies are not inherently inferior to the evaluation of a large sample through the use of inferential statistics. Instead, case studies are the preferred method, given certain types of hypotheses . . . . "[6]

But why choose Israel? Because the country has a number of advantages from the protest perspective. First and foremost, it has a relatively large number of protest events and a high rate of protest participation. Second, being a small country it has virtually no significant regional differences (from a cultural, and to a lesser extent socio-economic, perspective), so that almost all possible factors underlying protest are relevant to the (Jewish) population as a whole in relatively equal manner. Third, and closely related, with a unitary (nonfederal) form of government, there is virtually no political-institutional differentiation among subregions. Fourth and finally, Israel has been home to many of the objective elements mentioned as possible protest factors in the general literature: high inflation, frequent wars, ethnic pluralism, intense ideology, mass immigration, rapid economic growth, etc. In sum, Israel provides the clear fact of protest, many of the ostensible factors underlying protest, and the political conditions which enable us to test whether and how the fact and factors are related.

Have these factors been tested before? Has the enormous body of empirical research stretching back at least thirty years proven anything of substance in the realm of political conflict? Sadly, despite much effort and expenditure of time, energy, thought, and money, we are left today in a state of theoretical disarray which in a sense may be even more confusing than the relative non-empirically based received opinion on the part of the philosophical giants--Aristotle, Hobbes, Burke, de Tocqueville--of yesteryear.

A few summarizing comments of the experts in the field should suffice to present the fragmented and chaotic picture. Gurr actually begins his *Handbook* by declaring humorously and sadly: "The commentaries on theory reflect a level of contentiousness among conflict theorists that resembles their subject matter."[7] The rest of the *Handbook* is commentary on this basic theme.[8] Sanders, who looked at the related issue of political instability (and its underlying factors), surveyed the literature and concluded: "What emerges quite clearly from the empirical analysis . . . is that *considered in isolation* none of these theories (and they include both Marxist and non-Marxist theories) provides even a marginally adequate explanation of the cross-national incidence of political instability."[9]

Let there be no misunderstanding the situation in this field. The problem is one not only (or primarily) of multiplicity of theories and/or factors, but rather of contradictory empirical evidence regarding the relationships between the independent variables (social, economic, cultural, demographic, political, etc., factors) and the dependent variables being studied (protest, turmoil, war, etc.).

What, then, is to be done? Sanders provides one answer: "we can only *start* to explain why political instability occurs by drawing on a variety of different (and largely unrelated) theoretical propositions."[10] Snyder is even more specific:

> [T]he most serious impediment to further advances in theories of collective violence is the general (though sometimes implicit) assumption of universal applicability in each line of argument. Such assumptions appear untenable in view of contradictory empirical findings on the major approaches . . . [but] two alternative approaches are more promising[--] . . . theoretical integration of alternative approaches . . . [and] specification of the structural conditions or "critical dimensions" across which the validity of explanations varies . . . . Attempting to fit all results within one or another of the major arguments is simply not a tractable endeavor.[11]

It is at this point, however, that we come upon a serious meta-methodological problem. The standard and widely accepted approach to scientific study--even in the social sciences--is to present a priori hypotheses based on some overarching general theory, and then to prove or disprove these hypotheses using relevant methodological tools. But as was just explained, at this stage of the "conflict research" game we are in a triple bind. Not only are there an enormous number of hypotheses available, and not only can several factors be hypothesized to lead to opposing results, but most confusingly, the general findings of previous researchers in the main have been contradictory! On what basis, then, should we posit our hypotheses here? Carl Friedrich provides the answer:

> There exists today a widespread belief that scientific method is based upon the formulation of an hypothesis which then leads to the collection of data to test, to prove or disprove, the hypothesis . . . . [But] it is actually not a universally valid description of scientific inquiry and discovery . . . [for] as a matter of fact, there has also been a great deal of straight fact gathering with hypotheses for the interpretation of the facts growing out of the consideration of these data as gathered . . . . For neither induction nor deduction but a complex and multiform interaction seems to be the basis of scientific discovery . . . . [A]ny large-scale exploration of scientific data, whether political or any other, calls for open-mindedness as far as techniques of gathering them are concerned.[12]

This is not to say that the present study proceeded in gathering data without regard to theories of protest. It is to suggest that certain elements specific to the Israeli case were taken into account both in the data-gathering and also in the preliminary hypothesizing, while others were left out. It is important to understand the most significant of these.

To begin with, not all previous "conflict" studies have focused on precisely the same type of phenomenon. Indeed, the literature is traditionally divided into three conflict "dimensions": low-level *protest* (e.g. demonstrations), mid-level *turmoil* (e.g. riots), and high-level *revolution* (or internal civil war). Israel suffers not at all from the latter (our study relates primarily to Israeli citizens within the official 1967 borders), and not very much from mid-level turmoil either (see chapters 3 and 4). As a result, *the focus of data-gathering and analysis of the present study is mostly on low-level protest.*

Second, at least two prominent theories of protest were abandoned from the outset or soon thereafter as irrelevant to the Israeli case. Although a very prominent approach has been the relative deprivation (RD) and/or frustration-aggression hypothesis, the research efforts put in can be said to have produced somewhat minor results.[13] Nevertheless, a preliminary attempt was made to see whether there was cause to analyze this factor in the Israeli case. In the poll conducted for this study,[14] the following question was asked: "Is your personal economic situation average for people with your education, talents, and amount of work, or is your economic situation above average or below average?" A mere 12.1% gave the latter response, indicating that (at least as of 1981) RD could not be considered a very important phenomenon in Israel.[15] Nevertheless, we shall have occasion to show (in chapter 3) that at least in one central instance it may have played an important part in the Israeli protest drama.

Similarly, the theory which posits a nexus between governmental coercion and public turmoil was also removed from our general consideration for the reason that there is very little overt governmental coercion in Israel. Only in the case of the Israeli Arab community can it be said that until 1965 there existed overt coercion and thereafter some measure of covert coercion. This specific area will be qualitatively discussed in chapter 4 (with some empirical data as background), but as the Arab sector encompasses only a small segment (about a sixth) of the Israeli population with proportionately even fewer protest events scored, coercion was not tested in our statistical regression analysis which was based on *national* (and not local) data. True, such general indicators of coercion *capacity* as military-force size and budget expenditures have been used by several "coercion" theorists,[16] but there are many fundamental problems with such an approach which in the final analysis does not really measure coercion *in practice.*[17]

Beyond the remaining traditional theories that were tested through statistical analysis, a close examination of the Israeli case pointed to two additional areas where the protest literature is seriously deficient. This is not to say that nothing has been written about these two areas generally, or even in the specific case of Israel. Two students of Israeli politics in the past have noted that political culture[18] and blocked political communication[19] seem to be significant in Israel, but at best they are based on time-specific attitudinal information (or a few concrete examples) and are not longitudinal over time and/or founded on comprehensive aggregate data.

In the general literature, some reference is made to the "culture of protest [or] violence." In almost all such cases what is meant is that previous protest/violence may have a tendency to change or reinforce social norms which encourage further manifestations of the same phenomenon.[20] Barnes and Kaase, in their massive study of five Western democracies, sum up the general idea:

> Western liberal democracies are experiencing a process of change in political culture exhibited by, among other things, the increasing inclination of the citizenry to participate in such acts [protest, etc. Thus,] . . . slowly but surely during the last few years, the *idea* of uncoventional political participation as a legitimate resource of democratic citizenship has spread out into the wider political community.[21]

These few studies, though, are the exceptions, for overall political culture as an explanatory factor of protest and turmoil is mostly disregarded by the vast majority of the field's theoreticians.[22] An indication of this can be derived from the otherwise quite comprehensive review essay of Jackson and Stein which outlines the four main traditional approaches to the subject: economic, political, social, and psychological -- with no mention being made of culture as a possible approach as well.[23] Thus, if the whole field is marked by contradictory evidence, here at least is an area suffering from insufficient analysis and evidence--one worthwhile pursuing in a case-study context.

Such a venue has the additional advantage of affording an opportunity to pursue the "protest culture" hypothesis along paths heretofore virtually unexplored. The above studies approach the question of protest culture from one of two perspectives: either deducing that cultural change has taken place by *statistically* controlling (and accounting for the influence of) other independent factors, or by delineating the existence of a protest cultural norm through such indirect *attitudinal* questions as protest support, justification, and the like. In neither approach is there any attempt to address the issue from a *qualitative* standpoint, i.e., a more fundamental (perhaps historical, perhaps psycho-national) analysis of the cultural value elements of specific societies which may or may not drive that specific nation in the direction of protest, etc. Indeed, it is at this point that we can understand why "culture" has not been a central element in most previous protest studies: as they are almost all cross-national in scope it would be impossible to extract from the data qualitative culturally specific information which might explain the differences between the nations' protest behavior. Once again we see the need to start rebuilding the protest-theory edifice from the bottom up.

The second general theory which has not been given the proper attention due it in the general literature is that of blocked political communication which results from institutional dysfunction. As will be noted in chapter 7, a number of theories do touch upon this approach in several oblique ways.[24] However, especially in light of the great effort which has been given to *economically* based "frustration-aggression" theories, it is somewhat surprising at first to find that far less work has been done on a similar type of theory which emphasizes *political* "frustration-aggression." Here too a large part of the reason is methodological, for it is not at all easy to operationalize and quantify such concepts as systemic decay and blocked access.

Thus the need yet once more for a qualitative analysis (using appropriate quantitative data) of the existence and importance of such an otherwise incommensurable phenomenon as systemic petrification. By focusing on a single country we are able to bring together several elements which directly impinge on the specific hypothesis--elements and data which would be unavailable or noncomparable in a cross-national study: e.g., type of election system, party membership percentages, party control of socio-economic institutions, etc.

We have come full circle. If we started out with the desire to use the single-country approach in order to fill a number of holes which have been apparent in the theoretical field of political conflict, we now see that *the case-study approach may be unavoidable and absolutely necessary owing to the fact that certain theories cannot be adequately tested or (at least) explored in any other fashion.*

To be sure, this is not to suggest that the single-nation study is the only legitimate or useful type of approach (as mentioned earlier, it has its deficiencies as well), but rather that a full picture of the potentially useful theories and explanations cannot be acquired without extensive recourse to the investigation of many polities individuallyand (at least at first) singly. As Snyder concluded in his comprehensive critique of the conflict literature from the perspective of theory, data sources, and methodology (the subjects of our first two chapters):

> [The] collection of timeseries data on political conflict and other variables with the care and detail generally reserved for single nation studies . . . is required. But such efforts must be implemented for several countries in order to investigate the effects of institutional and cultural factors that cannot be captured in a single nation analyses [*sic*] . . . . More generally, these considerations suggest a partial moratorium on the use of widely available cross-sectional data and reorientation toward developing longitudinal information that will more appropriately address the substantive arguments.[25]

A very limited number of works have broken ground along this case-study path.[26] On the aggregate-data side, we find that only France, Germany, Italy,[27] and the United States[28] have been covered comprehensively. On the attitudinal side, just Britain,[29] the U.S., West Germany, the Netherlands, and Austria[30] have been extensively surveyed and analyzed from a protest perspective. Significantly, *not one study has combined these two approaches.*[31]

The present book, then, is an attempt to understand public protest by combining different types and levels of analysis. First, it is driven not only by abstract (previously posited) theory, but by the exigencies of the specific (Israeli) national case. In other words, it relies on the findings (and remaining questions) of prior conflict studies, as well as the hypotheses naturally generated by an *a priori* understanding of the Israeli situation. Second, both aggregate and attitudinal data are brought forth in the hope that in most instances they would tend to reinforce each other's data. Third, the analysis proceeds to combine quantitative and qualitative information wherever the former are unavailable and/or the latter can significantly add to our understanding of the specific problem. Fourth, while not precisely cross-national the present study attempts to be cross-comparative (as well as obviously being descriptive of the Israeli case) by drawing from previous international data and theories -- either building upon them or pointing out where the Israeli evidence raises serious questions as to their validity.

Fifth and finally, the exploration here of Israeli protest proceeds on a number of planes, from the micro to the very macro. As Gurr and Duvall strongly argued: "In general we think that the explanation of conflict within a social system lies at the junction of three paths, one from characteristics of its individual members, the second from its aggregate systemic properties, and the third from its external environment."[32] While not necessarily in that order, the thrust of this book is to follow that plan, thereby obtaining as rich and comprehensive a set of answers as possible to our central questions: Who in Israel protests? To what extent and when? *Why does s/he?* And with what success?

Chapter 2

Source Problems and Methodology

As we have just seen, the problems of faulty theoretical blueprint (theory) and/or inadequate tools (methodology) abound in the protest/conflict field of research. However, beneath them all may lie an even more basic problem--a lack of sufficient material with which to build this particular edifice.

The vast majority of past studies have tended to be international in scope--the more famous (such as Taylor and Jodice) cover up to 154 countries.[1] In order to come to grips with such a huge undertaking, the preferred vehicle for data collection is the *New York Times* (its Index--not a complete reading of the daily news!)[2] as the worldwide source, coupled with a regional reporting source (e.g., *Middle East Journal, Asian Recorder, African Diary*, etc.) as supplement. Other projects base themselves on such general reference works as *Deadline Data* and the *Yearbook of the Encyclopedia Britannica*. But even taken together, international and/or regional sources leave much to be desired, although for obvious reasons the researchers involved think otherwise as we shall shortly see.

Unfortunately, these works are beset by two critical problems which render their conclusions highly suspect. First, the data base is seriously flawed. A sample of the critiques leveled against them:

> Virtually all of the studies . . . reveal serious shortcomings in the attempt to operationalize and measure theoretically relevant concepts. Moreover, these shortcomings are often less the result of thoughtless and unimaginative operationalization or careless measurement than of the sheer inadequacy of the available data . . . . The raw data upon which these analysts base their data making and data analyses are sparse and generally of poor quality.
> [I]n marked contrast to census-type data there is no way of knowing whether the absence of reported events is a function of the absence of reporters or the absence of events themselves.[3]

Attempts have been made to statistically check whether, and to what extent, the lack of data distorts the results of such studies. Some can even be described as scholarly attempts at damage control. One such study, using three global and two regional sources, covering thirty African countries over a fifteen-year period, concluded that "the cost-benefit ratio of multiple sources may be unnecessarily high . . . . [as] the measurement implications of previously made distinctions between global versus regional sources and visible versus less visible forms of political conflict may have been overstated."[4] Another study came to a bit more of an ambivalent conclusion. On the one hand, it quite clearly showed the necessity for regional sources above and beyond the use of even several global sources which are far sparser in their reporting.[5] On the other hand, it found that "the tests for common structures of domestic political conflict events gathered from several sources indicate their strong comparability . . . [so that] *generally* whatever differences exist between the patterns do not manifest themselves in different substantive interpretations of the empirical tests."[6]

Nevertheless, this is a distinct minority view, contradicted by much evidence. For example, one post-mortem of the Feierabends' seminal work found not only that regional sources provide three times as many events as the international sources used, but that there was a distinct difference in the distribution of the type of events provided by these two sources, with the latter tending to be more violent. The defense of global-source data "representativeness" was found to be unjustified.[7]

Most interesting is the fact that almost no one mentions the use of local/national data sources[8]--for obvious reasons of cost and time expenditures. Indeed, while there have been a handful of longitudinal national studies using local sources for event information, none have attempted to compare their event totals with those of the cross-comparative studies which are based on the international/regional sources.[9] Zimmerman (in Gurr's *Handbook*) comes closest to suggesting the need for this but then backs off: "Obviously, when collecting conflict data one should use more than one source to control for potential single-versus-multiple source differences, and at least one regional or local source to take care of *global-versus-regional* [but not local] differences."[10]

There seems to be, therefore, a general (albeit not universal) assumption by those working in this area that the differences in event count between local and regional sources are no greater than the differences already discovered (whether theoretically significant or not, as noted above) between international and regional sources. To be fair, Taylor and Jodice do touch upon this possibility and even hint at the data riches to be uncovered. They further bring a couple of other arguments against local sources which are germane (in their own sphere) but hardly negate the oblique self-criticism:

> Of course there are alternatives to the elite-press, single-secondary-source approach. These alternatives are compelling for single-country studies and could supplement the data presented in the daily event files of the *World Handbook*. The first, and most costly, alternative is to code events from national language newspapers. *While this would produce a much larger dataset*, it would not resolve issues of editorial selection or official censorship. Indeed, there is reason to expect that national news sources will be more biased in their selection and reporting because of partisan interests in the issues at stake. Moreover, one cannot expect national newspapers to be free of reporting bias with regard to regional coverage or type of event. National language news sources are much more costly to code than the elite press or news compendia . . . .[11]

Such an argument just will not do. First, censorship is a problem only in some countries, not all. National language sources could give us a very accurate basis for cross-national comparisons in the free world. As to editorial selection, even assuming that the authors are correct, what is to be preferred: a source which is more impartial but reports only 10% of the events, or a relatively less impartial source which reports approximately 50-90% of protest/conflict reality? The question virtually answers itself. In short, costly, time-consuming, "exhausting" as it may be, the national language source is far superior to the international source (even when supplemented by a regional source as we are about to see). There is no choice but to travel this more difficult and lengthy road if any real progress is to be made in the field.[12]

As can be seen from Table 2.1, the gap between the results of the Taylor and Jodice survey--which presently serves as the benchmark for most cross-comparative work in the field--and those of the present study is huge, to say the least.

Table 2.1:
Comparison of Israeli Data Based on International/ Regional Sources vs. Local Israeli
Source, 1949-1977*

	Protest Demonstrations	Riots	Total
I/R Sources	136	80	216
Local Source	1,574	248	1,822
Relative Gap	1:12	1:3	1:8

*Protest Demonstrations: Includes "protest demonstrations," "regime support demonstrations," and "political strikes" as found in Taylor and Jodice, pp. 22, 26, and 31. For their definition of all these (and riots) see p. 19. The only (extremely minor) difference between their definition and mine is that they do not include protests against foreign governments which do not implicitly criticize the home government. At most, one might wish to reduce my "local source" total by 5%.

Riots: See Taylor and Jodice, p. 34. My parallel local source total (according to their definition) includes my three highest protest intensity levels (as defined in chapter 4).

Local Source: the *Jerusalem Post*

Relative Gap: Ratio of local source total compared to international/regional source total.

Using one national source[13] alone the present study found that *overall the local source reported over eight times as many events as the international/regional sources together*, with the low- level protest totals having a still larger disparity. Even when one looks merely at those "riotous" events (i.e., violent, by the Taylor and Jodice definition) which would have the greatest chance of being covered by the I/R sources, the local (national) source scored over three times as many such intense protests! These proportional errors are quite similar to those found by the Doran et al. study[14]--except that they compared regional to international sources. In other words, between a *local* source and an *international* one, there may exist disparities of up to 1:50!![15] Another study, focusing exclusively on the Middle East, and using the *Times'* Index plus two other general reference sources (*Keesing's Contemporary Archives; Facts On File*) plus one regional source (*Middle East Journal*), arrived at a total of 96 events, while our less inclusive study (it did not include bombings and assassination attempts) scored 815 events during the period 1949-1967--amazingly enough, the same (more than) eight- to-one difference in favor of the national data source.[16]

Of course a one-country comparison does not an overwhelming refutation make, but if anything the use here of Israel suggests that similar comparisons in other countries would be even more devastating to the cross-comparative data as collected in the past. The reason for this is that by all accounts Israel is one of the most "overreported" countries by the international media (especially the *New York Times*, due to its sizable Jewish readership). One can well imagine the even larger ratio gaps still to be discovered among "backwater" countries which are not consistently covered by the *Times* or even by the "regional" sources.[17]

What we are faced with here is no longer a matter of marginal difference; at some point overly flawed numerical counts irreparably undercut the soundness of the conclusions, regardless of the quality and sophistication of the statistical analysis (in which these works excel). Indeed, Taylor and Jodice themselves indicate as much: "The quality of the sources used invariably has an effect on the quality of specific conclusions drawn from the analysis."[18]

From this perspective alone, one must conclude that the general approach to understanding the phenomenon of protest around the world has heretofore attempted to build a strong edifice upon a very shaky, perhaps virtually nonexistent, foundation. In order to develop theory which is based on reality, we must have a far more precise idea of exactly what that reality entails. In short, such theory must be built from the ground up, i.e., from an accumulation of more detailed *national* studies. The present study constitutes a first step (at least for the contemporary period) in the direction of protest research based on indigenous, and therefore far more detailed, sources.

The second major flaw[19] of most previous studies, as we noted in the previous chapter, is also tied to the problem of quantification and statistical analysis, and it bears repeating in brief. When one comes to seek the factors underlying protest, the general lines of analysis tend to follow those aspects which are easily quantified as opposed to those which are more difficult to (or perhaps which we cannot at all) quantify statistically.

In sum, the welter of conflicting evidence in most cross- comparative protest studies may have to do more with the serious shortcomings in their data bases as well as their ignoring several not-easily-quantifiable factors than any other reason. The present work attempts to overcome these problems in a number of ways: using a more detailed and reliable source; assessing easily quantifiable elements as well as those less amenable to straightforward statistical analysis, each in respectively fitting ways. Given the incommensurability, however, of these methodologies and approaches, there is no possibility of assessing the exact weight of each factor underlying the Israeli protest phenomenon.[20] It will be enough to make a persuasive case for those factors usually shortchanged, thus ensuring that future studies will take into account the "soft" elements which are no less "real."

> Thus far in cross-national research, too little effort has been made in attempting to assess the degree of reliability of currently archived data. One of the more important tasks is to attempt to examine the reliability of data now used . . . .[21]
> To evaluate report reliability, I propose . . . to apply the general spirit and philosophy of statistical production quality control . . . . The general spirit of such quality control is to test regularly, by sampling methods, the hypothesis that something is seriously wrong with production methods.[22]

The above analysis of I/R data unreliability is but a first step. We must be equally forthright and critical regarding the reliability of the local data base upon which most of this study is based. Beforehand, however, a word about the data source itself is in order. On one thing everyone is in agreement. Virtually the only thoroughly accessible source for such a comprehensive survey is the daily newspaper. Here the Israeli researcher is in luck since all the major dailies are national in scope, thus covering virtually all the "significant" events throughout the country as a whole.

For the purposes of this study the *Jerusalem Post* was chosen as the primary source, while the three major Hebrew dailies were reviewed randomly as a control group.[23]

source, while the three major Hebrew dailies were reviewed randomly as a control group.[23]

Table 2.2:
Comparative Number of Protest Events Reported by
the Three Major Hebrew Dailies, 1956-1986*

Newspaper	Dec. 1956	July 1966	April 1975	Oct. 1986	TOTAL
Yediot Akhronot	1	1	1	2	5
Ma'ariv	1	2	1	4	8
Jerusalem Post	2	4	5	19	30

*One randomly selected month per year.

As Table 2.2 illustrates, the *Jerusalem Post* consistently scored higher than the two main afternoon papers on the reporting scale--at a rather astonishing ratio of between 2:1 all the way to 10:1. There is little doubt that over the years the *Jerusalem Post* has been the best single source for scoring Israeli protest data.

A far broader comparative sample study, albeit limited to one time period, was carried out as well--and it only further reinforces this conclusion. Here the eleven major daily sources of information--including print plus electronic media--were surveyed for a six-month period.[24]

Table 2.3:
Comparison of Protest Event Coverage among Eleven Daily Sources, November
1987-April 1988

Source	# Events Reported	Source	# Events Reported
Mabat (TV news; 9:00 P.M.)	31	*Erev Tov Yisrael* (Radio news; 5:00 PM)	17
Ha'tzofe	51	*Davar*	56
Ha'modiah	30	*Al Ha'mishmar*	59
Yediot Akhronot	35	*Ha'aretz*	41
Ma'ariv	91	*Hadashot*	21
Jerusalem Post	118		

Total actual protests (after accounting for duplication): 211

Once again, the *Jerusalem Post* turned out to be by far the most reliable national source of protest data in Israel, reporting 30% more events than the next best source (*Ma'ariv*). Of particular interest is the fact that the electronic media are among the *worst* sources. In any case, the selection of the *Post* for our study seems to have been a judicious one--at least insofar as protest *frequency* is concerned.[25]

Despite its being the best single media source, it is far from the only source in general. We would be remiss if we didn't at least try to come to grips with some other source possibilities. For example, in order to corroborate the reported protest events in the printed media it was thought that it might be useful to review the protest licenses which by law must be issued by the police to any and every protest group (over fifty individuals attending).

Nevertheless, an attempt was made to review all the relevant documents over a four-year period,[26] in the most important "protest city" in Israel--Jerusalem (capital city, home of the Knesset and the ministerial offices).

Table 2.4:
Jerusalem Licenses Issued and Protests Reported
by The Jerusalem Post (1977-1980)

Year	# of Licenses Issued	# of These Reported by J.P.	%
1977	46	9	19.6%
1978	61	11	18.0%
1979	67	15	22.4%
1980	62	14	22.6%
TOTAL	236	49	20.8%

The results of Table 2.4 show the dimensions of the reporting problems. One sees here a consistent pattern over this period of the paper's reporting on only about one-fifth of those protests which obtained a license. However, in point of fact the coverage is much better than that. First, many times a licensed protest does not in fact take place (so it could not have been reported by the paper). Second, there exists a journalistic inclination to report more on unlicensed protests since these are illegal and have a greater tendency to "action" (whether police-initiated or protest-group-initiated). On the other hand, the fact that we are talking about protests in Jerusalem--home base of the newspaper--suggests that the coverage situation may be even worse in other cities, and especially in the hinterlands where the newspaper may not have steady reporters on the beat. In any case, this extrajournalistic source of protest information indicates that the dimensions of Israeli protest (from the standpoint of number of events reported) are greater than even the large numbers included in this book. But any serious attempt to uncover *all* protest in Israel (and only the legally licensed events, at that) would entail the researcher having to read all the permit documents before the protest event, and then make sure that such events did actually take place--a rather imposing, if not impossible, assignment.[27]

A second oblique way of assessing the *qualitative* reliability of newspaper coverage is to attend a number of protest events and compare the goings-on as seen by the researcher's (relatively) objective eye to the reportage as it appears in the papers the next day. In order to shed some additional light on the overall problem,[28] a "modest" number of forty protest events were attended around the country, of varying size and on all different types of issues, from December 1985 until December 1986.

In Table 2.5 we get not only a clearer picture as to quantitative newspaper coverage but also the qualitative worth of its reportage. With regard to number of protests, on average a little under 50% (again, of the forty attended by the researcher) were reported upon in the papers. This time the two afternoon papers were found to be more reliable than the four morning ones, with the *Jerusalem Post* leading the latter group.[29] The overall journalistic situation is somewhat worse with regard to the number of protesters reported. Invariably, the numbers reported exceeded the actual extent of participation as seen by the researcher in the field.[30] The picture was only marginally better regarding the intensity of the protest as reported; here, too, almost invariably the reporting was of an oversensationalized nature.

Table 2.5:
Hebrew Newspaper Coverage of Protest Compared to Researcher's Eyewitness
Assessment at the Event*

Newspaper	# Protests	# Protesters	Prot. Intensity
Ma'ariv	3.25	1.75	3.75
Yediot Akhronot	4.25	3.25	2.50
Ha'aretz	1.50	1.25	2.00
Davar	2.25	2.00	2.25
Ha'tzofeh	2.50	1.75	2.00
*Jerusalem Post***	2.68	----	----
TOTAL	2.75	2.00	2.50

*Scale: from 1.00 = totally inaccurate, to 5.00 = totally accurate.
**The *Jerusalem Post* was not included in the original Berdugo study. A comparison was made between his forty events and the *J.P.*'s coverage of those events as derived from my comprehensive project.

Since the above study of forty protests was time-specific (only one year), and there existed a definite possibility of skewed protest event selection (they were selected at random, but from information gleaned from granted licenses and other public information sources),[31] one should be hesitant before basing any broad conclusions upon it. This is especially the case given the disparity between the results of Tables 2.2 and 2.3 on the one hand, and Table 2.5 on the other. In the former two, the *Jerusalem Post* scores far higher on the reliability scale (for number of events), whereas it lags behind the afternoon dailies in the latter comparative study.

Still, two additional questions need to be addressed at this point. First, why aren't more public protest events reported on in general? Are there any specific reasons for so many events not being included within the pages of the press? Second, how is the higher "inaccuracy" level of the internal variables to be explained? What accounts for the newspapers doing a relatively better job of reporting on the existence of the protest event than the several characteristics of each protest?

There are a number of possible explanations. To begin with (regarding the first question especially), one of the central "iron laws" of the newspaper world is the "90% syndrome." Almost invariably, papers have enough room within their prescribed set of pages (after the advertisements are apportioned) to include only 10% of all the raw material which reaches the editors' desks. Indeed, in many papers only 30-40% of the salaried staffs' daily output is ultimately used (the rest coming from news agencies, government offices, and other external sources). Thus, from the start protest events must compete for space with all other types of news; there is no automatic inclusion of a protest demonstration. But protest events do have a decided advantage in that they are "anti-," "action-filled," "confrontational," and/or "unusual"[32]--criteria which newspapers seek as at least one of the elements necessary for a story's inclusion.[33]

The problem of inaccurate reporting of the protests' internal variables has somewhat different origins. First, journalists are just as prone to error as anyone else, and occasionally even more so given the fluid environment of events (especially protests), and the ruthless time deadlines of the profession. Beyond this, however, are several factors found to be relevant by other researchers, all of which address the issue of "slanting" and "bias" (conscious or subconscious):

(1) The newspaper's socialization of its news staff;
(2) The routinization of work and accepted internal principles;
(3) The publisher's and/or paper's ideological stance;
(4) Recruitment and control practices of the editorial staff.[34]

Which of these factors are relevant to the protest reportage of the *Jerusalem Post*? In an interview with Mr. Ari Rath,[35] managing editor of the paper (with twenty-nine years' experience on its staff in various reporting and editorial roles), it became clear that only factor #2 is relevant here. To begin with, almost invariably it is the news editor (and not the specific reporter) who decides which protest events will be covered that day by a member of the journalistic staff. This tends, of course, to lend a semblance of consistency to the types of protest events covered by negating the idiosyncratic whims of any specific reporter (although the reporter always has the possibility of suggesting to the editor which protest event seems most "newsworthy"). With respect to the more important question of the criteria by which the editors decide on whether to cover a protest by sending a reporter to the scene, Mr. Rath was uncategorical in his reply: "in the case of a 'genuine' or 'justified' protest, we will cover it--regardless of whether we agree or disagree with the issue at hand." And such has been the paper's policy from the beginning, as far as he remembers.

The matter, though, becomes a bit more complex when it comes time to decide which articles will be included in the newspaper. Continuing the aforementioned policy, here once again the specific protest issue or protest stance is not determining: "there are no 'political' criteria for the *Jerusalem Post*."[36] What is of crucial importance in the final decision is the size and intensity of the demonstration--the larger (or higher), the greater the chance that it will be included.[37] Second, "repetitious" protests would have less of a chance of inclusion, according to Mr. Rath, although here a third element usually injects itself. Most groups indulging in "protest campaigns" tend to get "innovative" over time, trying to find fresh and even novel ways to get across their message--or at least, will use "pseudo-violence." From the paper's perspective, agrees Rath, "any demonstration which gets out of hand will be reported on; clever demonstrators will even use the 'violence factor' to get into the paper." In sum, he estimates that "20% of the nuisance and repetitive protests don't get into the paper, but a 'real' demonstration will not be skipped over."[38]

In short, with such selection criteria it is not surprising that the *Jerusalem Post* covers protest events more comprehensively than the other Israeli dailies. Regarding the question of protest report reliability, however, the matter is less clear. While Mr. Rath insisted that the editors will "challenge reporters" regarding the accuracy of their articles (and the exactitude of the numbers mentioned therein), this is usually done only after complaints are received or a problem comes to the notice of an editor, and not on any sort of ongoing basis.

It is clear from these studies, then, that in virtually all cases the use of newspapers as a data source is somewhat problematic, but in general less so for attaining a clear picture regarding the total number of protests than the internal variables within the protest events themselves. It is for that reason that most of the analysis contained in this book will be based on the number of annual protests and less on the internal aspects of such protest (discussed in chapter 4 mostly). It is primarily for this reason as well that our study (at the end of that chapter) will only cursorily formulate and analyze "magnitude" of protest, a combination of intensity, size, and duration.[39] Given that these indicators are less reliable to begin with, any unified indicator would tend to increase the inaccuracy.

To sum up, this study does not purport to be an exact reflection of the reality of Israeli protest. Rather, it marks one of the first serious attempts to go beyond highly flawed international/regional source material to a much more accurate but still not perfect national/local data source. Nevertheless, the fact that only one national newspaper was used throughout (still a vast improvement over studies done overseas utilizing only international and/or regional reportage, as we saw earlier) means that the total number of protest events reported (and used throughout this study) constitutes an underestimation. If anything, this merely strengthens the contention that the Israeli protest phenomenon is an important element in the polity; nevertheless, it does mean that the protest numbers as well as the regression analysis emanating from them are not precisely correct, and should be viewed as trustworthy (but not perfect) indicators.

How trustworthy? The approximate answer lies in the data presented in Table 2.3. Assuming that our comprehensive six-month survey of all the news sources is somewhat representative of other periods, and assuming as well that very few protest events were missed by all the sources put together, we find that the *Jerusalem Post* reports around 55% of all Israeli protest.[40] Whether such reported protest is "representative" of all protest (regarding the internal characteristics of the events) is very hard to say. The assumption here is that the reported protest events tend somewhat to overreport the following variables: high intensity, strong police reaction, large size, central geographic location, and Jewish nationality. The variables of organization, issue, level of authority protested against, duration, and type of protest are probably represented quite correctly in the reported data.

Despite the fact that using a local source for deriving aggregate data uncovered a huge number of protest events, and this in turn afforded the opportunity of viewing the overall phenomenon from a number of different vantage points, it must be kept in mind throughout that this picture is in a very real sense "second hand." The data are based on reports of those present, but not participating, in the demonstrations. Moreover, while several conclusions can be adduced from such statistical analyses, they still are not as strong as hearing it "from the horses' mouths." As a result, in order to complement and corroborate some of the points and conclusions made within this study, a random-sample public opinion poll was undertaken (see Appendix B).

The survey was conducted under the auspices of Dr. Mina Zemach (DAHAF Agency) in December 1981, not an altogether unusual period for Israeli protest (although the Yamit protests were beginning to unfold at that point in time). A sample of 1,250 Israeli adults were questioned from all population groups except the kibbutzim and the Arab sector (for budgetary and methodological reasons). The margin of error was 3%.

Obviously, such a poll significantly adds to our understanding of Israeli protest beyond what the frequency (and characteristics) of protest events can tell us. Still, there is a problem involved here as well. As it was virtually the first survey ever conducted in Israel on the topic of protest,[41] there is no basis for any longitudinal comparison backwards over time. In other words, whereas the survey of newspaper reports resembles a long-running film on the subject, with evolution and development evident over the whole period, our poll is more in the nature of a snapshot--albeit quite a detailed one. Any conclusions to be made from it are relevant only to the 1980s, and not to the entire period under review in this study.

More comprehensive conclusions were sought through other means. Despite the underlying hypothesis of this study that Israeli public protest is in no small measure influenced by political culture and blocked institutional channels of political communication--two factors not readily amenable to aggregate statistical proof--it could not be denied that other, more empirically quantifiable influences probably have had significant impact as well. Thus, in order to discover which (if any) of these potential factors are indeed salient in the Israeli context, a step-wise regression analysis was performed.

To explain briefly: in a step-wise regression, variables are entered into the regression equation in successive stages, one at a time. Each successive stage examines the relative potential contribution of each candidate variable to the overall explanatory power of the regression equation, taking into account the interdependencies existing between the explanatory (independent) variables. Concurrently, the possibility of deleting variables already in the equation is tested to find out whether their contribution to the multiple correlation has not become insignificant as a result of the entrance into the equation of other variables with which they happen to be correlated.[42] The regression equation is gradually built in this fashion, with variables entering the equation (or dropping out altogether) until the stage where addition of any further variable would not significantly contribute to the predictive power of the overall equation. Here the process stops, and the resulting equation is the one containing the variables which are most significant in predicting the variation in the dependent variable.[43]

Fifteen key economic (mostly), social, and political indicators were selected as the independent variables. They will be defined and explained in chapter 5.

Finally, despite the statistical exactitude of regression analyses there still exist methodological problems which were difficult to overcome. This was particularly true regarding the two important variables "election periods" and "war periods" for which different statistical techniques were employed.[44]

In summation, there are a number of general points which emerge from this discussion of the study's methodology. First, while the present approach is more multivaried than studies attempted heretofore, it can by no means be considered the final word (quantitatively, at least) for the Israeli scene. As in almost all scientific endeavors here too there is room for some incremental improvement and further fleshing out.

Second, while some of the statistical tools used in this study (e.g., regression analysis) give the impression of great exactitude, it must be kept in mind that such exactitude is relative only to the data at hand. As noted above, the study's protest-event figures scored for this study still fall somewhat short of the "reality." Thus, the study's statistical tools are more akin to powerful flashlights than pinpoint lasers, appearances of exactitude notwithstanding.

Nor should the reader be misled by another aspect of ostensible exactitude regarding the regression analysis. Such a statistical operation can only be as precise in its description of reality as the number of variables tested. It is a central point of this book that not all factors are easily quantifiable, and some important ones may not be at all. In addition, there is no doubt that the many quantifiable independent variables included in the regression analysis are not all which theoretically could have been included.[45] Thus here, too, to the extent that some other variables were not taken into account, the regression results are only approximations, albeit hopefully relatively close to "reality."

Third, although the aggregate data are very comprehensive, no effort was (nor could it have been) made to present all the statistical connections possible. Any attempt to do so would have seriously blurred the important interrelationships by placing all the data into one gigantic goulash. That would be tantamount in essence to an abdication of the researcher's obligation to separate the chaff from the wheat, in order to make the fare palatable and digestible. The book before you, therefore, may be relatively "short" (at least in light of its potential for quantitative monumentalism), but if it errs on the side of "brevity" it is for mostly positive reasons.

Fourth, even before we begin defining the variables (in the next two chapters) it must be noted that the ways of categorizing and defining the subject matter are not self-evident, and most thoughtful students of the topic will probably have a few quibbles. This is an inherent problem in the social sciences where values can hardly be divorced from "facts." It does not render the analysis overly subjective and biased; rather, it means that the arguments as presented in this book have been channeled in a specific direction through the choices made and criteria selected by the author. I do not think that the central conclusions of the work can be refuted (at least insofar as Israel is concerned), but I am certain that they can be augmented and even perhaps refined with a somewhat different set of definitional criteria used in professional and judicious fashion.

PART II:

The Typology of Israeli Protest

How has the public protest phenomenon developed and grown over the years? Did it reflect the major currents underlying Israeli society and polity during these years? What were some of the dominant characteristics of Israeli protest, especially regarding the central issues and the level of intensity? How large, how organized, and how long are most such events? To what level of governmental authority have they been addressed, and from which geographical location? What types of protest are most prevalent, and how do the police deal with the phenomenon in general? Is there an archetypical Israeli protester?

These and other aspects of the Israeli protest scene are described and analyzed in the following section, which constitutes the historical and factual basis upon which this book rests. Chapter 3 surveys Israeli protest through four differentiated periods during the years 1949-1986, presenting some preliminary theoretical explanations for the major discrete events and subperiod trends from the perspective of protest frequency, issues, and intensity. Chapter 4 surveys in somewhat schematic form eight other protest categories, ranging from police reaction to protester nationality. It then rounds out the typological picture from a somewhat different standpoint, analyzing the socio-economic demographics of Israeli protest participation, i.e., who is the Israeli protester?

Chapter 3

The Periodization of Israeli Protest, 1949-1986: Issues and Intensity

As one might expect, the development of Israeli protest from 1949 through 1986 has not been steady and gradual, but rather punctuated by sharp changes, at times even a regression of sorts. In this chapter we shall follow the broad outlines of such protest development with regard to protest issues[1] and protest intensity[2]--all in light of protest frequency over the entire era.

This chapter's survey of the protest phenomena and their historical background is not meant to be a definitive explanation of the factors underlying Israeli protest overall. Rather, it is intended to highlight some of the outstanding elements of such protest during the several periods and suggest for each period what the major direct, palpable causes may have been. A more detailed and comprehensive analysis of the *underlying* causal factors will be presented in chapters 5 through 8.

Given the fact that the frequency of Israeli protest has not been consistent over time, we shall divide the entire era into several internally homogeneous periods for purposes of exposition and explanation.[3] As can be seen in Graph 3A, from the perspective of protest-event frequency[4] the entire period can most usefully be divided into four separate periods. We shall call them:

1949-1954: The age of acculturation protest
1955-1970: The age of extra-parliamentary quiescence
1971-1978: The age of recrudescent mature protest
1979-1986: The age of protest normalization

The Age of Acculturation Protest: 1949-1954

Once the various stages of the War of Independence had been completed, Israel attempted to settle down and begin the work of national and institutional construction. Unfortunately, owing to the immediate problems the government did not have the leisure of orderly and gradual development. Two overriding areas of concern had to be dealt with immediately: the newborn country's severe economic straits, and settling the massive waves of immigrants entering the Jewish state, an immigration that increased Israel's Jewish population by well over 100% in the first five years![5]

From the standpoint of *number* of protest events, then, one is not altogether surprised at the "high" frequency of Israeli protest during this initial period. Indeed, while the numbers here are somewhat higher than in the ensuing "consolidation" period, the gap is even larger, for given the aforementioned huge population rise the seventy-three protest events of 1949 were per capita far more than three and a half times the twenty events of 1955. Second, in light of the still precarious security situation one would assume that protesters back then would have controlled their urge to indulge in any public activity that might undermine the legitimacy or unity of the government and/or state. That this was not so can be taken as testimony of the deeply felt bitterness of those protest participants. Third, as will be discussed at greater length in chapter 6, there was little acceptance by the Israeli public back then of even the legitimacy of peaceful protest. In short, the numbers for this early period probably

Graph 3A: Protest Frequency, 1949-1986

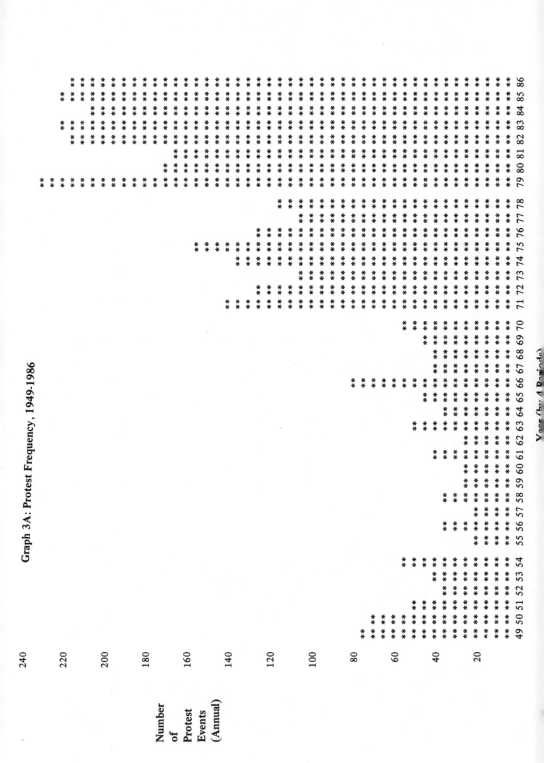

Number
of
Protest
Events
(Annual)

underestimate the importance of the phenomenon itself, not to mention the disaffection underlying it.

In addition, given the general hardship of the population at large and of the immigrants specifically, it also becomes obvious that at least for this period, problems of socio-economic modernization underlay much of its protest. The majority of immigrants arriving after the establishment of the State until the end of 1954 came from relatively socio-economically underveloped Arab countries (370,434 out of 716,587; or 51.7%), with a *weltanschauung* not quite modern from a social and political culture standpoint.

From the perspective of the Israeli authorities, on the other hand, there was "no choice" but to drag these "backward" immigrants into the modern age--as they saw it, for the (mostly economic) good of the State of Israel as well as the good of the immigrants themselves. Nachum Levine, head of the Jewish Agency's Culture Department in charge of immigrant acculturation and education, put it quite succintly (if a bit too openly and brusquely; he was subsequently fired). The Yemenites, for one, are "a very noble tribe . . . but also extremely primitive . . . . In the final analysis, our job and the job of the country is not to leave these (formerly) exiled people with their exile mentality, but rather to render them trustworthy partners in the great and noble Israeli revolution which has occurred . . . . "[6]

Inevitably, the immigrants began to resist in the only fashion open to a population not yet conversant (literally and figuratively) with the niceties of democratic political activity in general, and the intricacies of the convoluted Israeli system in particular. Thus, of the total 326 protest events during this period, there were 65 in which the immigrants constituted the sole or predominant presence.[7] What were they demanding? Among other things: more and/or edible food; better conditions within the ma'abarot ("temporary" transit camps of canvas huts and corrugated iron barracks) or transfer to other quarters; more say in the location of their ultimate homes; better health care; the right to religious education for their children; a fairer system of setting their wages; etc.

While the plight of the immigrants (especially those of Asian/African origin) was particularly difficult, as noted above during this period Israel as a whole suffered through inarguably its worst economic situation ever (colloquially called the tzena). For example, from 1951 to 1953 real per capita GNP plummeted by 14.3%, while real income fell by 10.6% in 1952 alone. Thus, it isn't very surprising that more than two-fifths of all protest events during this first period involved economic issues (Table 3.1). While unemployment was the chief problem ("Bread and Work!" was the standard rallying cry), there were several protests over such policies as consumer-goods rationing, too low price ceilings (from the manufacturers' standpoint), unfair allocation of scarce commodity goods, high tuition fees, government apathy toward the Black Market, high tax assessments, nonunion labor, and reduction of food subsidies.

The severe resource constraint under which the government was working also explains in great part the relatively large number of social-issue protests during this period. Of the 116 social protests, 41 involved demands of one sort or another for better housing (or any permanent housing at all), while another 18 related to poor quality of life and/or lack of adequate government services. As can well be imagined given the massive number of immigrants, there was no immediate solution possible to the housing problem. After the immigrant camps were filled to overcapacity already by the end of 1949, the authorities hit upon the expediency of building on a large scale

Table 3.1:
Annual Number of Protest Events by Issue,
1949-1954

Year	Political	Economic	Religious	Social	Total
1949	9	32	9	23	73
1950	14	32	7	16	69
1951	5	15	0	30	50
1952	5	10	1	19	35
1953	4	23	4	11	42
1954	4	21	15	17	57
TOTAL	41	133	36	116	326
(%)	(12.6%)	(40.8%)	(11.0%)	(35.6%)	(100%)

the *ma'abarot* which soon enough were overflowing themselves. Indeed, were it not for a large reserve of housing abandoned throughout the country by Arabs (as a result of their fleeing during the War of Independence), the housing shortage might have led to extremely serious social turmoil instead of the sporadically vociferous (and occasionally violent) protest which did in fact occur.[8]

Far less significant was political-issue protest in this early period. This may seem surprising in retrospect given the ideological divide separating the major party blocs even then, but a couple of factors tended to mitigate the potential for protest during these early years. The dominant Labor camp succeeded in forging a coalition government at one time or another in the 1950s with all the significant parties except the ultra-nationalist Herut on the far right and the Communists on the far left. Nevertheless, in light of the parlous state of Israel's security at the time, at least Herut was loath to endanger the nation's socio-political stability through extensive use of extraparliamentary protest.[9] Thus, with one great emotion-laden exception (the issue of accepting German reparations which led to a general riot on January 7, 1952 at the Knesset goaded by MK Begin, head of Herut; the party produced one other large demonstration two months later on the same issue), the large majority of political-issue protest events during these years was Communist Party-initiated (25 of 41). From a political-protest perspective, then, this period could well be described as the "Age of Fundamental Political Consensus."

The last issue area, religion, is interesting from several standpoints, both despite and because of the relatively small number of protest events in this category. Those religious-issue protests which did occur involved the modernization element once again, albeit with regard to two different groups entirely.

On the one hand, the Establishment's attempts at dragging the Asian/African immigrants into the modern age involved not just positive acculturation into the norms of Western, secular Israeli society, but first and foremost the eradication of those elements of their "primitive" cultural baggage which impeded the cognitive modernization process--chiefly religion. As a result, as even the government's own Official Investigative Commission admitted, there were systematic attempts at channeling the religious immigrant children into secular schools, preventing religious teachers from getting to their classes, cutting the sidelocks of the most devout immigrant youth (under the pretext of preventing lice), and other forms of subtle and not so subtle pressure to abandon their traditional practices--e.g., extra food and clothing were given only to those children attending secular classes; interruptions of prayer services; etc.[10] Outraged protest demonstrations were an almost inevitable outgrowth of the implementation of such an insensitive "modernization" policy[11]--and, one might add, would return to haunt Israeli society in general and the Labor Establishment in particular with even greater impact some two to three decades down the road as we shall see later on.[12]

On the other hand, the very existence of the newborn Jewish state and especially its nontraditional value system constituted an indirect, but no less serious, threat to the native ultra- religious segment of the population. Despite the "Status Quo" agreement entered into by the secular Establishment and the religious parties, the ultra-religious could not just stand by (indirectly suggesting approval of the new state of affairs) and give its own supporters the impression that a *modus vivendi* could be had with the nontraditionalist Zionist value system. Thus, carefully picking their issues (e.g., tearing down the flag on Independence Day; versus national army service for women; against boys and girls playing together in a working mothers' club; fighting public and/or official desecration of the Sabbath; etc.), these religious extremists were protesting in their own inchoate way against the "modernization" trends which threatened their traditional lifestyle and belief system.[13]

There is another important aspect at work in both these cases of religious antimodernization protest--the relationship between the formal and informal (parliamentary and extraparliamentary) forms of protest. Later on we shall discuss this point further, but it is worthwhile noting that such a relationship already existed during this early period. Of the two religious groups mentioned above, it was the new immigrant sector which should have accounted for the majority of religious-issue protest during the 1949-1954 period–from the standpoint both of population size and (perhaps) of strength of grievance. Such, however, was not the case. Why?

Despite their profound outrage, the new immigrants' religious problems quite early on were taken up by certain segments of the Establishment--chiefly the religious parties who were partners in the government during most of the period under consideration. One finds that the struggle over the secular immigrant education controversy entailed a full array of normal parliamentary tactics: questions put to ministers from the Knesset floor; a steady stream of articles and editorials by the religious newspapers; establishment of a public fundraising committee; convocation of a national rabbinical conference to discuss the issue.[14] With such broad and vociferous official support, the immigrants probably felt no overwhelming need to "man the barricades." Given a choice between parliamentary and extraparliamentary action, the new immigrants--like most Israelis thereafter--chose the former *as long as such was possible and/or effective.*

The religious extremists'[15] protest activity underscores this very point from the reverse vantage point. Here one finds a group which (of its own volition, in this case) removed itself from most contact with the normal channels of parliamentary and systemic-political communication, but still with a felt need (possibly for internal purposes as well) to protest. Thus, their protest expression of necessity had to be extraparliamentary, accounting for the rather high number of protest events relative to the very small size of the group. And as the modernization stimuli grew in number and "danger" over the ensuing decades there was, we shall see, not only a continuation but the eventual absolute and relative growth of this group's public protest.

Summing up this first protest period, one can assert with a fair degree of confidence that most of the extraparliamentary events resulted from the serious, and in many cases unavoidable, socio-economic problems of the newly established State of

Israel. In other words, the underlying factor was environmental, beyond the current power of the authorities and the political system to do much about. By and large, then, protest in this first period was a result not of systemic dysfunctionality, but rather of systemic poverty and/or overload. In those cases, however, where the protest emanated from governmental policy (or lack of), the protesters were invariably those "locked out" of the system for one reason or another (new immigrants, Communists, ultra-religious). Insofar as mainstream Israel was concerned, public protest was not a preferred, or a widely used, means of political expression.

The foregoing analysis explains in large part this initial period's deviance from other periods from the standpoint of a different category: the intensity of protest. Whereas 14.6% of all protest events in 1955-1986 involved some modicum of violence (vs. property, people, or general riot), during the 1949-1954 period 19.6% were violent in some measure. Having no recourse to following up their protest with effective parliamentary action, most of these outgroups not only had to gain the authorities' attention through protest exclusively, but had to make sure that their extraparliamentary pressure was of sufficient force to move those authorities to corrective action.

What specific type of violence was most prominent? Certainly not general riots, of which there were only two recorded cases over the six-year period. Rather, violence against the person was the norm (13.8% of all protests) compared with property violence (only 5.2%). While this seems particularly troubling, in retrospect it was not terribly problematic for a few reasons. First, of all the Jewish[16] protests, there were no fatalities during this period, so that there was a clear line of demarcation insofar as "acceptable violence" was concerned.[17] Second, much of this violence against the person was addressed to the police authorities who had obviously little experience in handling protest (those Jews who served in the British Mandate police force were not sent to quell Jewish protests for obvious reasons). As a result, this early period was marked by a tougher hand on the part of the authorities in the field vis-a-vis protesters, with the acceptable protest rules of the game still being developed by both sides. In a situation of such on-the-scene uncertainty, protest violence was more likely to ensue from misunderstandings and at times noncomprehension as to the limits of the permissible.[18]

Still, even an overall ratio of one violent protest out of every five is none too high, especially given the depth of the problems in the years immediately after Israel's establishment, and in light of the lack of a unified extraparliamentary political culture with accepted rules of the game. Having gotten through this most difficult period without severe social turmoil or even bloodshed, the Israeli polity was ready for some relief from citizen protest. As we shall see very shortly, however, this was no guarantee of quiet within other political venues--or of perpetual protest peace.

The Age of Extraparliamentary Quiescence: 1955-1970

By the mid-fifties the socio-economic atmosphere in Israel was undergoing rapid improvement. For one, the immigrant housing problem was finally coming under control (the huge annual waves had ceased already in 1952; the following waves were somewhat smaller in absolute numbers and far smaller relative to the total Israeli population). Even more important, the economy had begun to emerge from its Dark Age and was about to embark on an almost uninterrupted dramatic drive straight up for the next two decades (until the aftermath of the 1973 Yom Kippur War). Indeed, from the end of 1954 through 1970 real income rose annually 4% on average, real per capita consumption increased overall by 99%, and real per capita GNP shot up 128%! Israel had settled back to the normal state of nation-building with a vengeance.

This is not to suggest that the period was short of political controversy (I have called it "the age of *extra*parliamentary quiescence" for a reason). The Lavon Affair, for one, tore the government apart and led to Ben-Gurion's resignation and a serious (albeit in the final analysis temporary) split in the Labor camp. Nevertheless, with few exceptions (as described below) such internal government tempests did not spill over into the street. The public, while occasionally concerned (and always entertained) by the official brouhahas, was too busy to be overly moved by such goings-on, certainly not if it meant organizing demonstrations of overt public disgruntlement.

As can be see from Table 3.2 there was a marked decrease in the number of such protest events during this long period. Wheras the first period witnessed 54.3 protest events per year on average, this second span of time saw only 39.3 such events annually--a relative decline of almost 28%.

Perhaps the most striking thing which emerges from this table is the rough equivalency found among all four protest issue areas. Whereas the earlier period was dominated by economic and to a somewhat lesser extent social protest (the absolute gap between economic protests and religious ones was a whopping 29.8%), this second period evinces no such issue predominance (the largest divide--between social and economic protest--is a mere absolute 8.8%). In a sense, here at least public protest events take on a look of "background noise"--normal political static spread randomly throughout the body politic with occasional eruptions from one issue source or another.

To be sure, it is the eruptions which indicate the "highlights" of Israel's history during this period of national consolidation. A visitor from another planet could easily guess in which year the country suffered through a temporary economic recession (27 economic protest events in 1966). Similarly, someone not familiar with Israeli history would still realize that something of critical political importance occurred around 1967-68 with ramifications which extended onwards for at least a few more years (an average 24 political-issue protests for 1968- 1970 as compared with 8 per year until then during this second period).

More subtle, and probably hardly noticeable to anyone at that time (given the events of the subsequent third protest period it becomes relatively clear in hindsight), is the emergence of social issues as the dominant protest element in Israel. In this, easily the most consistent protest-issue variable from the late fifties onwards, one can detect subterranean congeries of social problems which were not being dealt with by the authorities.[19]

A loud clue of what was to come, albeit without any long- lasting political (or protest) effects, occurred on July 8-9, 1959. Far and away the most serious public disturbance of this entire second period, the riots which occurred in the Haifa slum area Wadi Salib were touched off by the police shooting of a bottle-throwing drunkard. The immigrant North African community exploded in a two-day rampage which the police were hard put to control. Nevertheless, other than the eventual depopulation of the area through an intensive slum-clearance program, no one seemed to sense the broader, more underlying implications of this particular tip of the iceberg. The ensuing decade was witness to further occasional social eruptions, but it was not until 1971 that the full dimensions of the problem as a whole became crystal clear--thereby inaugurating a new protest period of decidedly different proportions.

Table 3.2:
Annual Number of Protest Events by Issue,
1955-1970

Year	Political	Economic	Religious	Social	Total
1955	2	8	9	1	20
1956	4	12	11	6	33
1957	7	6	2	6	21
1958	4	4	19	9	36
1959	2	6	2	16	26
1960	3	7	3	13	26
1961	13	12	8	5	38
1962	3	12	4	8	27
1963	12	4	22	14	52
1964	11	4	7	12	34
1965	15	2	11	19	47
1966	18	27	12	19	76
1967	9	10	8	15	42
1968	20	2	6	14	42
1969	26	3	4	12	45
1970	27	8	8	13	56
TOTAL	176	127	136	182	621
(%)	(28.3%)	(20.5%)	(21.9%)	(29.3%)	(100%)

A partial list of such sporadic, yet relatively frequent, social protest in the 1960s
will be enough to provide a sense of *deja vu* to anyone even passingly familiar with
Israeli society in the seventies and eighties: lack of adequate housing and demolition of
illegally built structures; classroom overcrowding and lack of school space; poor social
conditions for development towns; school busing for the purpose of social integration;
violent Jewish reprisals against Arab citizens after bombing and/or killing incidents
where the victims were Jews; Israeli Jews demonstrating against racism in Israeli
society; demands for an official inquiry into the "kidnappings" of Yemenite children in
the early fifties;[20] and (well before 1971) overt discrimination against the *Edot
Ha'mizrakh* (e.g., April 11 and September 24, 1961).

As one can see, these are quite emotion-laden issues. Which leads to the question
of protest violence for this second period. Overall, there was a small but definite
decline in such violence (to 16.9% overall) relative to the first period. However, this is
only part of the story, for the latter part of the period had a significantly lower
percentage of protest violence--here too a harbinger of things to come. From 1967 to
1970 a mere 6.5% of all Israeli protest events involved some measure of violence.[21]

How can this best be explained? At least for the years 1967 through 1970 (and
again post-1973 for quite a while), the problematic national security situation probably
left its mark on the behavior of Israeli protesters. While unwilling to totally give up
their right to take to the streets (even during the 1968-1970 War of Attrition) the
Israeli protesting public showed remarkable self-control during their demonstrations.
In essence, the message being sent was almost a paraphrase of Ben-Gurion's famous
dictum regarding the British Mandate during World War II: the protesters were
cautioning that "we will continue to fight bad government policy as if there were no
war, but we will do nothing to endanger the government's stability in its efforts to win

the war." A rather high level of civic sophistication--to be repeated in the ensuing period.

Almost equally an augur of the future was the aforementioned sharp rise in political protest toward the close of the second period. The difference here between these latter years and the period's first decade could not be more marked. Until the Lavon Affair burst open in the early sixties there was almost no significant political-issue protest to speak of. Despite a fairly vocal Opposition (or was it because of such an Opposition?) the Israeli public felt no need to shatter what seemed at the time a much-needed political consensus. From this perspective, it was the Labor Establishment's own internecine fighting which paved the way for the public's subjective (psychological) readiness to step out publicly on political issues. With the Six Day War's conquest of the territories, the objective ground was laid for such significant political protest in actuality.

Indeed, paradoxically such political protest arose precisely at the time of the formation of Israel's first National Unity Government. Although one might logically assume that the wider the public's representation in the government coalition the less they would tend to protest, such was not the case regarding political-issue protest during the latter stages of our second protest period.[22]

True, part of this protest was directed at foreign governments (e.g., the French arms embargo; the Rogers Plan; Soviet policy on Jewish emigration), but fully a quarter of such protest can be traced to the "new" problem of the territories--with those in the forefront of protest being groups not part of the enlarged government (e.g., the extraparliamentary Left/*Siakh*; the parliamentary Communists/*Rakah*). Here we see for not the last time the relationship between formal modes of political communication and the informal (protest) mode. It may be precisely when there is little potentially effective voice of opposition to the government that (at least political-issue) protest becomes significant (1968-1970)--and vice versa (1955-1960). In any case, from the standpoint of political protest the Age of Extraparliamentary Quiescence ends somewhat early, and this coda is but a harbinger of more dynamic things to come.

Nevertheless, one ought not exaggerate the extent of protest during this rather long period. Relative to the tempestuous early fifties and even more turmoil-laden seventies, this second period was quite subdued from the extraparliamentary standpoint. Whether one views it as the calm before the storm or the pseudo- calm prefiguring the coming tempest is a matter of personal perspective. Be that as it may, Israel did enjoy a protest hiatus of sorts. It hasn't had another one since.

The Age of Recrudescent Mature Protest: 1971-1978

No one foresaw the veritable explosion of Israeli public protest which took place in 1971 and continued apace through the rest of the decade. In retrospect, however, one can offer a number of possible explanations for such protest recrudescence.

Table 3.3 makes clear the dimensions of the renewed phenomenon. The year 1971 was witness to a dramatic 139% rise in protest compared to a year earlier. The whole third period averaged 121.5 events per year compared to 38.8 for the second period-- more than a triple increase! Indeed, the "quietest" protest year during this third period (1973, a war year) had 25 *more* events than the "noisiest" year of the previous period (1966). Protest in Israel had returned with a vengeance-- catching both the public and the government by surprise.

Table 3.3:
Annual Number of Protest Events by Issue,
1971-1978

Year	Political	Economic	Religious	Social	Total
1971	25	13	31	65	134
1972	26	13	12	71	122
1973	34	15	7	45	101
1974	59	22	5	46	132
1975	59	17	13	61	150
1976	32	35	9	43	119
1977	29	9	8	56	102
1978	48	13	12	39	112
TOTAL	312	137	97	426	972
(%)	(32.1%)	(14.1%)	(10.0%)	(43.8%)	(100%)

What set off this major wave of extraparliamentary activity seemed, at first glance, to be a continuation of problematic conditions already found in the first period--inchoate social protest born of poverty, deprivation, and attendant frustrations on the part of those who had not succeeded in "modernizing," i.e., successfully entering the modern work force with its socio-economic benefits. The Israeli "Black Panther" demonstrators who initiated the deluge of social protest in the seventies were in fact the children of the first period's new immigrants, almost as if the protest "virus" had lain dormant until the next generation (merely a variant strain) was ready to erupt. The venue may have changed--now the central Jerusalem slums of Musrara instead of the periphery's ma'abarot of yesteryear--but the social conditions underlying the cry for help had not.[23]

Nevertheless, there were a couple of significant differences between the two generations and their protest. Much of the social protest of the first period came about as a result of the *means* of modernization and/or the very fact of modernization which is a disquieting process in any case. The third period's social protest, on the other hand, was due to the *results* of modernization. In other words, whereas the first immigrant generation opposed perhaps the fact and certainly the methods of the host society's modernization policy, their children (who had successfully internalized part of the modernizing culture and values) were frustrated and disappointed in not fully partaking of the fruits which the modern society had to offer. Put simply, the very success of Israeli society (both in advancing economically and in socializing the immigrants) led to large- scale social protest in the early seventies and beyond (when increasingly it turned "political" in character).

The second significant difference between the two generations' protest lay in the realm of political organization. The Black Panthers, with all their rough edges and uncouth external appearance, had successfully undergone the modernization process from another important standpoint: political socializa- tion. Whereas their parents may have been exploited on occasion by the political powers-that-be (whether of the Establishment or the Opposition), the Black Panthers and most of the protesters of different stripes and causes who followed in their footsteps understood quite clearly the rules of the political game and the ways to exploit the system for their own purposes.

Put another way, this was protest of a far more "mature" nature--to the extent that many such originally "spontaneous" movements were able to successfully penetrate (or from the reverse perspective, were coopted into) the formal political system, if not the ruling Establishment itself.[24] Indeed, in the first protest period only 14.5% of all protest was sponsored by an organization or institutionalized pressure group as compared to 41.7% in this third period. By the early seventies in Israel protest had become a professional business.

Perhaps the best example of this phenomenon, and arguably the single most important protest development of the entire period, was the extraparliamentary events in the aftermath of the 1973 Yom Kippur War. In early February 1974 a reserve soldier by the name of Motti Ashkenazi took it upon himself to demonstrate alone in front of the prime minister's office calling for Defense Minister Dayan's resignation. This solitary protest soon mushroomed into a nationwide movement leading ultimately (quite soon after, in less than two months, as a direct result of the Agranat Commission's interim findings) to the entire government's resignation and the departure of PM Golda Meir from the political scene. Nor was this the final effect of Ashkenazi's demonstration. That same movement soon institutionalized itself as *Shinui* (Change), eventually becoming a political party--one of the core constituents of *Dash* (the Democratic Movement for Change) whose appearance in the 1977 elections drew away enough previous supporters from the Labor camp to cause Labor's first ever electoral defeat and transfer of power to the *Likud*.

Of course, this is not to suggest that Ashkenazi's protest "caused" the downfall of the political Establishment; there had to exist the necessary environmental conditions for this to happen, not to mention the evident electoral decline of the Labor camp in the 1973 elections. His protest, though, was the spark which eventually set off the political conflagration. More important, it became a national symbol of what protest could potentially accomplish. As such, it constituted a continual shining model for anyone contemplating the risks/benefits of taking to the streets in the future.

The government's mishandling of the Yom Kippur War, to be sure, was not the only (or even the dominant) element in the continued increase of political-issue protest during this third period. It was more the success of the previous 1967 war which had shattered Israel's national security/foreign policy consensus. The first signs of rising protest in this formerly taboo area could be seen in the latter stages of our second protest period. Its full expression is felt in this third period with the increase of political protest over such issues as the sundry disengagement accords, West Bank settlement plans, and continuing attempts at finding a peaceful solution to the Arab-Israeli conflict in general.

In this regard, it is instructive to note the probable reason for the dramatic rise in protest events in 1971. While the ground had been laid over three years earlier, it was not until the end of the War of Attrition and the breakup of the National Unity Government in 1970 that the Israeli protest public felt comfortable enough to visibly attack the government. The fact that most of the 1971 increase was manifested in social- issue protest (with a boost from religious-issue protest as well) is beside the point. As we shall note on a number of occasions later on, objective factors in one issue area do not necessarily lead to a rise of protest only (or at all) in that same issue area. It may very well be (there is no way of checking this out empirically) that the Black Panthers, for example, did not feel "comfortable" expressing their frustration while soldiers were still dying on the front lines. As a prominent student of Israeli politics noted in the early seventies: "There is no doubt that a situation of political and military siege . . . helped greatly in the neutralization and freezing of feelings of frustration among certain groups."[25]

More generally, one might add another important factor facilitating protest in the entire third period--television. Introduced in 1968 (educational daytime TV arrived a few years earlier), this mass medium had a powerful impact on Israeli extraparliamentary activity from a number of perspectives. First, the 1969 election campaign was the first to employ television, thereby "intensively exposing to the campaign a larger percentage of the electorate than would normally be exposed,"[26] and possibly heightening the frustration of the public when campaign promises were subsequently not fulfilled (we shall more extensively analyze this point in chapter 8). Second, television invariably was used as a tool by the protesters themselves to publicize and magnify their activities and demands. This is not a phenomenon exclusive to Israel, of course. As Cantor noted elsewhere: "The rising effectiveness of protest movements runs parallel with the steady improvement in the means of mass communication. Television has been a big help, for protest feeds on publicity."[27]

Third, and perhaps most important of all, is the role which television may play in fostering and strengthening feelings of relative deprivation (RD) in society. Put simply: "The more facts of a social condition are known by the people, the greater will be the likelihood that they will learn to dislike it more (or appreciate it less)."[28] Israeli television, with all its shortcomings, certainly did significantly expand the number of social "facts" brought to the attention of the public.

But the whole notion of RD is extremely complex, lending itself to various explanations and interpretations. One of the most problematic aspects is the relative importance of subjective RD as opposed to objective RD, i.e., whether the critical factor in fomenting social envy is the *actual* economic gap between groups or the gap as *perceived* by the lower class. The Israeli evidence, at least insofar as the early seventies are concerned,[29] is clearly on the side of subjective RD, with television as the probable central "culprit."

One has to ask--as did the Israeli authorities upon the Black Panther eruption-- why all the fuss, and why now? A blue- ribbon commission set up by the government in 1971 in the aftermath of the riots found that *objectively* there was little to protest about:

> In the period under review (1963-1970), the standard of living of families of Asian and African origin improved relative to the standard of living of all families. This improvement found expression in higher income levels, in better housing, in a higher rate of ownership of consumer durables, in a decline in the proportion of Asian- African immigrants among lower-class families, and in an increase in the proportion of these families in the higher income brackets.[30]

But this was precisely the point. The RD was felt not by the whole lower class vis-- vis the middle class, but rather by the lowest stratum of that class compared to their upwardly mobile brethren. Put another way (in terms of synthesizing the theories of de Tocqueville and Marx), turmoil may erupt when things are getting better for the lower class in general (de Tocqueville's hypothesis) while at the same time getting worse (relatively or absolutely) for the lumpen subgroup within that broader lower class (Marx's hypothesis).[31] The Black Panthers indeed were the poor's poor (their Jerusalem Musrara neighborhood was one of the worst slums in all of Israel). For two decades they could "console" themselves with the thought that "we" *Edot Ha'mizrakh* as as a group were being deprived by "them" (the Ashkenazim), but by the early seventies with the advent of television's ability to visually show the strides which all of Israel's ethnic groups had made, it became clear that most of the "we" were reaching the level of "them."

And to this should be added one further element "introduced" into Israeli society in the late sixties and early seventies which only exacerbated the problem from a standpoint of the highest sensitivity. The huge wave of Russian immigration at this time, actively encouraged by the government through its diplomatic efforts (and duly noted by the media) as well as the economic benefits provided to the immigrants,[32] sharpened the sense of RD on the part of the slum residents who remembered only too well the lack of "adequate" care rendered them when they arrived some twenty years earlier. Worse, as a typical Black Panther poster succinctly put it, "New Immigrants Get Housing--We Get Nothing."[33] Money, they felt, that should have gone to alleviating their plight was being funneled instead to those Ashkenazi immigrants who hadn't as yet "paid their dues" within Israeli society. Overall, then, the slum dwellers' sense of tripled RD (vis-a-vis the Establishment, their ethnic "kinfolk," and the new upstarts) was too much to bear. Continual and occasionally violent protest ensued.[34]

It need hardly be said that this specific media effect was not exclusively felt by the residents of Musrara. It is quite probable that the huge explosion in social-issue protest through the seventies was at least partly due to television's (inevitably) corrosive impact on Israel's (already waning) egalitarian ethos. As a political scientist of note suggested back then: "The introduction of television . . . has been instrumental in heightening consumption expectations among all sectors of the population, and those who couldn't keep up with the Cohens became much more frustrated than they would have been without the goading influences of the TV set."[35]

A relatively short list of social protest issues during this third period should suffice to illustrate the point: decent (or in some cases, any) housing, especially for young couples; more doctors in outlying areas; improvement of poor school conditions; strengthening insufficent public transportation. Of special interest is the variety of "postmaterialistic" items (although their frequency is somewhat less than the "materialist" demands), suggesting that it was not only the poor who were taking to the streets: stopping urban renewal that upset traditional housing patterns; against building hotels in formerly pristine areas; versus setting up power plants in nature preserves; ameliorating the air and noise pollution effects of vehicular traffic (car and plane). If these issues seem to be taken straight from the American/European protest menu, that too is no coincidence. Israeli television did its share as well in bringing these "new" social issues to the consciousness of the broad, emerging Israeli middle class.

And indeed, herein lies the answer to one of the central paradoxes of this third protest period: while protest frequency was skyrocketing, protest violence was proportionately shrinking! A mere 9.4% of all protests in the 1971-1978 period were violent; and for the first time there were fewercases of the more severe bodily violence category than of property violence. How is this to be explained? Quite simply: as the protest phenomenon spread into the Israeli mainstream, middle-class people became much more involved in this mode of political expression. Consequently, the number of protests rose dramatically, but since violence was not a "proper" or "traditional" mode of behavior for that class, relatively fewer protest events were marked by property damage or bodily injury.[36]

In sum, the third protest period was both quantitatively and qualitatively different from its predecessors. To be sure, the frequency of public extraparliamentary events was far beyond anything Israel had encountered heretofore. More significant, though, was the way such protest was expressed and the impact which it had upon the governmental authorities. First, even protest which was originally inchoate, or at the least born of personal frustration (e.g., the Black Panthers; Motti Ashkenazi) soon developed into movements with great staying power (unlike Wadi Salib or the sundry ma'abara outbursts of the early fifties). Second, whereas the powers-that-be still looked upon public protest as something "abnormal" within the body politic, often they had little choice but to respond to the phenomenon in ways which at least addressed (if not completely resolved) the underlying grievance. Third, it soon became clear that despite the growing number of protest events the entire phenomenon did not constitute a threat to the society in general and to public order in particular. Quite the reverse, for as Israeli protest became more "mainstreamed," its less salutary aspects were diminishing. The protests were proving to be a headache for the government, but constituted no danger to the country.

Fourth, and finally, the entire period served as a breeding ground for the protest "super movements" which began to evolve in the mid-to late Seventies: *Gush Emunim* and Peace Now, to name two prominent examples. In this sense, the connection between the third and fourth periods is even clearer than that between the second and third. Whereas it was the absence of clear signs of public discontent (and concomitant governmental benign neglect of the problems lying just under the surface) in the second period which led to (at least many of) the third period's explosions, the protest group experience (plus occasional highly publicized successes) accumulated during this third period lay the groundwork for the events in our fourth and final time frame.

The Age of Protest Normalization: 1979-1986

As can be seen from Table 3.4, the year 1979 marked a new protest-frequency high for Israel, indeed an almost quantum jump from its predecessor. While a few subsequent years saw a return of sorts to the previous period's (upper) range, the post-1978 overall annual average of 202 protest events marked a huge 60% increase over the third period's 121.5 annual average. At this point protest ceased to be perceived as something "abnormal," and came to be viewed rather as a "normal" part of the political scene--a perfectly acceptable means of political expression on the part of the citizenry, and from the other side of the fence, one more pressure input which the system's institutions and leadership had to take into account in the regular course of the decision-making process.

There are a number of aspects that mark this as a period apart, above and beyond the sheer quantity of the events. Perhaps most obvious is the fact that for the first time it is political protest which leads the issue categories. Two distinct political issues are at work here which were responsible for this "unusual"[37] datum.

First, there was the extended and highly controversial peace process with Egypt, especially the withdrawal from the Sinai peninsula with all the attendant trauma involved in dismantling settlements and even one small city--Yamit.[38] Indeed, this could already be seen in the sharp rise in political protest in 1978 (48 events) compared to the previous year's total (28), as pressure began building on the government to first come to (or conversely, not to cave into demands for) a preliminary agreement (eventually the Camp David accords), and subsequently to conclude (or not) the peace treaty.[39]

Table 3.4:
Number of Protest Events by Issue,
1979-1986

Year	Political	Economic	Religious	Social	Total
1979	59	33	33	115	240
1980	45	28	22	71	166
1981	51	24	45	42	162
1982	115	37	25	35	212
1983	81	35	27	71	214
1984	68	57	34	39	198
1985	59	78	33	46	216
1986	84	53	36	35	208
TOTAL	562	345	255	454	1,616
	(34.8%)	(21.4%)	(15.8%)	(28.1%)	(100%)

Second, and even more outstanding, was the extraparliamentary explosion which occurred subsequent to the Lebanon War (officially called Operation Peace for Galilee). In 1982 alone, there were 115 political-issue protest events--virtually all relating to the war in one fashion or another. *This was the highest annual single-issue total in Israel's history.*[40] Nor was it merely a matter of protest frequency. The two largest protest demonstrations ever to occur in Israel took place after the outbreak of the war, with a reported[41] 200,000 showing up in Tel Aviv (July 17, 1982) in demonstrative support of the government's handling of the war. A couple of months later (September 25, 1982), a reported 400,000 antiwar demonstrators turned up to demand the establishment of an official commission of inquiry to investigate those responsible and culpable for the Sabra and Shatilla camp massacres (near Beirut) which were actually carried out by the Arab-Christian Phalange.

What explains this extraparliamentary outpouring while the war was still continuing? To begin with, it was not an "inevitable" war; while ostensibly there were legitimate reasons for its commencement (the gradual buildup of PLO arms over the border; continuing Katyusha attacks into the upper Galilee; and the assassination attempt on Ambassador Argov in London), other measures of defense and retaliation were available. Second, there existed fairly wide public support for the government's declared policy of "cleaning up" the enemy up to forty kilometers north of the border. However, when the army continued past that mark (arguably at the prompting of Defense Minister Sharon in defiance of the cabinet's earlier decision),[42] such widespread citizen support was seriously eroded--especially when it became apparent that an invasion of Beirut might take place, with incalculable casualties on both sides (especially civilian) a distinct probability.

Third, and not directly related to the events of that period but probably quite important in retrospect, is the experience of the previous war. Having had a tradition of nonprotest during times of war crisis, the Israeli public was quite loath to protest for a number of months after the Yom Kippur War until it became all too clear that serious failures marked the leadership's handling of that war. The subsequent series of protests in early 1974 psychologically paved the way for future "antiwar" protest in

Israel, as indeed erupted soon after the invasion of southern Lebanon. Here once again we can see how protest leads to further protest--especially when it comes to breaking an extraparliamentary taboo.

One further point regarding political protest during this period is worth mentioning, precisely because the relevant protest-frequency numbers are not unusual. No significant change in political-issue protest was registered after the establishment of the broad front "National Unity Government" in mid-1984. This is in contrast to the previous such government (1967-1970) which registered a significant rise as we saw earlier. Despite the fact that the central political issues remain the same (the administered territories and the nature of the peace process), it seems that after almost twenty years the country (divided almost fifty-fifty) has settled into a rather permanent dove/hawk cleavage.[43]

Extraparliamentary behavior on this issue, then, is no longer a function of who is in power. One could logically assume that with both central parties in the governing coalition, there would be *less* protest on such subjects, as each side is adequately represented parliamentarily and governmentally. On the other hand, one could just as easily and logically assume that political protest would *increase* in such a coalitional environment as each side tries to pressure its representatives within the government to advance the party line. In the event, though, no change can be discerned in going from an ideologically (relatively) unidimensional government situation to a bi- ideological one. Rather, political protest in the mid-eighties on the central issues is a function of specific items which appear on the current political agenda, and less a matter of who is running the show.[44]

When one turns to social-issue protest, a quite different phenomenon appears. We have already mentioned in passing that protest in one issue area may be a reflection of a problem in a different issue area, i.e., there is a "spillover" effect of protest into issue areas which are not directly connected. The huge rise in social protest during 1979 (115 events compared to 39 in 1978) is an example of this. This was the first year in Israel's history in which inflation hit *triple* digits. One might assume that such a development would engender massive economic- issue protest against government policy, but as can be seen from Table 3.4 such was not exactly the case. While there was a significant increase in economic protest, it fell far short of the explosion occurring in the social-issue realm.

What explains such a development? The deleterious consequences of inflation are felt quite clearly, and perhaps most strongly, on the social side--especially for the poorer classes who (despite indexation) usually suffer the most from this "economic" blight.[45] Housing, for example, became virtually unaffordable for those entering the market for the first time (real-estate prices almost *trebled* in real terms between 1978 and 1980). Thus, extraparliamentary pressure, in the case before us at least, addressed the symptom rather than the underlying cause–but the amount of protest was impressive nonetheless.

Very ironically (but not at all surprisingly, given the above analysis), economic-issue protest *rose* precisely when the government began to really address the underlying causes of the economic malaise! As can be seen from Table 3.4, it is during the last three years that economic-issue protest doubles in number, at a time when inflation was being stopped in its tracks (especially 1985-1986): dropping from over 400% annually to less than 20% in the space of only one year! Why, then, the economic protest reaction? Because of the price which had to be paid for slashing the government's budget--closure of bankrupt factories instead of the traditional bailout which had come to be expected in Israel's formerly paternalistic economic environment. The workers at such large plants as ATA Textiles, Soltam, Solel Boneh, and Israel Shipyards were shocked when the government announced that it would not step in to save their jobs. Here, then, was an economic issue with a clear "culprit," and the workers did not hesitate to protest long, hard, and loud. Such a radical policy development could not have been taken lightly by those affected, and the economic protest frequency especially during 1985-1986 bears this out. Social-issue protest, meanwhile, for the first time since the recession of 1966 was actually less evident than its economic counterpart, a sign that the society at large had begun to appreciate (and perhaps even reap) the benefits of lowered inflation.

Finally, the religious-issue protest numbers for this fourth period would seem to be incorrect for anyone having lived through these years. This is one of our rare distorted results as a result of a methodological quirk. As explained in the next chapter, any protest which turned into a "campaign" whereby the protesters would return on a set, repeated basis to the same place on the same issue, was scored as *one* protest event (although they may have appeared numerous times in total), albeit of *long* duration (even if each episode lasted only a short while). This was precisely the situation for much of religious-issue protest during these years. To take but one example, the ultra-Orthodox appeared like clockwork every Friday night in Petach Tikva for over a year to demonstrate against the opening of a cinema on the Sabbath. This would appear in our scoring as one, or at most a few,[46] protests.

Thus, religious-issue protest may actually have produced the highest number of actual events of all the issue areas during this fourth period. Certainly the list of (mostly)[47] ultra-religious demands (almost all in Jerusalem) is impressive: prohibiting Sabbath traffic on the new Ramot Road; blocking the construction of a soccer stadium in Shuafat; stopping the archeological dig of "David's City"; ceasing and prohibiting post-mortem autopsies; passage of the new "Who Is a Jew?" bill; stopping cinema screenings on the Sabbath; preventing a Mormon university from being built. And compounding this was the fact that most of these protests were far more violent than protests on other issues. Talk of a *kulturkampf* (culture war) was now beginning to be taken seriously as the pre-State religious "Status Quo" agreement collapsed on all fronts, rendered void by the "advances" of both the religious and secular camps on different religious topics.

Indeed, such religious-issue protest violence accounts for almost half of the increase in overall protest violence during this fourth period (16.5%) compared to its relatively placid predecessor (9.0%). Put another way, fully 38% of religious-issue protest during the years 1979-1986 contained some measure of violence, while all other protests at this time had only a 13% violence rate, i.e., protest over religious issues was three times as likely to be violent as other protests. It is little wonder, then, that religious extraparliamentarism came to dominate the Israeli headlines except in times of acute military or economic crisis. And the zero-sum game nature of both sides' demands suggests that unlike other types of commensurable matters (wages, housing, even military security as measured in terrorist incidents, etc.), future Israeli governments will be hard pressed to resolve the basic issue easily, if at all.

Conclusion: The Dominant Elements and Trends, 1949-1986

Although this historical description of Israeli protest is relatively lengthy, it is at best a selective survey of protest highlights. Still, from the jumble of events, numbers, and names, one can easily lose sight of some of the main elements of Israeli protest overall. We turn now to a brief enumeration and discussion of the dominant general points as a way of summing up the data.

First, some measure of public protest has been part of the Israeli political scene from the State's inception, and significant numbers of protest events have been in evidence for about two-thirds of all the years under review (1949-1954; 1966; 1971-1986). To be sure, the immediate cause of such high levels of protest activity differed from time to time, but the continued existence of such intensive extraparliamentary behavior over such a long period suggests that it is not a passing phenomenon by any means.

Second, and contrary to Israeli conventional wisdom, it is not political issues but rather *social* issues which have most concerned the average Israeli extraparliamentary activist. Exactly one-third of all Israeli protest (33.3%) was over social issues of one sort or another, with political issues not too far behind (30.8%). On the other hand, it is true that political-issue protest has shown a steady rise through our four periods and did take over the number one spot in the last period. Running well behind were economic-issue protests (at 21.0%), although they were the most prominent issue area in the first period. Finally, religion–despite the impression of inexorable frequency over the years--is the *least* protested issue (14.9% overall), although it somewhat makes up for this low frequency in other ways.

Which brings us to the third point: Israeli public protest by and large is not violent and on only very rare occasions threatens the public order in any serious fashion. As can be seen from Table 3.5, overall only 15.1% of all events had a measure of violence,[48] with the worst period being the first when a large number of protesters were recent immigrants who had not yet "learned" the rules of the Israeli protest "game."[49]

Table 3.5:
Protest Intensity through the Four Periods*

Level of Intensity	'49-'54	'55-'70	'71-'78	'79-'86	Total
Peaceful	149	408	687	947	2,191
	45.7%	65.7%	70.7%	58.6%	62.0%
Disrupt./Obstruc.	113	108	194	395	810
	34.7%	17.4%	20.0%	24.4%	22.9%
Viol. vs. Property	17	35	39	124	215
	5.2%	5.6%	4.0%	7.7%	6.1%
Viol. vs. Person	45	41	27	122	235
	13.8%	6.6%	2.8%	7.6%	6.7%
General Riot	2	29	25	28	84
	0.6%	4.7%	2.6%	1.7%	2.4%
TOTAL	326	621	972	1,616	3,535

* Percentages are vertical (by period) and not horizontal (by level of intensity).

Nor is all violence to be viewed in a completely negative light. Especially in a society where rates of general violent behavior are relatively low (such as Israel),[50] occasional violent protest may serve a long-term constructive purpose despite its short-term threat to the public order:

[V]iolence, the complete antithesis of the spirit and nature of the democratic ethic, is nonetheless a necessary part of the democratic process. Harmful and costly in its immediate effects, in the long run it may serve as a catalyst in the operation of the necessarily imperfect democratic society. In forcing the system to a reexamination of its weaknesses and to a readjustment of its values, violence thereby performs a useful function which is therapeutic to the body politic.[51]

Such was the case in Israel on at least a few occasions as we have seen--the turmoil surrounding the new immigrants' absorption (especially the religiously traditional ones); the Black Panthers' explosion; the post-Yom Kippur War political protest; and the mass demonstrations during and after the Lebanon War hostilities.

Fourth, and perhaps most important, public protest in Israel has reached such numerical proportions--especially in the last two decades--that it has become a "normal" part of doing political business in Israel today.

Is this good? There are two answers: on the one hand, clearly, the Israeli public (or at least a relatively broad segment) is not apathetic and does not suffer from a "subject" political culture but rather has quite a deep "participatory" one (as can be seen as well in the high rates of voter turnout through the years). On the other hand, extraparliamentary protest is usually not the most efficient or ideally preferred mode of political activity in a democracy, and its great frequency in Israel might attest to some deep-rooted problems within the body politic--as will be analyzed in chapters 7 and 8.

The conclusion at this stage of our study is that Israeli public protest until now has not endangered the social or political order (perhaps quite the opposite). Perhaps, however, such protest is symptomatic of something rotten within the social and political system. One thing is certain: there are no signs that the phenomenon is waning in strength, while there are many indications that it is gathering steam as time goes on. Before we turn to a more in-depth analysis of the factors behind the protest phenomenon, though, we should first try to understand some of the other elements involved in extraparliamentary protest. Our next chapter is devoted to a dissection of such additional variables.

Chapter 4

The Categorization of Israeli Protest:
Variables and Demographics

As we shall be analyzing eight protest categories (plus several demographic aspects) in this chapter, the discussion of each will necessarily focus on the major points. Several categories will be covered more indepth in later chapters where they are relevant to the analysis.[1]

Reaction of the Authorities

We have seen that the level of protest intensity over the years in Israel has not been particularly high. Can the same be said for the strength of the reaction by the police (and occasionally other forces, e.g., the Border Patrol, the army)?[2] It is obvious that police reaction is the only category almost completely dependent on another category (protest intensity), so most of our discussion will relate one to the other.[3]

Over the entire period, strong physical force was employed by the authorities in the field only 5.1% of the time, while in a mere additional 0.8% (27 cases in 38 years!) were guns fired, almost always in the air. Of all *Jewish* protesters,[4] only one died as a result of police reaction (an ultra-Orthodox Jew in 1956). In addition, in just 11.9% of the cases were arrests made. At the least, all this is hardly an indication of an overly strong hand in the field.[5]

The real question, however, is to what extent such reaction fitted the intensity of the protest. In order to ascertain this, two relatively simple methodologies were employed. First, the authorities' reaction was cross-tabulated with the protesters' intensity (Table 4.1); second, an Index of Reaction (IR) was developed.[6]

In order to get the sum total of overall "appropriate" reaction one draws a diagonal line from the upper left to the lower right corners. The result: in 71.3% of all the events the police authority in the field reacted to the protest intensity as they should have. When the reaction was not altogether appropriate, in 12.2% of the cases it could be termed too strong whereas in 16.5% of the time it was too weak.[7] As the gap between the latter two is quite small, it can be posited that in general there is no specific policy of "strong hand" or "weak hand," and in the large majority of the cases the handling of protest in Israel is quite satisfactory.

There is some indication that this is a function of experience in the field, for the "appropriate reaction" percentages gradually increased over time: 59.5% in the first period, 69.2% in the second, 76.1% in the third, and a small decline to 71.6% (precisely the overall baseline average) in the fourth period.

How can this generally satisfactory record be explained? As a result of constant involvement, the Israeli police (especially)[8] have developed a comprehensive strategy for dealing with the country's sundry forms of extraparliamentarism. These include training in democratic norms; preprotest intelligence gathering, setting guidelines with the protest leadership, and tactical preparation; measured escalation of reaction during the events themselves (warnings, followed by light force, and then arrests, etc.); postprotest feedback and evaluation.[9]

Table 4.1:
Cross-Tabulation of Reaction by Intensity
(# and %)

	Peaceful	Disrup.	Prop. Viol.	Pers. Viol.	Riot	TOTAL
No Reac.	2,006	250	36	16	2	2,310
(%)	(56.7)	(7.1)	(1.0)	(.5)	(.1)	(65.3)
Reac.	130	347	72	40	8	597
(%)	(3.7)	(9.8)	(2.0)	(1.1)	(.2)	(16.9)
Arrests	46	169	85	95	26	421
(%)	(1.3)	(4.8)	(2.4)	(2.7)	(.7)	(11.9)
Force	9	40	20	73	38	180
(%)	(.3)	(1.1)	(.6)	(2.1)	(1.1)	(5.1)
Shoot	0	4	2	11	10	27
(%)	(.0)	(.1)	(.1)	(.3)	(.3)	(.8)
TOTAL	2,191	810	215	235	84	3,535
(%)	62.0	22.9	6.1	6.6	2.4	100.

Note: Percentages are proportional to total sample of 3,535. Minor percentage "errors" due to rounding.

This is not to say that such protest handling is consistently applied across the board. The most interesting and blatant example of inconsistently handled events relates to the specific *issue* of each protest. Over the entire period, the authorities respectively underreacted (U) and overreacted (O) to issue protests in the following manner: (a) political--9.0% (U) and 15.1% (O); (b) social--17.4% (U) and 10.4% (O); (c) economic--17.9% (U) and 8.5% (O); (d) religious--28.0% (U) and 15.2% (O). In other words, political protest is dealt with overly severely, social and economic protest quite softly, and religious protest very weakly.

Nor is the protest *issue* the only determining factor. In order to determine whether there might not be a *political* factor underlying the overall underreaction to religious protest (by far the most violent of all protest issues), a subdivision by periods (accurate to the day) was undertaken. The most significant turned out to be related to coalition membership as can be seen in Table 4.2.

Table 4.2:
Index of Reaction--Religious-Issue Protest by
Religious Party Coalition Affiliation, 1949-1986

Protest	Total	NRP-/AY-	NRP+;AY-	NRP+/AY+	NRP MoP
Religious	-0.21[a]	+0.21	-0.16	-0.08	-0.34
(SD)	.933	.579	.991	.762	.940
Other	-0.03	+0.09	+0.03	-0.10	-0.06
(SD)	.639	.569	.664	.674	.710

Code: NRP: National Religious Party (and predecessors); AY: Agudat Yisrael (including Poalei and Shas); (-): In opposition; (+): In governing coalition; MoP: Minister of Police; SD: Standard of Deviation
[a]Index goes from -4.00 (total underreaction) to +4.00 (total overreaction), with 0.00 being correct reaction.

There is a fairly consistent positive relationship between religious party representation within the coalition and police underreaction to religious-issue protest. Whereas the police overreacted to religious-issue protest when both major religious parties were in the opposition, they increasingly underreacted (albeit not totally consistently) as those parties' representation within the coalition became more pronounced. In addition, this trend was far more evident than that regarding the other issue protests during these periods (only during the NRP+/AY+ period was nonreligious protest handled more lightly than religious protest). This relationship reached its peak under Dr. Yosef Burg, the only NRP politician to ever be minister of police (1977-1984), when the index reached -0.34.[10]

How is one to explain this? Gamson and Yuchtman noted the strong links between the ostensibly (politically) neutral police and their civilian (political) superiors. Owing to the historical development of the Jewish police force under the British Mandate, "since the inception of the Israeli police, political criteria have been central in the selection of higher officers . . . . Thus, when an issue has implications for national policy, it is natural for top police officials to assume political orientation at the outset."[11]

Through an investigation of police archival material (Jerusalem, 1977-1981) and discussions with high-ranking police officers, it became clear, however, that no specific politically oriented directives or instructions are sent from the minister (or cabinet) to the police authorities. Rather, the blatantly inconsistent and seemingly politically motivated underreaction is due to the great political sensitivity of the Israeli police. As Arye Ivtzan, a recent police inspector-general, publicly admitted: "The police do not act on the basis of political pressures or guidelines from higher up, but according to the law, except in cases of special populations, such as in Me'a She'arim and Bnei Brak [where the ultra-Orthodox are concentrated]. There the police are guided by their discretion."[12] At worst, what we see here is not political manipulation from on high but rather self-manipulation from within.

This is not to suggest that the political authorities cannot leave an imprint on police protest-control behavior. Two different approaches tried to test for such "political control": differences in the IR under the Labor and *Likud* governments; and between locally addressed and centrally addressed protest.

Under Labor (1949-1967; 1970-1977), the IR was -0.01 for all protest, as close as one can come to perfect (on average) handling of protest. Under the *Likud* (1977-1984), the IR rose to -0.10, a very mild average underreaction. When both these parties ruled together (1967-1970; 1984-1986), the IR was -0.06 (a seeming corroboration of the difference between the two dominant parties). In sum, a difference yes, but not very significant.

The other test was far more telling. In Israel, the police force is a national one, with the local authorities having very little control over the police within their territorial jurisdiction. If political control over police handling of protest exists, then one should expect to find a difference in the respective IRs. But in which direction?

Regardless of protest issue, the IR for local protest was always significantly lower than for national protest! The protest-issue IR breakdowns were as follows: central/political +0.10, local/political -0.48; central/economic -0.06, local/ economic -0.20; central/religious -0.13, local/religious -0.28; central/social 0.00, local/social -0.15. The major conclusion of this rather startling finding is that *the Israeli police, left to themselves without any political control, normally tend to underreact to the intensity of the protesters* (overall local IR = −0.20). It is when they must answer to their civilian political masters (the central authorities) that a tougher, but completely balanced, hand is displayed in dealing with protest (overall central IR = +0.01). Once again, this is most probably a function of political sensitivity on the part of the police, rather than specific directives received from the government or particular minister of police.

On the whole, though, the Israeli authorities in the field have not lost control of the situation despite the rising number of protest events with which they have had to deal. On the contrary, their handling of extraparliamentarism has somewhat improved over the years because of the increase in protest frequency. Taking the relatively huge numbers of protests into account, the rather low totals of arrests, injuries, and certainly fatalities are ample testimony to the fact that those in charge of controlling Israeli extraparliamentarism are not adding fuel to the fire--despite some measure of inconsistent handling along a few variables.

Size

Relative to Israel's population size, the average number of protest participants is about what one would expect.[13] Over the entire thirty-eight years, 37.5% of the events were found to be small (under 100), 45.6% medium (100-999), 13.3% large (1,000-9,999), and only 3.6% huge (10,000+). Far more interesting is the fact that despite a septupling of the general population, the only steady increase in protest size is to be found among the "huge" events, ranging from 1.8% in the first period to 4.4% in the fourth.[14] In short, whatever the influence of population increase on protest *frequency*, our evidence suggests that there is little impact on the actual size of the protests themselves.

Are there differences in protest size relative to the issues? Most certainly, with political-issue protest being large or huge 22.1% of the time as compared with social-issue protest only 11.3%, while between them lie economic and religious-issue events with similar high participation 19.5% and 16.6% of the time, respectively. The latter is especially impressive given the fact that religious Jews constitute only about 20% of the general population, and yet are able to mobilize large numbers of their adherents relatively frequently. It also indicates the type of problem the Israeli police have to deal with on occasion regarding this protest group which is the most violence-prone.

Size as a variable also has an impact on the level of intensity of the protest event. Taking all the protests together, the larger the number of participants the more peaceful the event tends to be. Thus, whereas 55.8% of the small events were peaceful, the next (ascending) size categories registered 58.9%, 82.0%, and 91.3% on the lowest intensity category. Conversely, when looking at the truly problematic events (violence vs. property, person, and general riot) we find that they constitute 13.9% of the small events, 19.0% of the medium (a reverse bulge), 7.9% of the large, and 5.5% of the huge protests.

This is an extremely important element regarding the danger which extraparliamentarism constitutes for the peace and order of Israeli society. Not only do the "problematic" protests constitute a small minority of all protest events, but when violence erupts it tends to be in a demonstration of manageable size from the police authorities' perspective. (This obviously further adds to our understanding of the police's satisfactory handling of most events overall). As far as this study could ascertain, for example, only seven"huge" events were of a riotous nature in the entire period under review--an average of one every five and a half years. "Large" riots averaged only one a year. This is not the stuff of significant and deeply threatening internal turmoil. Whether protest size is equally connected to the outcome (governmental output) side of the question shall be ascertained in chapter 9.

Organization

As already noted, the tendency among Israeli students of protest is to concentrate on protest *movements*, i.e., "professional protest groups" which are institutionalized in some ongoing, permanent fashion.[15] Peace Now, Gush Emunim, the Black Panthers are but some of the more famous. While there is certainly no doubt that they are a significant part of the Israeli protest landscape, our data suggest that they are not the dominant organizational element in the Israeli context.

Overall, such institutionalized protest groups initiated only 36.2% of all protest events, as compared to 56.3% emanating from "ad hoc" groups (or on rare occasions, spontaneous protest/turmoil). The remaining 7.5% are accounted for by political-party-organized demonstrations.[16]

The reasons for high "ad hoc" and relatively low "pressure group" frequency are twofold. First and foremost, by its very institutionalized nature the latter will usually have greater resources and political ability to transmit "protest" messages through parliamentary channels, thereby reducing the need at times for extraparliamentary action. Suffice it to say at this point (see chapters 7 and 8) that precisely the population sectors not "connected" to the Establishment are the ones which tend most to establish *temporary* organizations for the purpose of getting their protest message across.

Second, while Israelis tend to be highly involved in their politics and society (see chapter 6), up until recently there has not existed in Israel the sort of institutionalized volunteer group system as is found in America, for example. This is mostly because of the highly encompassing control of Israel's political parties and governmental institutions, as will be discussed in chapter 7. Indeed, in our 1981 poll it was discovered that a minuscule 1.9% of the respondents were "active members of a pressure group," with another small 3.8% being "independently active" (e.g., involved in community affairs). For most protest-minded Israelis, then, extraparliamentary activity is a specific action taken on a specific issue for a specific purpose, and not necessarily part and parcel of a greater social involvement as expressed through volunteer/pressure group membership.[17]

Be that as it may, it is obvious that political protest is the most "organized" in Israel: of all the events on that general issue, 44.2% were initiated by "pressure groups" and another 18.1% by the political parties.[18] Only religious-issue protest was close (49.9% and 3.4% respectively). Economic (39.1% combined) and social protest (25.0% combined) were far less "institutionalized." The relatively low level of economic-protest organization might seem surprising in light of the fact that Israel is extremely highly unionized, through the umbrella trade organization called the *Histadrut*. However, this is precisely the point, for when economic demands were made, the great power and intimate political connections between the *Histadrut*'s leadership and the Labor Party always ensured that the message came across, and usually meant some sort of acceptable response would be forthcoming. Indeed, of those economic protests which did erupt, many were spontaneously generated--directed against the *Histadrut* itself for "abandoning the workers"!

Unsurprisingly, "ad hoc" protest tends to be rather more intense than that initiated by "pressure groups": 18.6% of the former vs. 10.3% among the latter are violent in one form or another (55.6% vs. 70.0% are peaceful).[19] Given that virtually all established organizations have more to lose by transgressing the law (they may also understand the law's requirements better), the natural tendency on their part is to avoid severe conflict with the authorities. Of greater interest is the fact that political-party protest is somewhat *more* prone to violence (13.2%) than that of the nonparty pressure groups! This probably has to do with the fact that such protest is usually initiated by the most extreme parties of both right and left--*Kach* (Kahane's anti-Arab fringe party) and *Rakah* (the Communists, especially among the Arab population) are two contemporary parties which can serve as examples.

In short, Israeli extraparliamentarism may be very *widespread* and perhaps even a *normal* part of the Israeli political scene, but its major thrust--both quantitatively and qualitatively--is not dependent on the more organized sectors of society. As a result, one can add as well that it is a natural element within Israel's political society--not born of "artificial" demands by self-declared interest group leaders, but rather an outgrowth of true grassroots needs and demands.

Level of Authority

Israel is a unitary state with federal division of authority almost nonexistent. This explains why overall the majority of protests have been addressed to the central government and its multifarious institutions (60.5%), and far less to the local authorities (30.1%). The rest (8.6%) is directed at foreign governments and bodies (e.g., the U.N.)--also not very surprising given the Jews' concern for their overseas brethren (such as in the Soviet Union), and also in light of the amount of unwanted foreign political pressure directed at Israel on occasion.

As chapter 8 will analyze at length this "level of authority" category,[20] our remarks here will merely supplement that discussion. First, the relative gap between the first two addressees has *increased* markedly over time (50.9% vs. 42.3% in the first period, 68.9% vs. 25.9% in the fourth), while protest against foreign authorities started low (6.8%), almost doubled in the middle two periods (averaging 12.5%), and then returned to its original small proportion (5.2%).

This "foreign protest" bulge in the middle two periods is to be explained wholly in terms of pressure regarding "undesirable" peace proposals being pushed by external sources. Thus, for instance, during the post-Six Day War years (1968-1970) protest against foreign powers accounted for an astounding 36.4% of Israeli protest (in 1969, the year of the Rogers Plan and Gunnar Jarring mission, such protest constituted *more than half* of all Israeli protest)! A decade later, the Sadat visit to Jerusalem brought in its wake a 15.2% foreign protest proportion (addressed almost exclusively against America in 1978)--five times the previous year's relative rate.

Second, there are some remarkable differences in protest intensity along this category. Whereas only 11.2% of all "centrally addressed" protests involved some violence, 25.3% of the "local authority" protests were violent in some measure. This is in part due to the fact that fully 58.3% of religious-issue protest (by far the most violent issue category) is addressed to the localities who decide on such things as whether to open a mixed-bathing public swimming pool, cinemas on the Sabbath, etc.[21] It may also be in part a function of greater proximity to the protest addressee, who (or which) makes an inviting target for violence. Many protests against the central government do not take place near its important offices (31.7% of such protests occurred in areas other than the three largest cities), whereas on the municipal level the event almost always is at the site of the "problem."

The intensity level of "foreign" protest is even more interesting. While the general impression world-wide is that when the native population gets its dander up versus foreign governments, such protests (at the foreign embassy, for example) on numerous occasions end violently, this is certainly not the case in Israel where a mere 5.6% of all such demonstrations involved violence. Out of sight may not always be out of mind; but in the Israeli case it almost never gets out of hand.[22]

Duration

As we have no duration data regarding a third of all protest events, we can only chart the general outlines of protest duration.[23] Indeed, when one adds the fact that the police authorities forcibly dispersed the protest in another 17.5% of the cases, we are left with just half of all protests having a reported "natural" length. Of these, the split between short, medium, and long was almost equal--34.9%, 36.4%, and 28.7%.

Israel has been witness to an astonishing array of protest events of remarkable duration (and durability)--both sequential and unitary in character. The former have included religious protests such as those on Jerusalem's Ramot Road over the span of a few *years* in the late seventies (including life-threatening "symbolic" rock-throwing at cars every Sabbath), and a year-long assembly of demonstrators in Petach Tikva (in the mid-eighties) against the Friday night opening of a local cinema. Even more impressive (and consequential) have been a number of unitary demonstrations of lengthy duration. Perhaps the most important was the protest "vigil" held continuously for months in front of Prime Minister Begin's residence which tallied the slowly increasing death toll of Israeli soldiers throughout the War in Lebanon.[24]

Statistically, however, it is *social*-issue protest which registers the highest long-duration rate. Indeed, while the three other issue categories exhibit a decline in event numbers as one moves from "short" to "long," social protest actually increases steadily --27.2% short, 34.5% medium, and 38.3% long! Numerous examples of the latter could be brought: young couples without financial means demonstratively squatting in newly built housing during the early seventies; slum residents establishing "tent cities" in central squares in both Tel Aviv and Jerusalem later in the decade; almost uncountable numbers of parental school boycotts around the country because of a lack of adequate (or dangerous) facilities; etc.

In short, duration of protest is not a function of whether the problem is utilitarian or a matter of high principle. When different segments of the Israeli population feel strongly enough about almost any issue, they are willing to sacrifice large amounts of their time, energy, and comfort for the sake of extraparliamentary expression and pressure. Here then is but another indication of not only the important part which protest has played on occasion in past Israeli politics, but also the importance of the protest tool as viewed by the protesting public itself.

Type

By far the most preferred type of protest in Israel is the "open-sky" demonstration (most do not take place in the street, but in public squares, parks, etc.).[25] Over 70% were of this type, as compared to 12% for politically motivated strikes, a bit over 4% for indoor protest assemblies, with the remainder being "miscellaneous."[26]

These dry numbers, however, present only a fuzzy general picture. Far more interesting are the colorful ways in which many such protests are expressed. This is not merely a matter of human interest, however. In many cases, for the protesters themselves the form of the protest is crucial not only in clarifying their message but to ensure that it will reach its intended target altogether. For in a situation of ever-increasing protest frequency (from the seventies onwards), the competition between the numerous protest groups and events for the attention of the media has grown quite heated. When protest becomes a "normal" part of the political environment, when reporters (and their readers/viewers) become increasingly jaded, the task of grabbing everyone's attention becomes that much more difficult. The Israeli protester, though, by and large has been up to the challenge.

Any complete list of such protest pyrotechnics would fill up another book. The following are but a sampling of the variegation to be found in the Israeli context:

(1) Ultra-Orthodox Jews displaying a severed human hand in protest against unnecessary autopsies.

(2) Leftist demonstrators putting up a green "fence" many kilometers in length between Israel and the territories in protest against the gradual elimination of the "Green Line" (Israel's official map border) through the government's "creeping annexation" policy.

(3) Tomato growers handing out free tomatoes to passersby in protest against the authorities' lack of agricultural planning.

(4) Jewish slum residents marching to the office of the International Red Cross to seek asylum as "homeless refugees."

(5) Scores of truckers tying up highway traffic for hours by driving their rigs in tandem at very slow speeds, in protest against the government's vehicular tax policy.

(6) A "sea demonstration" by dozens of swimmers off Israel's southern Coral Island, against Egypt's breaking a "free zone" tourist agreement.

(7) Fifteen hundred kibbutz members releasing doves opposite the prime minister's office in an antiwar (Lebanon) event.

(8) Five hundred deaf people standing in eerie silence at the entrance to the Knesset, in protest against the government's neglect of their problems.

(9) The Kiryat Shimona Town Council holding its weekly meeting on the sidewalk outside the Interior Ministry's offices in Jerusalem to highlight the financial plight of the town.

(10) The Committee of Concerned Citizens wearing blank masks at a demonstration outside of the Knesset to dramatize the facelessness (and lack of accountability) of the country's elected representatives.

In short, in Israel it is not always enough for a protest to have an important message; it helps greatly to add some style which not only concretizes the message but also attracts the attention of the public bearers of that message (the media). If a picture is worth a thousand words, a good protest gimmick may be worth at least another few pictures and thousand words being published and televised about the event and its goals.

Location

The following table outlines the *place* where Israeli protest occurs.[27] However, it is not as clearcut as it appears.

Table 4.3:
Geographical Location of Protest, 1949-1986

	'49-'54	'55-'70	'71-'78	'79-'86	Total
Lge.City	239	428	699	1045	2411
	73.3%	68.9%	71.9%	64.7%	68.2%
Town	73	144	193	324	734
	22.4%	23.2%	19.9%	20.0%	20.8%
Rural	14	49	80	247	390
	4.3%	7.9%	8.2%	15.3%	11.0%

Note: Percentages are relative to the period, not the location.

Table 4.3 seems to suggest that there has been only minor change over the years regarding the geographical location of Israeli protest. But this is far from the case once we consider some other variables.

The only steady trend that can be easily discerned is the relatively sharp rise in rural protest. There are a few reasons for this trend. First, as a result of the Six Day War, a large additional amount of territory (the West Bank, Gaza, and Golan Heights) came under Israeli rule. While the Palestinians' protests were not included in our study, the lack of Jewish settlement policy engendered such movements as *Gush Emunim* which in the mid-seventies began to protest through quasi-mock settlements in the territories (mostly, but not always, in the uninhabited parts of the area).

From the start, these served a dual function: to attract the media's attention (la other "exotic" protests which we just discussed), and to force the authorities to deal with them physically--something which the latter were loath to do, given the settlers' "pioneering" and idealistic image ("settling the land" strikes a deep resonance in the Zionist psyche of whatever ideological stripe). The advent of television, then, was a second factor which served a crucial purpose, for without that medium it is doubtful whether the message could have hit home (in the government and public at large) with the same force. Indeed, once television appeared on the scene in Israel, rural protest had much less problem transferring its message altogether. In other words, in the television age there is less need for protesters to travel long distances in order to physically appear before the addressee (in the case of *Gush Emunim* they actually went in the reverse direction!). It is sufficient to attract the media's attention for the message to get through.

Far more significant than the rural protest trend is what happened--or did not happen--in the smaller cities and towns. The virtual stability of the proportional rate (approximately 20%) is in actuality a huge relative decline when one takes into account the fact that the population of these municipalities has grown tremendously vis-a-vis the other two geographical units under consideration. This category constituted only 30% of Israel's population in 1950 and well over 60% by the mid-eighties. Thus, stability of [rotest frequency in such a situation really represents a real 50% decline given the population trend. Conversely, because the three major cities suffered a proportional decline from half to a quarter of the country's population, the relative protest stability of the large cities really represents a dramatic increase.

How is this to be explained? First, we have already noted that the central government over time increasingly became the focus of protest attack. Notwithstanding our above comments on the use of the media,[28] standing in front of the Knesset is still more effective than in one's hometown. Second, the dramatic increase of private car ownership in the last two decades has enabled many potential protesters to travel distances in order to protest in the heart of the country. Third, the increasing organizational strength of certain protest movements (Peace Now, *Gush Emunim*) has enabled them to sponsor massive *busing* of periphery population groups to the central cities for their protests.

In short, the widespread suburbanization of Israel has not led to a geographical dispersal of protest. The increasing sophistication of Israeli protesters has led them to make very rational calculations regarding the place of protest, taking all other factors into consideration. This, of course, works to the protesters' benefit as it maximizes impact. It also, however, makes things easier for the police authorities, as the brunt of the protest phenomenon can be borne by those who are most experienced handling it.

Nationality

This book focuses almost exclusively on Israeli Jewish protest, as it accounts for 88.8% of all Israeli protest. However, combined Jewish/Arab protests have added another 2.7%, other ethnic/religious groups (Druze, Christian, etc.) accounted for 1.0%, and Israeli Arabs 7.4%. We now turn our attention to this latter group--keeping in mind the problematic nature of the totals.[29]

It is clear from the data that Israeli Arab protest can be split into two periods. During our first three periods (1949-1978) such protest accounted for 4.0%, 4.2%, and 4.7% of all Israeli protest, while during the fourth period it skyrocketed to 11.0%. More precisely, the clear divide occurred in 1976. The years 1973-1975 averaged four annual events, while in 1976 fifteen were registered, mainly as a result of Land Day–the massive set of demonstrations and riots at the end of March, protesting against expropriation of Israeli Arab lands by the Israeli authorities.

Here once again--as with the Black Panthers five years earlier--we find that a specific protest explosion can serve as a springboard for continued future extraparliamentarism on issues not totally related to the original eruption. From that point onwards, Israeli Arab protest remains quite high, reaching a pinnacle of thirty-two events in 1982, or 15.4% of all Israeli protests that year.[30] Thus, it can be said that as of late, Israeli Arab protest has become more or less proportional to the country's Arab population (about 14%). Paradoxically, then, Israeli Arabs' very intensification of protest against the Jewish authorities is a sign of the former's increasing acculturation into, and acceptance of, the political norms of Israeli society!

This latter point must be expanded, for it provides a double explanation (still only partial) for the increased Arab protest within Israel. On the one hand, just as increasing protest activity in the Jewish sector eventually led to a change in the Jewish population's perception of protest legitimacy (see chapter 6), so too this heightened Jewish protest activity eventually began to change both the norms and culture of Israeli Arab direct political action. On the other hand, after close to thirty years of living within the State of Israel (which by now obviously was not going to be destroyed by the surrounding Arab countries), Israeli Arabs--perhaps especially those who had been born after the State's establishment--had begun to take seriously Israel's creed of liberty and general legal, social, and political equality. Given the blatantly different socio-economic situation in which Israel's Arabs found themselves, strong feelings of relative deprivation could not be long in awakening, or in being actively expressed publicly (despite, or perhaps because of, the tremendous economic strides made by them over the whole period)[31]--much the same as occurred with the Black Panthers (despite several important other differences).

To these two factors we must add several more. A rapidly growing intellectual class among the Israeli Arab population constituted a social and ideational spearhead for organizing such protest. Whereas in 1949 there were a mere 300 teachers in the Arab educational system, by 1975 their numbers had surpassed 6,000. Whereas in 1970 there were only 645 college students among this sector, in only five years their total had increased to 1,500.[32] For these people, having come into close contact with Israeli society during their university stay and then having to go back to their own society where the opportunities for professional advancement were minimal at best, the feelings of relative social deprivation could only have been greater.[33]

The evolution of a new generation of leaders can be seen from another perspective which also had profound impact on Israeli Arab protest. During the mid-seventies, a number of local Arab organizations emerged with loose ties across the country as a whole: the national committee of Arab high school students arose in 1974, the national student union of Arab collegiates came into being in 1975, and (most important of all) the national committee of municipal heads of Arab townships in 1974. All these served as organizational networks which could initiate and lead Arab protest on a significant *national* scale.

The latter point is critical to an understanding of the rise in protest found over the last decade. The traditional Arab political unit has almost always been the *hamula*-- the extended family or local "tribe."[34] Given the traditional *weltanschauung* of the mukhtar (the local leader), he had very little incentive (and much to lose) in fomenting protest of whatever nature as long as the Israeli authorities left local politics well enough alone (which they were only too happy to do). The younger generation, especially the new elite, had a double reason for initiating protest--both as a tool for strengthening the Arabs' demands for equal treatment on the part of the Israeli authorities, and as a way of undercutting the traditionalist leadership by changing the political focus from a local to a national one.

A number of "external" factors can be adduced as well. By the seventies it was becoming clear (and publicly spoken of in the Jewish press) that the age of Jewish mass *aliyah* to Israel was over, and that a developing "demographic problem" was in the offing given the large gap between Israeli Jewish birthrates (low and dropping) and Israeli Arab birthrates (dropping too, but still much higher). By the year 2000 the latter sector might constitute close to a fifth of all Israelis, with greater relative increases further down the road. This was somewhat of a psychological boost for them, after they had been numerically decimated (mostly as a result of outmigration during the War of Independence). The post-1967 incorporation of another million or so Palestinian Arabs could not but further add to the self- confidence of Israel's native Arabs who could now at least envision the possibility of a future internal balance of demographic and (in a democracy) political power.

Furthermore, the economic integration of the West Bank and Gaza into Israel, and the continued political stalemate regarding these territories, engendered occasional severe outbreaks of protest in those areas. This too undoubtedly had a reinforcing impact on the Israeli Arab populace who could not be seen to be trailing their brethren in protest, especially considering the fact that the former had the full legal right to do so in Israel. It could hardly be considered a coincidence that a mere two months after the serious riots in the West Bank in January 1976 (tied to the U.N.'s debate on the Palestinian problem), Israel's own Arabs exploded on their Land Day commemoration. The same held true in early 1988 when a complete one-day general strike was successfully held by Israel's entire Arab population in sympathy with the ongoing *intifada* ("uprising") of their Palestinian cousins a few kilometers away over the Green Line.[35]

Finally, it was around the mid-seventies when it became clear that the former consensus among Israeli Jews (regarding the Arab-Israeli conflict and its resolution) was not only permanently shattered but that the internal ideological divide was rather deep. From this perspective, the 1967 Six Day War was far less important than the 1973 Yom Kippur War and its aftermath, for whereas the former merely placed the territorial issue on the national agenda, it is the latter which sundered the country's Jewish citizenry into two irreconcilable camps. While most of Israel's Arab protest did not directly involve this specific "external" issue, there is little doubt that the lack of Jewish solidarity emboldened the country's Arab population to more forcefully express its own needs and desires.

In short, for several important reasons Israeli Arab protest over the last decade reached the same proportion as that of the dominant Israeli Jewish population. But this is not the only similarity. Even more significant is the fact that the *goals* of their protests are of the same level of oppositionism: in most cases, they do not have the intent of toppling the State of Israel or even the Government in power, but rather demand equal treatment to that given the Jewish population.[36] Indeed, a clear indication of this can be gathered by the fact that overall Israeli Arab extraparliamentarism on *social* issues (47.0% of all their protests) actually exceeds their *political* protest (43.5%)! When one adds to the former another 8.8% for economic issues, nonpolitical demands end up constituting a clear majority. (It is a measure of the religious freedom granted in Israel that over the entire thirty-eight-year period only two religious-issue protest events emanated from the Arab sector.)

This is not to suggest that Arab and Jewish protest in Israel has been similar in all characteristics. Three differences stand out: Israeli Arab extraparliamentarism was a lot more violent, tended to be larger, and was somewhat less organized (the former being a function of the latter, in part). Whereas Jewish protests involved some form of violence 13.7% of the time, Arab protests were violent at a 26.3% rate–virtually double. To a certain extent this may be a result of slanted reporting, with a tendency to play up Arab violence and downplay Jewish violence, but there is little doubt that Arab protest is more violent, for cultural as well as political-communications reasons. The problem of communicating from "afar" (institutionally-politically, as well as geographically) also may explain to some extent why Arab protests were bigger than those of their Jewish counterparts: 21.4% "large" vs. 12.4%, and 6.9% "huge" vs. 3.4%. respectively. This is especially impressive given the far smaller population base of the Arab community in Israel.

Given the nonformal organizational nature of Arab society as described above, it is not surprising to find that Arab protest is less "pressure group"-initiated than that of Israeli Jews: 26.3% vs. 37.5% (although the gap has been narrowing recently as noted above). However, this is somewhat compensated for by a higher political-party proportion (9.9% vs. 6.9%), a function of the Israel Communist Party having constituted the Arabs' almost sole vehicle of organized oppositionist expression for almost thirty years. Should many of the internal and external political trends mentioned above continue to hold sway, then we can expect Israeli Arab protest to "normalize" itself from the organizational, size, and (perhaps even) intensity perspectives as well in the near future.

Magnitude of Protest

At the conclusion of the previous chapter, and at various points throughout this one, we have noted that Israeli protest is not very violent, nor does it usually constitute a threat to orderly society. In order to show this more clearly, a composite variable–"magnitude"–was devised which combines a few categories in order to show the "strength" of Israeli protest. Such a composite variable is quite normal in the conflict literature, although in most cases it includes different criteria (e.g., deaths and injuries) from those used here. For our purposes, the equation will be *Magnitude* (M) = *Intensity* (a score of 1-5 for variables 1-5) + *Size* (a score of 1-4, corresponding to variables 11-14) + *Duration* (variables = score: 25 = 1, 26 = 2, 27 = 3, 28 = 1.5, 29 = 2).[37]

The overall M is 5.67, or less than 2 for each constituent variable on average. Interestingly, no significant changes in M were found over the four periods (5.51, 5.77, 5.70, and 5.64). Nor overall were there real differences in central (M = 5.74) as opposed to local (M = 5.67) protest, although foreign-addressed protest was quite lower (M = 5.28).

Important differences were found to exist, however, in some other categories, in many cases reinforcing some of the points brought up in this chapter. For instance, political (M = 5.52), economic (M = 5.66), and social (M = 5.54) issue protests were almost identical, but religious protest had a much higher magnitude (6.29). In addition, a clear difference appeared between central city protests (M = 5.59) on the one hand, and town (M = 5.82) or rural (M = 5.89) on the other. Once away from the media centers, greater "strength" is necessary to attract attention. Peripherality also explains the large gap between Jewish (M = 5.60) and Arab (M = 6.39) protest (combined Jewish/Arab events scored M = 5.93).

The one surprise category turned out to be "organization," with ad hoc (M = 5.47) and political-party (M = 5.48) registering much lower strength than pressure-group protest (M = 6.02). Upon closer inspection, this turned out to be a function of the latter's ability to get out a far greater number of protesters than ad hoc or political-party protest events. Almost a third of pressure-group events were "large" or "huge" in size, more than making up for somewhat lower intensity (duration was about equal across the board).

A final measure of the relatively benign presence of Israeli protest can be seen in the very low number of events whose magnitude score was 9.00 or higher (i.e., averaging violent + large + long). Only 3.5% of all Israeli protest events had such a seriously disruptive M (286 events altogether, on average about 7.5 per year). In short, from a public protest perspective Israel is certainly no tranquil oasis, but neither is it even close to resembling a socio-political maelstrom.

In these two chapters we have covered the when, what, where, and how of protest in Israel. We are still left with the question of who actually does the protesting (the why will be analyzed over the next four chapters). Such a question is important for a number of reasons.

First, aggregate protest-event frequency data do not enable us to make comparisons with other nations because of huge differences in population size. Second, there remains the problem of the breadth of extraparliamentary behavior within any given nation. One nation may have a small hard core of protest activists who demonstrate on a regular basis, while another country may have fewer protest events but with a broader base of participants. Only with the additional data regarding the proportional number of actual participants can we fully understand the phenomenon and its impact on the country's politics.

Let us then be clear at the outset regarding the comparative place of Israeli protest relative to the rest of democratic western civilization: *Israel leads the democratic world in protest participation per capita*. In order to understand how such a statement can be made we must turn for a moment to one of the central comprehensive research studies undertaken in the past number of years.

In their massive project published in the late seventies, Barnes and Kaase extensively polled the population in five Western democracies: the U.S., Great Britain, West Germany, the Netherlands, and Austria.[38] Of the many questions asked, one queried the extent of participation in what the authors called "unconventional political behavior," per specific activity. Our Israeli poll, *in an earlier question* (see Appendix B, question #1), listed most of these activities as definitions of "general protest," and then went on to test the extent of "protest participation" (question #2). Thus, in order to compare the results between the different polls we must first agglomerate all the positive responses in the Barnes and Kaase study and place them opposite the one result of the Israeli poll. This is done in Table 4.4. It must be kept in mind, however, that the overall score which we derive from the five-nation study is *too high*, as it is very likely that some participants in such behavior were involved in more than one specific type of protest. As a result, the Barnes and Kaase national scores include some overlap and probably are a few percentage points lower in reality.

The comparison between these countries is striking.[39] Other than the U.S., there is no country which even approaches Israel in the breadth of public protest participation. And one must keep in mind that Israel's poll was taken *before* the tumultuous and massive extraparliamentary events of the summer of 1982 when antiwar protest erupted in dimensions heretofore unseen in the country.

Who are these protesters? What, if anything, characterizes them socio-demographically? Table 4.5 provides the answers. There are a number of interesting variables at work here, some of which are not necessarily "logical" (at least at first glance) but nevertheless are connected to our larger theory of Israeli protest (as will be more fully explicated in the following chapters).

Table 4.4:
Comparison of % Protest Participation between
Israel and Five Western Democracies

	Austria	Germany	Britain	Nether.	U.S.	Israel
(1) Lawful demonstration	6	9	6	7	11	|
(2) Unofficial strike	1	1	5	2	2	|
(3) Occupying building	0	0	1	2	2	|
(4) Blocking traffic	1	2	1	1	1	|
(5) Damaging property	0	0	1	1	1	|
(6) Personal violence	0	0	0	0	1	|
TOTAL	8%	12%	14%	13%	18%	21.5%

First, it is clear from Table 4.5 that a few socio-demographic variables are unimportant in influencing protest participation, while a few have some impact. Israelis of all ages, for example, have protested in similar numbers.[40] The same is true by and large regarding "religiosity level"--the gap between the Orthodox and the secular population is a mere 3%, and even this might not be completely accurate (it is most difficult to interview the ultra-Orthodox, and impossible to get to the *Neturei Karta*, groups with high levels of protest participation). In addition, political-party affiliation seems to have no influence on extent of protest participation. This is strikingly apparent with regard to the supporters of the two major parties--their participation is *exactly* the same (22.5%)![41]

The connection between residence and protest participation seems at first glance to be somewhat stronger, but this may be a result more of ease of access to the central government offices and the media centers than of anything intrinsic to the type of residential area per se. In any case, it is clear that those residing in the major cities do participate in protest at higher levels than their brethren in the periphery.

When we come to "ethnic origin" we find the connection to be more complex, but highly interesting. To begin with, it is apparent that those born within the Arab world are more "conservative" in protest than their brethren from the West (although this may be in part a result of their lower socio- economic condition as we shall see in a moment). However, when we look at the native-born children of both these groups we immediately see a marked increase in protest participation–a relative rise of 23% in both cases. This is most probably a result of the modernization success (political and socio-economic) which we spoke of in chapter 3. By the time we arrive at the second native-born generation, a middle point is reached between the two ethnic-origin groups, very close to the entire sample's overall percentage.

Sex also is somewhat of a strong determining factor. Women in Israel tend to protest less than the men, and certainly there are far fewer "active protesters" among the female population. This is unsurprising given that virtually everywhere in the democratic world women overall are more "conservative" in their beliefs (except with

Table 4.5:
Socio-demographic Elements of the Israeli Protester (%)

	Participated Once	Partic. More Than Once	Never Partic.
Age			
18-22	13.6	10.1	76.3
23-30	8.5	11.3	79.1
31-40	13.1	9.9	76.2
41-50	10.6	11.2	78.3
51-60	7.4	15.4	76.5
61+	5.3	13.2	81.5
Education			
Elementary	5.7	7.5	86.2
Part H.S.	9.3	7.0	82.6
H.S. Matric.	9.6	10.2	80.1
Higher Ed.	14.5	18.3	66.6
Ethnic Origin			
Asia/Africa	9.9	6.9	82.8
Eur./America	8.3	13.3	77.8
2d-Gener. Isr.	7.9	14.3	77.8
1st-Gen. Is. A/A	12.9	7.8	79.3
1st-Gen. Is. E/A	12.3	14.2	73.5
Religiosity			
Orthodox	8.3	11.8	78.7
Traditional	11.1	8.4	80.0
Secular	10.0	13.1	76.5
Income			
Lower	7.7	8.8	83.5
Lower/Middle	9.4	7.3	82.2
Middle	11.9	12.6	75.1
Upper/Middle	9.6	13.9	76.1
Upper	13.6	16.9	69.5
Residence			
Large City[a]	10.7	16.5	72.8
Mid-size City	10.2	8.9	80.1
Town/Village	9.1	9.7	81.2
Sex			
Female	10.2	8.1	81.2
Male	10.0	15.2	74.2
Party Support			
Labor	8.4	14.1	77.3
Likud	12.6	9.9	77.0
Other	10.1	11.2	78.7
TOTAL[b]	10.2%	11.3%	77.9%

[a]Jerusalem, Tel Aviv, Haifa
[b]Percentages are not 100% owing to some nonanswers on the question of protest personal participation.

regard to war and peace issues) and more restrained in their political activity. The Israeli woman is no exception, but one need not exaggerate the disparity between the two sexes on the matter of public protest participation.

Most salient of all the independent variables, and obviously interconnected, are level of schooling and personal income. Here the trend is clear and virtually straightforward: the *higher* the education level and income level, the *more* likely is protest participation. The gap between the extremes is huge: only 13.2% for those with elementary schooling compared to 32.8% for those with university education (a relative gap of almost 150%); only 16.5% for the low income group compared to 30.5% for those in the upper income bracket (a relative difference of almost 85%). This stands in contrast to the Barnes and Kaase findings where three of the five countries surveyed had a *negative* correlation between education and protest, while only Austria evidenced a slight positive one (Britain was curvilinearly correlated).[42]

These latter two interconnected findings of our poll are of great significance. For one, they belie the conventional wisdom that it is the "riffraff" or "exploited workers" who take to the streets in protest. Quite the reverse, it is the more politically sophisticated citizen (and the one with more spare time from work and other personal chores) who tends to protest in Israel. This suggests that as a whole, "relative deprivation" may not be a very salient causal factor–at least in Israel. Indeed, another question in the poll specifically tested for this factor and the results were quite revealing.

To repeat and enlarge: the question put to the respondents was: "Is your personal economic situation average for people with your education, talents, and amount of work, or is your economic situation above average or below average?" Overall, 7.7% answered "above average," 76.0% "like the average," and 12.1% "below the average"–hardly a statement of widespread relative deprivation (4.2% did not answer).[43] Indeed, not a whole lot more relative deprivation could be found within those groups where we would most expect to find it: of those in the lowest income group only 26.4% chose "below the average." Put another way, close to three-quarters of Israel's "poor" do not feel relatively deprived! Of those born in Asia/Africa only 20.1% answered likewise;[44] and those with elementary school education replied "below the average" at a mere 19.5% rate.[45]

Another nail in the coffin of RD as an explanatory factor of protest (at least in Israel) was derived by cross-tabulating "protest participation" with the above "relative deprivation" question. Of those responding "below the average," 21.9% had participated in Israeli protest (12.6% once, 9.3% twice or more). This is *almost exactly* the national average of 21.5%, and well below the 32.3% response rate of those answering "above the average"! It might perhaps be worthwhile to develop a "relative prosperity" theory to explain protest participation.

To return to the implications of the higher education result, we can note already at this stage a point which will be developed later on in the book: Israeli public protest is a political tool which *complements* the more "normal" parliamentary modes of political communication, and not one which is used to take the place of the latter. That this is so becomes obvious when we consider that it is precisely the more educated members of society who know how to use the formal system (not to mention being closer to the political Establishment, and thus able to use what is called in Israel *proteksiah*). Were protest a replacement mode of political expression, then we should find it more among the less sophisticated members of society. Instead, it is precisely those who in principle know how to manipulate the system formally, but find themselves unable to do so (for reasons to be discussed in chapter 7), who turn as a supplementary measure to extraparliamentary forms of behavior in order to get their message across.[46]

As stated above, the nexus between personal income and protest participation in Israel is also relatively strong and statistically positive. Here one may ask whether this does not stand in contradiction to the general analysis contained in chapter 3 regarding the early *ma'abarot* turmoil and the later Black Panther demonstrations. The answer, of course, is no--our poll does show that one out of every six poor Israelis has protested in the past, enough of a population group to include both those economic protest phenomena. What our demographic percentages do suggest is that the *general* tendency of the poor is not to participate in protest (whether out of innate conservatism, political apathy, or lack of time and/or knowledge as to the availability of such an option), but given special circumstances such protest will appear nonetheless.

What special circumstances? One could perhaps speak of "critical mass"--either residential or economic. In a slum, where the poor live in concentrated fashion, there is probably a far greater likelihood of an "explosion" than when the poor are relatively dispersed. The former was the case in the early fifties in the *ma'abarot*, in 1959 with Wadi Salib, and during the early seventies with the Black Panthers living in the rundown Musrara section of Jerusalem and its other slum areas. Likewise, during the *tzenah* of the early fifties, the economic downturn of 1965-1966, and the recession/high unemployment years of the mid-eighties, one finds large-scale protest participation on the part of the lower class workers who were directly hit by the economic problems.[47]

It is not, then, that poor Israelis do not protest; rather, they will usually tend to protest only when the issue affects them most directly and palpably. When the connection between their economic lot and government policy (or lack of) is either indirect or not altogether clear, lower-class protest tends to wane. In such a situation (most often the case in reality), it is the middle- and upper-class segments of the population which pick up the protest slack–better perceiving and understanding the source of their, or the country's, economic travails.

To sum up, who is the "average" Israeli protester? He (more likely than she), of any age, any party (but slightly leftist), and any religious bent, is highly educated, resides in one of Israel's three central cities, is making a good livelihood, and tends to be of European/American extraction. At least in some of these elements this is not the standard picture we usually envision when thinking of an "average" demonstrator. The young (and especially the students) do not stand out here; neither does the "embattled" religious sector; the poor and uneducated are actually underrepresented; the geographical periphery does not rail against the center; the *Edot Ha'mizrakh* are not leading the way in attacking the powers-that-be; nor are *Likud* (and other Opposition) supporters in the protest forefront against Israel's traditional Labor Establishment. However, above and beyond the socio-demographic differences (a few significant, most only tangential) in the Israeli protester's profile is the fact that they are to be found in all walks of life, in all places, of all ethnic and educational backgrounds, with all ideological and religious beliefs, and at all ages. In the final analysis, just as Israeli protest existed during all of Israel's four-decade history, it is also to be found among all segments of the Jewish population. Both chronologically and demographically, therefore, it is clear that public protest is a universal (albeit not all-encompassing) phenomenon in Israel.

Part III:

The Environmental Bases of Israeli Protest

Having delineated and described at some length the facts of Israeli protest, we turn now to an analysis of the environmental factors which may have influenced such extraparliamentarism. A number of the economic, social, and political factors in the Israeli context that have been found to be influential in other national and cross-comparative contexts are tested in this section. The goal is to assess the relative importance of these variables in Israel, as well as to lend support to and/or undercut several of the alternative theories previous works have developed.

The central approach in chapter 5 is a step-wise regression analysis which initially incorporates many elements to be winnowed down to the most significant ones. In addition, because of some methodological problems a few additional statistical analyses are carried out regarding some other empirical variables. However, public protest cannot be understood solely in terms of statistically testable data. Thus, chapter 6 focuses on "political culture" as a significant environmental factor. While some empirical data is brought to bear, here the brunt of the analysis is historical and qualitative in nature.

Chapter 5

Economic, Social, and Political Bases of Israeli Protest

This book began with the question of "why do people protest?" We turn now to a more finely tuned statistical approach: step-wise regression analysis, which is particularly useful where at least interval data are available.[1] Unfortunately (albeit understandably), such data are almost exclusively economic in nature--which is why so many theories of conflict are economically based. Social and political data are either harder to obtain, cardinal in nature, or entirely nonquantitative. Nevertheless, an attempt was made here to include some social, political, and "environmental" variables,[2] both within the regression (Gini Index, cabinet size, plus population data and a "period" indicator) and independent of it (election periods and war periods).[3]

Before we turn to the findings, three important explanations are in order. First, a reminder that no attempt will be made here to hypothesize initially a specific theory. Rather, the present regression analysis includes data which are related to virtually all the major "economic" theories regarding public protest. The choice of data was driven by two considerations--previous theories incorporating them, and statistical availability in the Israeli context. In any event, in light of the next important point it would have been impossible to hypothesize *a priori* a specific theory to account for all the protest frequency data.

Why? Because *this chapter constitutes a pioneering effort to understand the relationships in far more detailed a fashion than has been attempted by others--by conducting a regression analysis not only for protest as the general dependent variable, but also respectively for each of the protest-issue categories.*[4] The reason for this is simple (and therefore it is all the more surprising that other researchers have not considered it): different factors may influence the citizenry to protest on different issues in dissimilar ways. To take but two examples among the many possible--income tax rates may well be related to economic protest but not to religious protest; inflation could easily be correlated to social protest but not to political-issue protest; etc. In short, we shall be analyzing five regression runs: overall protest frequency (PROT) and the four specific issue categories respectively (POLPROT; ECOPROT; SOCPROT; RELPROT).

Third, and finally, while the analysis in chapters 3 and 4 was based on the simple annualized protest-frequency totals (i.e., how many events occurred each year), it was decided that for the purposes of the present more sophisticated analysis the dependent variable would be protest frequency *per capita*--because many of the independent variables were per capita as well. It was expected that this would neutralize the effect of population growth over the years,[5] but as we shall see, a few surprises were in store in this regard as well.

Findings: Economic Variables

Table 5.1 presents the results of all five regressions within one table. We shall, however, discuss each one separately, focusing first on the economic factors, and then on the socio-political ones.

Table 5.1:

Step-Wise Regression Results for Five Categories
of Protest--Adjusted R^2

PROT[a] (R^2)	POLPROT (R^2)	ECOPROT (R^2)	SOCPROT (R^2)	RELPROT (R^2)
PER[a] .35	POP .73	UNMP .38	POP .14	PER .19
(6.94)[b]	(9.62)	(3.54)	(5.16)	(3.90)
INTX .57	----	INF .54	INTX .31	UNMP .28
(4.23)		(3.49)	(4.42)	(2.99)
----	----	----	UNMP .47	GNPPC .37
			(-2.94)	(2.35)
----	----	----	CABSZ .52	----
			(-2.06)	

[a]Variables are in the order that they entered the model.
[b]t-value

OVERALL PROTEST: At first glance, it is surprising to find that only one
economic variable was found to be significant regarding protest as a whole over the
years. However, in light of the more specific protest-issue results, this "surprise"
strongly indicates the need for more discrete protest analysis.

To further elaborate: protest as a general socio-political phenomenon cannot be
viewed as a homogeneous reaction to the national "condition." The exact reverse may
be the case: *protest activity may well be a function of heterogeneous clusters of protesters
reacting to disparate issues.* This is by no means illogical; on the contrary, nothing could
be more commonsensical. It is unlikely that any society should have a large body of
"professional protesters" who take to the streets no matter what the issue. Rather,
most (potentially activist) citizens are galvanized into protest when the issue is of
specific concern to them. In the Israeli context, for instance, those who tend to protest
on religious issues do not usually demonstrate over economic policy; settlement hawks
probably don't get much involved in social issues.[6]

If all this is indeed the case, *we have here another possibly very significant reason for
the lack of consistent evidence supporting any specific theory in the vast protest literature.*
As all previous research works on protest and conflict view protest (or riots, turmoil,
etc.) as one unified phenomenon to be explained by several possible independent
variables, such variables which may indeed influence different issue types (respectively
in different fashion) could either cancel each other out, weaken each other's effect, or
even heighten a factor's strength, when jumbled together into such a gross variable as
overall "protest."

Our PROT result clearly shows two of these effects. Virtually all of the economic
variables found to be correlated with specific protest issues are removed when all
protest issues are agglomerated together. INF, UNMP, and GNPPC all disappear in
the grossness of the dependent PROT variable. Far more surprising, even paradoxical,
is the fact that INTX explains more variance in PROT than in SOCPROT, even
though it appears in none of the other three discrete issue variables! Be that as it may,
the conclusion is obvious: *research into all types of conflict must go back to the drawing
board in order to more finely delineate--along an issue axis--the types of dependent
variables which are to be taken into account.*[7]

In the Israeli case, the level of income tax is the only economic variable of significance in PROT, accounting for 22% of the variance. Given the relatively high rates of taxation and the fact that income taxes affect virtually the entire population, such a finding is not altogether surprising. To this we might add another point mentioned in the previous chapter--Israelis in the higher income brackets tend to protest far more than those in the lower brackets. As Israeli income tax has been traditionally highly progressive in its rate structure, it is obvious that such a burden has a decided effect on those most affected, and most able to protest.[8]

More interesting is a general important aspect of protest which comes to light here. Logically, one might think that economic variables would affect those types of protest in which economics (one way or another) is a palpable element. It would hardly be surprising if INTX were found to be significant in ECOPROT or SOCPROT. But why should there be a relationship with protest overall?

The answer (valid for other independent variables "unrelated" to their protest, as well) lies in the general nature of this variable--high taxation is a widespread burden which causes the population to live under continual stress (i.e., trying to make a living). Such stress may express itself not necessarily (or exclusively) in protest against the tax rates themselves (viewed perhaps as a necessary evil), but in other spheres unrelated to taxes. In other words, noneconomic protest may occur not only because of the specific issue, but because the tax pressure (for example) pushes the protester past the psychological point at which s/he might otherwise grudgingly have accepted noneconomic policy with which s/he disagreed.

POLITICAL PROTEST: No economic variable was found to be significantly correlated with political-issue protest. This does not contradict the point just mentioned, but merely suggests that in the Israeli case at least no "general" economic variable extends into the specific political-issue realm.

This is not surprising, for most of the critical political issues are quite divorced from economics (at least on the face of it)--war and peace, foreign policy, even the settlements in the territories are not usually considered by the government or by the public at large in terms of their economic impact. And when a clear conflict between the two is evident, economics usually is given secondary emphasis.[9] Especially over the past twenty years, the major salient ideological divide in Israel has been hawk/dove (political issues) and not left/right (socio-economic ones). In short, more than any other protestissue it is POLPROT which is highly issue-specific--standing independent of all "extraneous" economic factors.

ECONOMIC PROTEST: The only two variables entering the ECOPROT regression model are economic ones, and they are the two indicators most usually associated with economic protest specifically, and protest in general. The only surprise is that the "narrower" variable UNMP explains more of the variance (38%) than INF (an additional 16%) which has a wider impact.

This is possibly due, paradoxically, to the relatively low levels of unemployment found in Israel over the years. As a result of the country's general Socialist ideology and particular Zionist principle of gainful employment for all, the public's sensitivity to unemployment in Israel has been particularly acute--manifesting itself in economic protest whenever so much as a minor deviation from full employment is apparent.

This was especially the case in the earliest, the middle, and the latest of those years under review. Large-scale unemployment as a result of mass immigration led to widespread demonstrations in the early fifties ("Bread and Work!"); the severe recession of 1965-66 brought in its wake a sharp rise in economic protest; and the removal of government subsidies and general liberalization of the market in the mid-eighties led to a relatively large number of corporate bankruptcies with ensuing higher unemployment, immediately accompanied by fairly unruly demonstrations on the part of the newly unemployed (ATA Textiles, Israel Aircraft Industries, Alliance Tires, etc.).

That INF entered the model was to be even more expected, given the high rates of inflation in the first and fourth periods (although this was not a function of the "periods" themselves), and the concomitant high levels of economic protest during parts of those periods.

But more significant is the fact that *inflation seems to have no independent influence on any other type of protest!* If any variable undercuts our above comments relating to the cross-cutting nature of certain variables, it is inflation. Not even SOCPROT is affected in Israel by inflation, nor are POLPROT and RELPROT. In brief, inflation explains some of the ECOPROT variance as was expected, but unexpectedly has no impact on other protest issues.

Why not? And why does INF explain less of the variance than UNMP? The answer most probably lies in Israel's extremely sophisticated and widespread system of index linkage, running the gamut from automatic[10] wage increases to similar rises in welfare payments, subsidies, and other types of government transfers. This has significantly cushioned the devastating effects of rampant inflation (although it probably also significantly contributed to the upward inflationary spiral), thereby dampening a good measure of its otherwise potentially large impact on ECOPROT specifically and PROT in general.

SOCIAL PROTEST: Despite social protest being a rather complex affair (or perhaps because of this), only two economic variables managed to enter the regression model for SOCPROT. Making matters worse, one of them did so in quite illogical fashion.

Once again, INTX appears as an explanatory variable--indeed with the highest additional explained variance of 17% (although not the first to enter the step-wise model). We need not explain this here, having already discussed its impact above.

UNMP too enters the equation again (explaining 16% of the variance), but this time with a *negative* coefficient: the less unemployment, the more social protest! What could account for this? Some *post facto* explanations can be entertained, speculative as they may be: (1) When unemployment rises, those who are unemployed tend to protest almost exclusively over their unemployment (defined by us as an "economic" issue), thereby sharply reducing social protest, normally this population group's natural province; (2) Given Israeli society's great sensitivity to unemployment, the entire population (even those securely employed) and/or the mass media may be focusing almost exclusively on such a painful economic "human interest" issue, relatively avoiding more "normal" types of social issues; and (perhaps least convincing) (3) Those potentially threatened by unemployment may be too wary of that specter to "indulge" in any form of social-issue pressure which may force the government to divert its resources from aiding employment to resolving social problems.

In any case, at present this anomalous UNMP/SOCPROT finding stands without a definitive explanation. As we shall now see, it is not the only one.

RELIGIOUS PROTEST: Of all the protest-issue categories, one would least expect to find correlations between RELPROT and economic variables. The fact that two did emerge as significant (although not extraordinarily so: t-values under 3.00; additional R^2 only 9% per variable) is only half surprising.

There does not seem to be any logical connection between UNMP and RELPROT, especially considering that about half of such protest emanates from the ultra-Orthodox who are not employed in Israel's "mainstream" economy, and are thus probably less affected by the official ups and downs.[11] There is always the chance that this result is purely a statistical anomaly. No other explanation comes to mind.

GNPPC, one of our national economic indicators, appears here for the first and only time. How could this be connected to RELPROT? Two different processes may be at work--the one socio-cultural in origin, the other more economic.

First, the entire ultra-Orthodox community is caught in a bind, as the dominant surrounding culture is not only secular but increasingly so as the country has become more materialistic (GNPPC!) as time goes by. Thus, here religious-issue protest is genuine, a reaction to the greater national wealth which brought in its wake public "hedonism" which could not be countenanced by those religious communities. One graphic example of this was the spate of advertisement vandalizations in the eighties directed against "immoral" public ads featuring scantily clad models, etc.

The second possible explanation lies in the internal dynamics of the non-Zionist ultra-Orthodox community (although not the anti-Zionist *Neturei Karta*). A good portion of its protest is based on the collective need for funds for its *yeshivot* (religious schools) plus other religious institutions, and on the specific competition between subsects (of which there are many, usually quite antagonistic to each other) for the same ends. We may be witness here to a kind of *corporate relative deprivation*: as Israeli secular society grows wealthier, there is increasing pressure within the ultra-religious community to fight for a growing share of the government pie. However, as ostensibly these Jews are motivated by religiously "pure" motives, their protest cannot be couched in utilitarian economic demands; rather, the pressure is indirect (religious protest) but not any less understood by the governing authorities. An excellent example of where this community's true concerns lie can be seen in the fact that while the *Agudat Yisrael* party would not (for ideological "principled" reasons, at least before 1988) join the cabinet, in the eighties they had no hesitation in supporting the government while receiving in return the chairmanship of a Knesset committee--not Interior (where religious legislation is drawn up), but rather Finance!

In short, religious protest in Israel is not altogether as cut and dried as it may seem. The issues at stake are certainly important for the actors involved, but the specific timing of the sporadic RELPROT eruptions may have more to do with economic factors than strictly religious ones.

A few additional words are in order regarding what is missing from all the above findings. First is the fact that four of the nine economic variables tested did not make it into any of the regression models at all. GNP is least surprising in that it was accounted for by GNPPC for SOCPROT. More interesting is the failure of INTXNI to show up, as this indicator is not highly related statistically to INTX (-.5148 simple correlation).

Of greater importance, though, is the nonappearance of both private consumption indicators. Despite the attempts to artificially raise consumption during election periods (the 1981 elections being only the most notorious case), and even our earlier comments about relative deprivation in an increasingly conspicuous consumption society, this does not seem to be a very salient factor in Israel--for good or bad.

In general, and in conclusion, high levels of income tax and of unemployment turn out to be the most significant economic factors underlying the Israeli protest scene. However, our initial hypothesis that protest cannot be viewed as some monolithic entity was a correct one--no economic variable was found to be significant in all protest issues, and no two protest issues had the same significant combination of economic factors.[13] The only surprise is that previous researchers should have assumed, and acted, otherwise.

Findings: Socio-political Variables

As can be seen in Table 5.1, only three of our six noneconomic independent variables managed to enter at least one of the regression models. As a result, we shall not discuss each of the dependent protest variables separately, but rather will address the three significant independent variables one after the other.

The two most significant variables were POP and PER. As the simple correlation between them was extremely high (.9468; significance = .0000), the two could not practically enter the same model simultaneously. Taken together, however, they entered all the regressions except for ECOPROT. PER was found to be significant both in PROT and RELPROT (once again, with greater explained variance in the former all-encompassing category than in the narrow latter one). The PROT/PER relationship is especially interesting.

Such a finding, explaining over a third of the variance of all Israeli protest, suggests one of two (and possibly both) things. First, as mentioned earlier, there may be some unique unquantifiable (or unaccounted-for) factors within some of the four periods. The mass immigration and accompanying difficult socio-economic integration (causing high ECOPROT and SOCPROT) of the first period are one possibility. During that same period, the very tenuous security situation probably accounted for the relatively low level of POLPROT. The breakdown of national security consensus in the third and fourth periods (leading to high POLPROT) is another possibility, to which one may add the fourth period's historic reversal of political fortunes (Labor in the Opposition for the first time).

Second, and a point to which we shall return in the next chapter, is the possibility that the specific average level of protest in any individual period produces a "cultural" norm regarding the "accepted" or "conventional" amount of protest in society. Put simply, the citizenry learn one from the other not only what types (and/or intensity) of protest are acceptable, but also how much protest is acceptable or considered normal during that particular "period."

The protest-frequency figures suggest quite strongly that once a certain new plateau is established, protest frequency tends to continue within the parameters of that plateau until something significant happens to change it (either up or down). The plateau can be considered the extraparliamentary baseline for that period, from which protest frequency does not deviate much from the norm. As such, PER is a "silent" but important cultural variable circumscribing the extent of protest (i.e., setting a ceiling and a floor) for the time being, although by itself PER cannot stand in the way of stronger social phenomena which can shatter its underlying impact on occasion.

Explaining POP is a more difficult matter. Read simply, it means that regarding SOCPROT (to a small extent; R^2 = .14) and POLPROT (to a very large extent; R^2 = .73!), as the population increases, the frequency of these protest-issue events increases even more (again, we must keep in mind that the protest-frequency figures are per capita and thus already account for population in one way).

On the face of it this would seem to make sense for SOCPROT, as the range, variety, and complexity of social problems may increase in geometric fashion compared to "arithmetic" population growth. This is especially the case for those periods in which mass immigration is significant, for the added population groups have social problems far in excess of their "normal" population contribution (and may also indirectly cause an increase in feelings of social envy and/or persecution for some "native" groups). Our problem, however, is that if all this were true, then the resulting correlation should have been between SOCPROT and *POPIN* (or *POPIPC*), i.e., the *increase* in population from year to year, and not the absolute number of residents in the State.

The very high POP-explained variance for POLPROT does not seem to lend itself to any causal explanation whatsoever, and attempting to force a Procrustean Bed causal link would be pointless. A *logical* (not causal) explanation, however, is easily available. POLPROT skyrocketed in the latter two decades (when the territories and other national security issues became controversial topics), precisely at the time of Israel's highest population. If this is the underlying reason for our strong POLPROT/POP (and perhaps also the weaker SOCPROT/POP) correlation, then it is merely a historical artifact, from which nothing of theoretical worth can be learned.

Indeed, to return to the earlier point, the fact that POPIN and POPIPC did not make it into *any* of the models would seem to indicate that population increase in and of itself has no independent impact whatsoever on Israeli protest. Immigration per se is not a factor underlying Israeli extraparliamentarism--a conclusion which may be theoretically relevant to other countries. Here, however, one must be very careful not to jump to any preliminary cross-national conclusions, for the fact is that in contrast to the situation in most other countries (excepting perhaps the U.S.), a central principle of Israel's existence is "ingathering of the (Jewish) exiles"--the moral obligation to accept immigrants and aid in their social integration. Antiforeigner movements which constitute a good part of extraparliamentarism in many countries are virtually unknown to Israel (with absolutely no public legitimacy whatsoever), and so our "reverse" finding here may not be strictly applicable to other nations.

CABSZ appears in only one model (SOCPROT), and even there with an additional explained variance of only 5%. Thus, we should not attempt to build a theoretical mountain out of this statistical molehill. Interestingly, though, the coefficient here is negative--the smaller the cabinet, the greater the protest. The explanation probably lies in the realm of political communication[14] which will be addressed in far greater detail in chapters 7 and 8. Here we have perhaps the first (albeit rather small) sign that political communication is a weighty factor which may not easily be accounted for by a regression analysis based only on hard annualized data. Other approaches may be necessary to draw out the full impact of such a factor.

Finally, we come to GINI. As noted earlier, a separate step-wise regression run had to be performed for the eighteen years for which the GINI data were available. This is a relatively good, and straightforward, indicator of *objective* relative deprivation as a factor underlying protest. In the event, *GINI did not appear in any of our five models*.[15] There is little one can add here, other than to say that above and beyond other indications we have for the overall insignificance of relative deprivation in the Israeli context,[16] our nonfinding constitutes additional proof that this famous theory finds no support in Israel at least.

Although we have now covered the *fifteen* independent social, political, and especially economic variables which were entered into the regression analysis, there are two additional political variables which should be tested, given their importance in the general conflict literature: elections and wars. This was done through an Analysis of Variance (AV).[17]

The hypothesis behind the elections variable was the following: protest frequency should decline during the election year for two reasons. First, the government tries as much as possible to fit the election cycle to the economic/business cycle, thereby presenting the voters with a good economy during election time. If this were to show up in our AV, then it would be especially prominent regarding ECOPROT (which should be very low). Second, if the potential for open political communication is a factor underlying public protest, then elections–the most "open" period in a democracy–should be marked by low-grade protest relative to other periods. The postelection year, on the other hand, should show the converse as the economy must pay for the pump-priming and as the voters become frustrated once again in their political-communication efforts.[18]

As to the war factor, the hypothesis is even simpler: during times of national crisis the nation tends to unite, and not harp (through protest among other things) on its problems. The postwar period should evince a significant rise in protest both as a result of the delayed protest pressure now giving full vent, and perhaps owing as well to some of the deleterious consequences of the war itself. In both cases, it was assumed that the greatest variance would appear in POLPROT.[19]

The results here too were extremely "disappointing": *not one AV for any of the twin combinations or for any of the protest- issue variables was found to be significant.* In other words, at least through this statistical technique there was no support whatsoever for any of the election- or war-related theories and hypotheses which have been brought forth in the literature. How is this to be explained?

The answer most probably lies in the way the data are scored. All past research studies in this field have used annualized data regarding both the dependent variables (protests, riots, etc.) and the independent variables. This is highly problematic, however, for the following reason. If an election occurs near the beginning of the year, then the *post*election protests are still scored as election-year events, even though tough economic measures and/or political-communication blockage may be in force during this calendar postelection period. If a war should occur near the end of the year (it happened twice out of our four cases), then all that year's prewar protests are scored as "war-year protest" even though no one is aware during that time that a war will occur later on. In short, annualizing protest events is far too gross an approach for phenomena as time-specific as elections and wars.[20]

What, then, can be done? In both cases, a more discrete and pinpointed (albeit less statistically sophisticated) analysis should be able to suggest whether any connection exists. The way to do this is by looking at the protest frequency levels during exact periods of time before and after the occurrence of war or elections, and comparing the differences. If a pattern of "pre-" decreases or "post-" increases emerges, then one can say with some assurance that there is a connection--in the direction hypothesized-- between the factors "war" or "election" on the one hand, and extraparliamentary activity on the other. The "war" results will be discussed here,[21] while we shall leave the more complicated "election" findings to chapter 8 where they fit into a broader analysis.

As can be seen from Table 5.3, there are strong but not unambiguous indications that over the short term protest does decline markedly after the outbreak of war. This was true for three out of Israel's four postIndependence wars--precisely those which were considered by most of the public to be "*ain brairah*" (no choice). The last one, Operation Peace for Galilee, was controversial from the start, and as there was no real threat to Israel's existence at the time (Egypt and Jordan staying out), the "war" factor did not dampen protest even at the start.

Table 5.3:
Pre- and Postwar Protest around Four War Periods[a]

Period (Months)	1956 #	1967 #	1973 #	1982 #	Total
Pre- (6)	17	31	61	91	200
Post- (6)	10	17	43	113	183
Change (%)	D (41)	D (45)	D (30)	U (24)	D (9)
Pre- (12)	33	65	110	188	396
Post- (12)	21	36	115	226	398
Change (%)	D (36)	D (45)	U (5)	U (20)	U (.5)

[a]The protest events of the month in which war broke out have been deleted.

Over the longer term, i.e., twelve months, the effect of war seems to wear off somewhat. This was especially true regarding the aftermath of the Yom Kippur War (1973), when significant protest reared its head not against the war per se, but against the government's handling of the war (the *mekhdal*). As noted in chapter 3, this broke the taboo of Israeli antiwar protest which burst forth in full force during the 1982 Lebanon campaign.

In short, hard and fast conclusions *cannot* be made on the basis of this small sample. At best, the data here suggest that while war *does* have a dampening effect on protest, the extent and duration of such a factor depend on two things: the universal acceptance of the war and its conduct, plus the degree of threat to national existence (or sovereignty, in most other national cases) of each specific war.

Conclusions

If we compare the results of our economic variables with those of the socio-political ones, a number of interesting things emerge. To begin with, in both cases only about half of the independent variables succeeded in entering any of the models (5 of 9 among the economic ones, 3 of 6 among the socio-political variables). However, somewhat surprisingly it is the group of socio-political variables which seem to be more significant in explaining Israeli protest than their economic counterparts. This can be seen in two ways: in four of the five models[22] it is the socio-political variable which enters the regression equation first, and in the five models taken together the socio-political variables explain 146% (mean = 29.2%) of the variance, compared to 127% (mean = 25.4%) on the part of the economic variables.[23]

This is particularly important when one considers a number of points. First, socio-political variables might in truth be even more significant than evidenced here, as they are not only outnumbered in the regression analysis, but are missing two variables (war and elections) which for methodological reasons (only) were not included as well. Our more discretely scored analysis of "war" suggests that given the proper statistical formulation it might add to our overall variance; we can already divulge that the same might be true regarding "elections" as a significant socio-political variable (and not economic, as will be explained later on).

The general thrust of the protest/conflict literature to concentrate on economic variables (for understandable, but not necessarily acceptable, methodological reasons) to the detriment of social, and especially political, factors, receives no support from the regression analysis presented in the above two chapters. Greater efforts must be made to find ways in which socio- political data can be included in such wide-ranging sophisticated statistical analyses–or investigated in other, more novel, fashion.

Such a conclusion receives extra support from another aspect of our regression findings. Overall (whether looking only at PROT, or at the mean for all five models together) the adjusted variance explained reaches 57%--certainly not bad, but far from ideal (no one today expects absolute completeness). There is obviously more at work here than the fifteen empirically testable factors which were entered. Perhaps other testable variables could have been included (although there is no end to this). The assumption, however, by which we shall continue in the following three chapters, is that the real significant additional explanations must be sought in other directions by other means.

Chapter 6

A Stiff-Necked People:
The Cultural Bases of Israeli Protest

All the traits that we found in Judaism--the "intimacy" between Man and God, the foundation of the Covenant, the absence or weakness of a creed of mediation . . .--all these lead to a sharpening of political conflict intensity; of the emphatic belief on the part of various groups and even individuals that they hold the correct solution for the question of fashioning the social and political order; to the tendency of not accepting authority of any kind, whether due to "higher conscience," tribal solidarity, or to the idea that everyone possesses enough personal authority.[1]

Throughout Jewish history, there has existed a "culture of oppositionism" that has manifested itself in various guises and forms.[2] There is little reason to doubt that this underlying perspective continues to thrive within the Jewish State of Israel.

To be sure, "oppositionism" in the Jewish political tradition does not imply that it doesn't exist in other peoples' heritages in some measure as well.[3] One can say that: (a) the *quantity* of such "oppositionism" throughout Jewish history is quite high; and more important, (b) the Jewish heritage developed an imposing qualitative set of norms and rules which in essence *routinized, institutionalized, and even (in certain circumstances) encouraged various forms of "oppositionism."*[4]

What are these "oppositionist" forms? They can be subsumed under four graded elements: argumentativeness, protest, disobedience, and rebellion (see Appendix A for a list of biblical examples).

Argumentativeness is an *intellectual* quality, a mindset which at base is skeptical of received truth, which perceives things not monistically but *dialectically*. Whatever the conventional coin of wisdom at the moment, an argumentative mind tends to flip it over in order to reflect upon the obverse side and argue over its merits.[5]

Protest is more of a *moral* quality, whereby one's voice is raised against the action, and not merely the thought, of another. Conversely, it may manifest itself in ways other than the purely verbal, expressing a sense of injustice (and not just the possibility of "another way") while demanding actual redress, not merely reconsideration. Finally, as in argumentativeness the element of protest may be directed at one's peers as well as a higher authority.[6]

Disobedience is in practice a stronger expression of opposition to the powers-that-be, yet philosophically presents less of a threat. Whereas protest is addressed against the authority's opinion on a matter, but the directive of that authority is not transgressed, with disobedience one enters the realm of "illegal" action. However, disobedience does not always carry with it a "political" statement, i.e., the perpetrators may know that they are going against the authority's will but may have no intention of sending any sort of "message" regarding the transgressed law. With protest, though, the adversarial position vis-a-vis the leader(ship) is patent from the start, and thus demands more of a reasoned response on the latter's part. In any case, outright disobedience was far less acceptable in the Jewish tradition, but did occur (and was even semiofficially sanctioned) on numerous occasions.[7]

Rebellion transcends lower-level legal/political matters; it is ultimate oppositionism on the constitutional plane. Here the legitimacy of the leader(ship) and/or type of regime is under attack, i.e., modern "revolution," almost always involving bloodshed. Judaism severely frowned upon this ultimate form, and little official sanction can be found. This, however, did not prevent numerous rebellions from occurring in the monarchical period of early Jewish history (Appendix A, #31-33; 36).

But even if such a categorization and the existence of Jewish "oppositionism" is accepted, can it still be valid for the modern State of Israel? As we shall shortly see, many of the same "oppositionist" characteristics which were to be found among premodern Jewry are evident in contemporary Israel as well. True, this does not prove any direct cultural nexus, but the evidence (even if only circumstantial) strongly suggests such a link. As one of the premier students of the Jewish political tradition has argued:

> It is always a mistake to underestimate the continuity of culture. Individuals are formed early in their lives by the cultures into which they are born. So, too, is a people. The seeds of whatever Jews are today were planted in us at the very birth of the Jewish people . . . . In sum, when the Jews were formed as a people, they acquired (or already had) certain characteristics that have persisted over time. Despite all the differences, the similarities and elements dating back to or deriving from those original conditions have had an amazing persistence.[8]

The modern *secular* State of Israel may be somewhat of a novum in Jewish political history, but the political culture animating it has roots deep in the past. Regarding "oppositionism" specifically, the cultural manifestations within Israeli society may be even more variegated than in the past, with some new wrinkles thrown in for good measure, as we shall see shortly.[9]

Polling on this question of national-cultural continuity has found consistently strong self-identification with Jewishness among the Israeli (Jewish) population. In a 1974 poll, Israeli eleventh-graders were asked: "In your opinion, is the State of Israel a continuation of Jewish history?" Fully 85% answered "yes, of all periods," while another 11% responded "yes, only of the period when Jews lived there." Only 4% felt that "no, it has opened a new page of history."[10] Around the same time, a survey of Israeli adults found that only 6% of the population felt that there was no connection whatsoever between Israel and Judaism, while a further 18% did not think that the state should live in accordance with Jewish tradition. On the other hand, 11% felt that there should be complete accord between (Jewish) religion and state, while fully 65% saw the necessity of Israel continuing to have a Jewish essence, albeit not necessarily based on strict religious practice.[11]

Much more recently, a similar type poll asked the following question: "There are those who see themselves as more Jewish than Israeli and others who see themselves as more Israeli than Jewish. How do you view yourself?" The results show no change at all from the previous decade: 34% "see myself first as Jewish and only then as Israeli"; 28% "first as Israeli and only then as Jewish"; 27% "Jewish and Israeli in the same measure"; 4% "only as Israeli"; and 3% "only as Jewish" (4% had no opinion). In short, a sizable majority view their Jewishness as important, with only an extremely small minority disregarding their Jewish national-cultural identity entirely.[12] Whether or not a significant cultural continuity from the Jewish past actually exists in Israel, there is little doubt that the Israelis themselves believe in such a general connection. But even if they didn't (especially regarding the more specific question of protest),[13] we are about to see that there is little doubt as to the existence of such an "oppositionist" cultural proclivity in Israeli society in any case.

The idea of a "tradition of conflict," of course, is not altogether new in the general theoretical literature. As Eckstein notes in his review essay on the factors underlying conflict in general and protest specifically, there seems to be some evidence that conflict in the past leads to higher levels of conflict in the future. This is mostly a result of the establishment and reinforcement of a political culture which, if not justifying and encouraging such activity, at least views it in a "normal" light.[14]

However, we must note that in most cases this historical learning and/or imitation process is relevant only to the most intense forms of conflict, i.e., those involving high levels of violent behavior. The cultural factor has been found to be (if at all) significant when dealing only with such types of "extraparliamentarism" as revolution, civil war, and the like. As one of the handful of researchers on this topic concludes: "the 'culture of violence' hypothesis is inadequate vis-a-vis the Collective Protest dimension of violence. High Protest in the recent past does not increase the likelihood of [H]igh Protest in the current period. But this is not the case in the Internal War equation, where lagged Internal War is estimated ... to have a substantial impact."[15]

Insofar as Israel is concerned, there is not much reason to search out a "culture of violence," as socially violent behavior in general, and politically violent activity specifically, does not exist on a high level there compared with most other countries.[16] The question to be addressed in the present chapter is the existence (and extent) of a norm in Israeli society which justifies and/or encourages two things on which political extraparliamentarism may feed: complaining against and circumvention of the formal system--whether social, economic, political, or general.

If such a contemporary proclivity exists, it is not necessarily exclusively historically based (pre-State in origin), although as was suggested above Jewish history most certainly had, and continues to have, a significant effect.[17] Nevertheless, it is possible to point to a few additional post- State factors which further reinforced this specific Jewish *weltanschauung*.

For one, paradoxically enough the very importance of the Zionist enterprise (especially the problem of fashioning and safeguarding the State after its establishment) may have been cause for internal conflict. As Coser argues: "in relationships in which the participants are deeply involved, in which they are engaged with their total personality rather than with only a segment of it, there will probably arise feelings of both love and hatred, both attraction and hostility."[18]

Second, while Jews from the Arab world constituted approximately 15% of the pre-State *yishuv*, the overwhelmingly dominant culture among the Zionist pioneers was Central and Eastern European. With the mass immigration of Jews from the Levant after the State's establishment, and with their far higher birthrates, a situation of demographic parity was eventually achieved, with a strong push for greater Levantine cultural as well as political expression on the national level--with much potential for points of conflict, which did indeed erupt from time to time in the seventies and eighties especially. Here it was precisely the population group with the most authoritarian/obedience-oriented politico-cultural baggage (having come from countries with no semblance of a democratic system) which "socialized itself"[19] into the "culture of oppositionism."[20]

Third, as long as the Jewish leadership in the yishuv (under the British Mandate) did not have ultimate sovereign decision-making powers, a number of central issues did not have to be dealt with. Once the State of Israel came into being, such issues could no longer be avoided. Chief among them, of course, was the problem of "religion and state"--to what extent would official public behavior and policy be grounded in Jewish religion? As we saw above, significant differences of public opinion have existed from the start, not only from a macro-philosophical perspective, but especially regarding those specific policy points on the border between religious dominance and democratic freedom (Sabbath, religious education, etc.). Once again, here we find the more "authoritarian-oriented" Israelis (the religious Jews) who had to fight for their rights (as they perceived them), pushing them in a direction of political (or at least extraparliamentary) oppositionism which may have been against their "normal nature."

In sum, not only the appearance of certain new objective conditions but even the very establishment of the State further reinforced the Israeli Jewish population's traditional "culture of oppositionism." However, as we shall see, its manifestations do not appear only in extraparliamentary activity. The entire social structure is imbued with such antiauthority behavior and attitudes.

High Political Interest, Low Political Tolerance

At first glance, the Israeli public seems to have a dual attitude to its democratic political system. On the one hand, there is a very high level of interest in all things political; on the other, there exists fairly widespread skepticism as to the worth of Israel's democratic institutions, and a large measure of intolerance to opposing ideas and beliefs. In political-culture terms, there seems to be a strong democratic norm regarding political participation but a weak democratic norm regarding political toleration–a perfect recipe for protest.

From a participation standpoint, voting percentages in national elections hover around the 80% mark.[21] More informally, various polls highlight the intense interest which Israelis display toward public issues. A 1969 study, for instance, found that 67% were "very" or "somewhat interested" in social issues, 69% in economic topics, and 87% in security/foreign relations subjects. Moreover, 65%, 63%, and 85% of the respondents discussed such issues "frequently" or "from time time."[22] In 1970 it was found that 77% of the adult population read a newspaper every day (up from 63% in 1960), while 86% read at least one daily newspaper on occasion.[23] A more recent study put matters into a comparative perspective: "we found . . . that 57% of the Israelis talk about politics every day or once a week, compared with only 33% of the Americans. On political information questions, an average of 87% among the Israelis knew the right answer, compared to 53% among the Americans."[24] In short, Israelis are cognitively and verbally very much involved in their politics.

Their attitudinal relationship to groups with which they don't agree is another matter. In a sophisticated analysis of political intolerance, Shamir and Sullivan found that whereas 21% of Americans are "strongly intolerant" (of groups with which they seriously disagree), the comparative number in Israel is 32%. And while such American intolerance is diffuse (projected against many targets), in Israel it is far more focused (mostly against groups on the left).[25] A similar exclusively Israeli study quite recently discovered much the same thing, with the entire population (on average) exhibiting "moderate intolerance."[26]

Indeed, so problematic had the intolerance phenomenon become that we find a nonpolitical organization being set up for the specific purpose of fighting intolerance. In 1982, *Sovlanut* ("tolerance") was established as a result of the (perceived) rising tide of political violence in Israel--with such luminaries on its board as a former president of Israel, Supreme Court justice, mayor of a large town, etc. As Yeshai Almog, the organization's director, noted of the Israeli political scene: "We tend to see everything in black and white. Whoever is not for me is certainly against me. This even leads to the feeling that whoever doesn't support the government is an enemy of the state . . . ."[27]

One might think that the latter point would tend to dampen actual public criticism and protest, but the former two attitudes are too strong. As every policy of every party is viewed by the supporters of others as being wrong, if not satanic in intent,[28] the charges of "political treason" only tend to reinforce the initial perception--leading to further criticism. "There is no room for the neutral or for the careful analysis," Almog concludes. In short, owing to the very nature of the Israeli as a highly political animal, as well as the ideological and attitudinal divide separating citizen from citizen, protest is an almost inevitable result of the general Israeli political culture environment.[29]

Israeli Nonformalism and Illegalism

Attitudinal and political demonification, however, by themselves do not necessarily lead to extraparliamentary behavior. Theoretically, one could hold such attitudes and express them through the formal system of politics. Indeed, there is no dearth of examples of such mudslinging, accusing, satanizing, etc., within the halls of the Knesset itself.[30] What does lead to extraparliamentarism on the part of the public is a more general political-cultural approach of bypassing and/or undercutting the formal institutions in whatever sphere.

One of Israel's more prolific political scientists, who also serves as a member of Knesset, perhaps put it best:

> There is great similarity between the behavior of the policymakers and the behavior of a large part of the public, from the standpoint of accepting the legitimacy of "flexibility." Both of them do not attach great importance to sticking to the formal rules of the game . . . . Perhaps this is the reason that there is a measure of legitimacy for deviance. Finicky "letter of the law" types, who are utterly attached to the traditional framework and to the formal rules of the game, not only don't succeed in government but are considered by many to have failed because of their "inflexibility."
> It is hard to determine the source for this ambivalence vis-a-vis the governmental institutions. On the one hand, one finds active utilization of the opportunities which these institutions provide . . . and on the other hand, systematic circumvention by all parties involved. This is conscious dissonance between the structural and the functional. *In great measure this quasi-anarchic approach has traditional roots, but it is also novel in its own right.*[31]

Having spent centuries in constant efforts to outsmart the Gentile authorities and the alien system in which they lived in the Diaspora, the Jews' *"yiddische kopf"* (Jewish cleverness) mentality continues apace within their own institutional framework--with some new manifestations in light of the different context. At times such behavior is merely amorally functional; in other cases it is downright illegal.

One of the most widespread examples of the former is the existence and broad extent of *proteksia*--circumventing the formal requirements of statutory law and/or bureaucratic procedure through the utilization of "connections" with which one is personally familiar. In a study of the phenomenon in Israel, Danet found an interesting disparity between the public's perception of the legitimacy of *proteksia* and their actual use of it.[32] When polled, only 29% of the public thought that it was "sometimes [or] almost always OK" to use *proteksia*. However, when queried as to whether they had actually used *proteksia* during the preceding year, 20% answered in the affirmative. Given that many, perhaps most, citizens had not had any need for special, "unusual" requests over the previous twelve months, this latter percentage is far higher than it appears. This only further reinforces the conclusion that while Israelis feel themselves to be law-abiding, when need be there is little hesitation to bypass the formal rules of the game.

As a result, near-anarchy existed within the Israeli bureaucracy for over two decades. In an attempt to more adequately serve the public and mitigate the need for such circumvention, the Knesset passed into law in 1971 an amendment to the State Comptroller statute which added a further responsibility to that august office: public ombudsman, i.e., the address for public complaints against bureaucratic high-handedness and unfair treatment. His comments in the first annual report shed additional light on the Israeli culture of "protest," albeit in this specific case admittedly through the most formal of means:

> What has characterized the complaints, from the time the Office of Ombudsman began working, is the large number arriving from every part of the country and from all segments of the public as well as the variety of the subjects . . . . *The Israeli ombudsman receives a larger number of complaints than his counterparts overseas, not only proportional to the size of the population but even in absolute numbers.*[33]

Thus, extraparliamentary protest is not the only thing in which Israelis lead the world; in formal, bureaucratic protest they are in the forefront as well. While no direct comparisons can be made between these two somewhat different types of public complaining, there seems to be little doubt that they both in part stem from the same culturally based mentality.

Another "recognized" form of public expression of discontent, this time economic, is through work stoppage, i.e., the strike. Here Israel is not in the very forefront, but does rank among the world leaders. A cross-comparative study conducted over the years 1960-1969 found that among the sixteen nations tested for, Israel ranked fourth in number of salaried employees (per 100,000) who went on strike.[34] Significantly, and quite in line with our protest data, when it came to the intensity of such strike activity Israel ranked near the bottom (in twelfth place).[35]

Perhaps even more significant, and disturbing, is a related phenomenon which has come to be called (in Israel) "illegalism." Sprinzak has devoted a short book to this phenomenon, highlighting the general (anti-)norm from a number of perspectives. His definition: "An orientation which does not view obedience to the law or the idea of rule of law as a fundamental value, but rather as a form of behavior according to which one behaves, or doesn't behave, depending on criteria of utility."[36]

In his view, the phenomenon in Israel can be seen on four planes: (a) the ideological, whereby parliamentary democracy is not necessarily denied, but justifications are brought forth for disobeying or disregarding specific laws based on a "higher law" or a more just cause;[37] (b) illegal extraparliamentary activity, systematically undercutting the law in an inexorable progression toward violent and even terrorist activity (e.g. the "Jewish Underground" of the mid-eighties, against Palestinian Arabs; see his chapter 8); (c) personal corruption on the part of public officials (numerous major scandals in the seventies and eighties; his chapter 7); (d) extended political patronage, i.e., an entrenched system of party and personal favoritism--a sort of super-proteksia infiltrating virtually every corner of Israeli society (his chapter 6).

What is important to note here is that there seems to be a significant difference between Israeli "illegal" public and private behavior, for while "illegalism" seems to have become so rampant in the public domain as to almost have turned into an accepted, if not acceptable, norm, Israeli social behavior in private life is still quite law-abiding by international standards.[38]

Of course, it is not always easy to clearly demarcate the line between public and private illegalism. Two interesting and further illustrative examples (not touched upon by Sprinzak) of Israelis' penchant for systemic circumvention bordering both spheres are the "Black Market" and the "Black Economy." The former is a relatively mild sort of illegalism having a clear quasi-public sanction. As a result of strict foreign currency restrictions, a flourishing market of "black dollars" has existed in Israel for decades, known to the police authorities who have almost never done anything to stop it. So widespread and accepted has it become that the daily newspapers actually report the going "black market" rate for the dollar along with the other official, legal rate!

More insidious is the underground economy, i.e., market activity on which no income is declared or taxes paid. Official statistics are obviously nonexistent, and even serious academic attempts at measuring the phenomenon around the world are to be considered general estimates at best (as the authors themselves admit). Nevertheless, here too Israel ranks in the upper echelons. One recent study placed Israel tied for fifth among twenty nations, with its underground economy constituting some 10-15% of GNP.[39] Using a somewhat different methodology, another study found that by 1977 Israel's black economy was 15% of GNP as compared to the approximate averages of 3.5% for England, 3.6% for Sweden (with even higher tax rates than Israel!), 4-10% in the U.S. (most estimates), and 15% for Belgium.[40]

In sum, when it comes to behavior in the public domain Israelis seem to take almost perverse pleasure in either "beating the system" or "bashing the system"-- whether it be in the political, social, and/or economic spheres of life. One could add to the above examples others just as widely known and "accepted"--pushing to get to the front of the line; massive networks of "pirate" cable television (many of whose subscribers are reportedly policemen and other public officials); quasi-institutionalized "black medicine" (i.e., paying doctors privately to move up one's operation date in public hospitals); "grey education," whereby private lessons (after regular class hours) are given by public school teachers *within the school premises*; etc., etc., almost *ad infinitum* and certainly *ad absurdum*. To be sure, each and every single example by itself proves nothing. The large number and wide-ranging characteristics of these "circumvention" and "complaint" phenomena, however, clearly indicate the existence of a deep-rooted "public culture" of a decidedly antisystem nature. Just how this is expressed in terms of a "political protest culture" we shall now see.

The Political Culture of Israeli Extraparliamentarism

From the standpoint of the Israeli public's attitude to its rulers, we can broadly divide Israel's short history into two distinct periods: pre-1967 and post-1973, with the intervening period marking the changeover. Before the conquest of the administered territories in 1967 and the subsequent breakdown of national consensus on the critical issues of security and defense, little significant criticism against the authorities in general was to be heard. True, as we saw in chapter 3, the very early years were marked by raucous protest on the part of the newcomers over socio-economic problems, but this was the exception that proved the general rule. Indeed, so powerful was this sense of keeping criticism to a minimum that anyone today reading the Israeli newspapers of the fifties would find it hard to believe that it is the same press which has fired away at will from 1973 onwards.

The Yom Kippur War of that year, and the revelations as to the government's unpreparedness, broke the camel's back. To be sure, an eruption of protest had already occurred in 1971 over (once again) socio-economic issues. But with the newfound evidence of serious political/security mistakes, the dam burst open-- eventually ushering in the period of huge protest waves along all issue fronts.

Why the digression here regarding this historical political revolution, in the context of a discussion of Israeli *culture*? Because of an interesting anomaly in the meager attitudinal data which we have on the subject of protest culture. In the only question of its kind to be asked during *thirty* years of intensive Israeli polling, a 1950 survey queried a representative sample of the adult population (N = 2369) with the following: "Do you think that demonstrations on the part of unemployed people are justified?" An astounding 56% answered in the *negative*, while only 37% responded in the affirmative (the rest did not answer).[41] And this at a time when Socialist ideology was at its zenith within Israeli society, while unemployment was quite a serious social problem!

Our 1981 poll asked the exact same question, and this time the numbers were more than reversed: 61.4% answering "justified" while 34.1% replied "unjustified." What accounts for the dramatic shift? To begin with, the security (and overall national) situation had dramatically improved, thereby removing a strong psychological impediment to protest. Probably more important is the fact that although the Israeli-Jewish mindset was already culturally prepared for protest from the start, it took actual significant protest activity among a few peer groups to set it off--both attitudinally and practically. In other words, while the Jewish historical culture of oppositionism formed the underlying basis of Israeli protest in the seventies and eighties (it existed, albeit dormant, before then), such a cultural inclination became conscious under the impact of protest in the field. In answer to the old chicken and egg problem, in Israel the culture of protest preceded the act of protest, but it was the act of protest which enabled the culture of protest to emerge full-blown.

This can be seen indirectly in some relevant attitudinal data which we have from 1972 (once again, unfortunately, no results previous to this period are available, excluding the one above-mentioned 1950 survey): by then, already 67% of the population felt that it was "very important or important to criticize the government when its actions are unjust."[42] When another poll that year asked underprivileged respondents their opinion regarding the Black Panthers, 59% felt that their demands were at least partly justified, but only 23% considered their (occasionally violent) tactics to be justified. We have, then, some indication here that a "culture of protest" is emerging but it is not yet at this historical stage fully mature.

By 1981 it can be seen in full regalia. When asked whether they justified a number of extraparliamentary activities, 76.1% responded in the affirmative to "nonviolent, licensed demonstrations" (among them 21.8% justified nonviolent, *unlicensed* demonstrations too; see Appendix B, question #1). How does this compare with other democracies? In their five-nation survey, Barnes and Kaase (et al.) found the "approval" rate of "lawful demonstrations" to be the following: the Netherlands, 80%; the U.S., 73%; Britain, 65%; Germany, 62%; Austria, 58%.[43] Israel, then, places second among this august group of contemporary democracies in its citizens' attitudinal perception of the place of extraparliamentarism within the body politic-- quite a long way from its initial reaction to public protest in 1950.

Another question, designed to measure the level of democratic sophistication regarding the protest phenomenon, was included in our poll: "In your opinion, do nonviolent public protests strengthen or weaken Israeli democracy?" A comparison between the results of the first two choices is the key to this question from an Israeli perspective:

Strengthen 42.5%
Weaken 13.7%
Strengthen and weaken 11.2%
Don't strengthen/don't weaken 29.2%
No answer 3.4%

Fully three times as many Israelis see public protest as a positive addition to the country's political system as view it in a negative light. Thus, a significant minority of the population do far more than justify such activity from a democratic philosophical perspective; they see it as a wholesome practical contribution to the citizenry's political repertoire and/or the system's ability to function democratically.

When one adds to this large minority opinion (42.5%) the fourth group which sees no harm whatsoever emanating from protest (29.2%), it emerges that fully 71.7% of adult Jewish Israelis see no utilitarian (not to mention moral-philosophical) reason to oppose extraparliamentary activity. And if one considers the third group of respondents (11.2%) as also viewing the bottom- line implications of protest as neutral, we are left with quite a small segment of Israeli society which sees significant harm in the general phenomenon.

In conclusion, then, while the actual number of protest participants in Israel is low (but still leading the world, as we saw in chapter 4) compared to those merely justifying protest, these extraparliamentary activists are today working in a political-cultural environment of broad public support and, to a somewhat lesser (but still significant) extent, public encouragement. Given all that we have seen regarding the Israeli penchant for complaining and circumvention--not to mention the forceful weight of historical Jewish activity and culture in this respect--it is hardly surprising, then, that Israeli public protest has taken on the large dimension which it has.

PART IV:

The Structural Bases of Israeli Protest

Despite the wide-ranging analysis of the many factors underlying protest (in Part III), our understanding of the causes behind the phenomenon in Israel is still not complete. We turn in this section of the book to another important area which, as political culture, also does not lend itself to precise statistical quantification: systemic dysfunction of Israel's polity, especially regarding political communication. This, however, is a more "concrete" element which at least lends itself to some indirect empirical analysis.

Chapter 7 surveys the history and causes behind systemic political decay in Israel, and provides the theoretical underpinning for the connection to public protest. Chapter 8 then goes on to show in somewhat roundabout fashion--but from a number of different perspectives, using some of the same protest data brought forth in Part II-- how such protest does indeed stem from Israel's political communication breakdown.

Chapter 7

Bottle-Necked System: Israeli Political Blockage and Decay

If Israeli Jews are culturally inclined to argue, complain, and otherwise stand up to authority, why need we go further and seek out additional factors which may be at play? Because such a cultural tendency by itself does not explain why Israelis gravitate to the specific mode of extraparliamentary protest. Indeed, as we saw in the case of personal problems with the bureaucratic apparatus, when Israelis are offered an institutionalized and orderly means of registering disapproval (e.g., the ombudsman), they will eagerly use such an "official" approach. The Israelis' proclivity to circumvent the system, then, is not necessarily their preferred modus operandi, but results (at least in part) from a lack of other systemic alternatives.

In a democracy, of course, such formal alternative approaches exist--at least theoretically. The election system is usually the major channel for registering "protest" or other kinds of political messages to the authorities. Israel's unique system of national proportional representation, though, does not afford the public the opportunity to elect specific candidates; rather, one votes (without possibility of deletions or additions) for a straight party list which represents the country as a whole, and not any single district or region. Indeed, even the nominations process is far removed from the electorate as the central party apparatus (in almost all cases) decides on its party nominees. In short, Israel's members of Knesset are beholden to the party leadership and hardly at all to their erstwhile voters. As a result, "[t]hose who are elected to the Knesset frequently do not know who their voters are, and the voters do not know whom they have elected."[1]

Even if this were not the case, it is generally recognized that voting once every few years does not afford enough of an opportunity for political communication in an advanced society with a relatively high participatory political culture. This is certainly true of Israel where, as we have already seen, the civic level of political knowledge and interest is quite high. For a polity to function well, to allow for citizens' political input on a regular basis, other channels of political communication must be developed or at least be inherent in the system itself. That such is not the case, indeed that the situation has been getting steadily worse over time in Israel, will be shown in this chapter.

Beforehand, a few words are in order from a theoretical perspective. Surprising as it may sound, in the vast literature of protest and turmoil there is extremely little which has been done or written regarding "blocked political communication" as a dominant factor stimulating or underlying extraparliamentary activity. As Eckstein notes in his wide-ranging review essay: "The matter of alternative channels would seem immediately vital for anyone who considers all collective actions a set, or repertoire, of equivalent events. However, astonishingly little has been done with the subject . . . [which] cries for far more investigation by all inquirers into our subject."[2]

The reason for this is most probably methodological in nature: there are no easily quantifiable ways of measuring such systemic blockage. Given that most cross-comparative studies in this general area are based on readily accessible data, the "blocked polity" theory cannot be added to the statistical pot of other theories which are based on objective facts and phenomena.[3]

This is not to say that no theoretical foundation exists upon which to draw. Huntington's seminal work *Political Order in Changing Societies*[4] constitutes a good starting point, although his discussion is not starting point, although his discussion in not about protest per se. In analyzing the reasons for political conflict and instability, Huntington posits (among other "laws") the following:

> The stability of any given polity depends upon the relationship between the level of political participation and the level of political institutionalization . . . . As political participation increases, the complexity, autonomy, adaptability, and coherence of the society's political institutions must also increase if political stability is to be maintained.
> [P]olitical participation becomes the road for advancement of the socially mobilized individual. Social frustration leads to demands on the government and the expansion of political participation to enforce those demands. The political backwardness of the country in terms of political institutionalization . . . makes it difficult if not impossible for the demands upon the government to be expressed through legitimate channels and to be moderated and aggregated within the political system.[5]

Here, then, is a theory which sees a direct connection between the inability of the political system to absorb political messages from the public (low institutionalization; high participation) and political instability. But it is very important to note that Huntington seems to view the chronology or development of such an imbalance in only one direction. In other words, in his view the problem results from either institutionalization or participation progressing at a faster (or slower) rate than its partner. This is what he defines as "political decay" as is usually found in developing societies.

However, as Pirages notes, "Huntington does not apply his analysis to more highly developed countries, but it would seem possible that political decay can take place in industrialized societies as well."[6] In other words, there exists a possibility which is logically *more* probable from a long-term historical perspective but is, in fact, relatively rare among modern democracies: countries which at some stage of development reach relatively complete political institutionalization as well as high levels of participation, and then begin to *regress* in at least one of these two spheres of political life. Weimar Germany, France's Fourth Republic, and contemporary Italy are some possible examples of such regression--especially with regard to the increasing inefficiency of their political-institutional frameworks. To these may be added Israel.

We have here, then, a somewhat special case--something akin to a corollary of Huntington's law--of "political decay."[7] Theoretically, there need not be that much difference in the outcome of such a decoupling of the two political planes, for if an imbalance exists why should the instability be dependent on the direction from which either of the two planes (d)evolved? It need not, although in Israel the "instability" has been expressed heretofore in relatively low-level extraparliamentary protest, and not in the more destabilizing forms of coup d'etat, insurrection, and/or revolution. In any event, the present chapter should serve the additional purpose of providing a start for investigating the utility of Huntington's thesis for developed polities moving in the "reverse" direction.

That Israel is indeed moving backwards from an institutional perspective (on the national plane; see chapter 8 regarding Israeli local politics) has been noted by other students of its political system. Eisenstadt speaks of "petrification" of the elite leadership while Shapira analyzes the lack of elite generational continuity; Medding noted the "increasing tendency towards the formalisation, bureaucratization and centralisation of political, social and economic activities" after 1948;[8] while from a purely political-institutional perspective Weiss (already in 1974, and still valid today) summed it up best:

> Virtually all the central government institutions retained their basic structures [after 1948]. The Knesset remained at the 120 member level despite a tripling of the voter population [today quintupling; S.L-W] .... The basic structure of the court system didn't change .... One can say the same about the religious courts .... The institution of the Prime Minister hasn't surrounded itself with advisory and liaison bodies .... His office doesn't coordinate interministerial activities .... The institution of the Presidency hasn't changed at all ....[9]

It may seem somewhat strange that as "young" a country as Israel should be suffering from political-institutional arteriosclerosis, especially when one considers that it doesn't even have a constitution which might tend to stultify institutional development. However, the Israeli polity is quite a bit older than the State itself. While 1948 marks the official year of sovereign independence, institutional autonomy already existed from the early 1920s and (in some respects) even before then.[10] Still, seventy years is not exactly old age for a polity; the more fundamental reasons for such ossification lie elsewhere.

Before we turn to an examination of these causes, however, one very important point must be noted. Not all theorists would agree that a certain amount of blockage within the political system is necessarily a bad thing. Kornhauser, in his trenchant analysis of "mass society," describes the possible deleterious effects of too open a political system: at best, mass pressure causes the political leadership to make unwise policy; at worst, the leadership itself emerges from the incompetent masses. A system which blocks a certain amount and specific types of political input paradoxically may actually serve to preserve freedom specifically and the democratic system in general![11]

Almond and Verba make somewhat the same point albeit from a different perspective. In their typology of "political culture" the authors conclude that the ideal form is not the "subject culture" whereby the citizen passively accepts the dictates of government, but neither is it the "participant culture" through which the citizen is moved to express relatively frequently personal wishes, opinions, and demands to the elected leadership. Rather, the "civic culture"--a combination of the two--is most preferred: normal passivity coupled with civic action when the situation is exceptional.[12] The reason is that the former allows for no input into the system which eventually must suffer from lack of renewal and adaptation to challenges, while the latter becomes equally paralyzed as a result of *too much* input, either through information overload or overly numerous cross-purpose pressures.[13]

Given what we have seen about the high level of interest and participation among the Israeli public, one could theoretically make the argument that any political blockage is probably conscious (on the part of the authorities) and certainly salutary for the continued functioning of Israeli democracy. However, as we shall see, neither is the case. On the one hand, the petrification of the system was (and continues to be) mostly a matter of inertia and personal self-interest, and certainly was not due to any worry about systemic overload.[14] Indeed, the signs of, and trends toward, ossification in Israel commenced well before any problem of information overload could have existed. On the other hand, by almost all accounts[15] the functioning of the Israeli polity is seriously flawed, with a greater danger emanating from blocked communication than information overload.

Political Party Atrophy in a Changing Society

Among the sundry political institutions in any modern polity whose function is to deliver "input" into the system from the citizenry, perhaps the most important is the political party. As Kaase notes, political parties in democracies are the "core mediating element between the governors and the governed."[16] It is hard for someone outside of Israel, however, to comprehend just how pervasive and central the party, as an institution, is in that country. Indeed, Israel has rightfully been called a *parteienstaat*[17]--a social, economic, and political system of the parties, by the parties, and for the parties. While a certain decline in their overweening predominance has occurred over time, Israel's parties still constitute the focus and fulcrum of the entire national framework. It is for this reason that we shall concentrate on the ossification and degeneration of the parties as channels of political communication in general, and the traditionally dominant Labor camp (*Mapai*) specifically, in our analysis of the last central underlying cause for Israeli public protest.

Already during the *yishuv* period,[18] the political parties functioned as far more than mere electoral mobilizing agents. As Medding points out, "party control also applied to employment, housing, health services, trade unionism, and in general to the provision of most of the significant instrumental needs and demands of the new immigrants,"[19] who constituted the vast majority of Israelis at least until the late fifties. In such a situation it is not surprising that party membership was quite high, e.g., a ratio of one card-carrying *Mapai* (Labor) member for every three citizens who voted for that party.[20]

Membership numbers by themselves are not the whole story. What marked the political and party system in the yishuv period especially was the *openness* to input and feedback between leaders and led. Indeed, to a certain extent even "the boundary between elite and non-elite, rulers and ruled, became blurred as well."[21] In the specific case of *Mapai*: "As a democratic socialist party it emphasized the individual participation of members in policy discussion and policy decision," Medding notes, adding, though, that "[i]t is therefore somewhat surprising that a party cast and moulded in this tradition should develop structures that we have defined as political machines."[22]

But such a development was not limited to *Mapai*. Already in the late sixties Eisenstadt noted that "the major test . . . is in the degree of new vision, new routes for leadership development, and new forms and systems in most of the parties," which until the late fifties had been doing fine along those lines. "But from then on there are numerous signs that this ability has become progressively weaker," he concluded.[23]

What happened along the way, especially sometime after the establishment of the State of Israel?[24] What accounted for the steady ossification of the party over time? There were a number of factors at work here, which we can divide into two general categories: trends and phenomena "external" to the political parties, and developments within the internal organizational structure and relating to the processes of the parties themselves.

EXTERNAL FACTORS: (A) *Statism*--Almost immediately after the State was established, Israel's first prime minister, David Ben-Gurion, inaugurated a policy of *mamlakhtiut*: the transfer of functions from the partisan political parties to the central governing authorities and their several institutions.[25] In a number of spheres this was, of course, necessary, e.g., security and defense (there were at least three party-based militias in the *yishuv* which were not enthusiastic about giving up their organizational autonomy entirely) and education (several party-oriented school systems existed at the time).

Nevertheless, such a Statist policy--especially when carried to systemic extremes-- was completely at variance with the Jewish political heritage which was based on "a system of dispersed decision-making with different tasks assigned to different bodies."[26] Thus, *mamlakhtiut* constituted a double problem. On the one hand, it attempted to foist on the Israeli public a relatively imposing and artificial political construct instead of the paternal communal/corporate party within which each member could feel at home, and (as befits any member of the family) was able to communicate relatively freely. On the other, by stripping the parties of many of their former functions the State would naturally draw away from those bodies many members who could now see no instrumental reason for continuing to pay dues, etc. In the end, of course, such a move was a mistake from the political-communication standpoint as each citizen was now up against a distanced Big Brother (the government) instead of the familial and more familiar paternalistic pseudo-father (the party) who had provided for most previous needs.[27]

(B) *Periphery*--One of the clearest examples of the State's predominant control of life in Israel is the policy of land settlement. Unlike in the American West where individuals moved and settled on their own initiative, from the start of the post-State period[28] it was the Israeli government and subsidiary organizations which directed and channeled settlement (for positive reasons of population dispersal and security) in the direction they wished to see it go.

Unfortunately, the vast majority of those resettled were the relatively poor *Edot Ha'mizrakh* new immigrants, who were asked to pioneer in establishing "development towns." Whether this was a wise choice from an economic or social perspective is beside the point here; what does matter for our purposes is that through this process a territorial/economic/ethnic "periphery" developed over time--easily controlled politically by the government while physically divorced from the party power centers in the older urban (or kibbutz/moshav) areas.

Thus, as Sheffer remarks: "With the benefit of hindsight, one can now see that these trends . . . eroded both the government's and the political parties' ties with the grassroots and led to the center's loss of direct contact with the periphery."[29] In other words, it was precisely those most in need of communicating with the political system who were least able to do so because of the lack of physical closeness to the party core, an inability which was to cost the parties dearly in lost membership over the ensuing decades.

(C) *Voluntarism*--There was another by-product of *mamlakhtiut*: the decline of a spirit of voluntarism which had marked the pre-State period. If the State now declares itself responsible for guaranteeing the basic needs of its charges, there is little felt need for voluntary organizations to duplicate what tax money is already providing. To be sure, such a decline is almost inevitable in any situation of nation-formation, but in the Israeli case the policy of government paternalism certainly added force to such a withering of voluntarism.

Indeed, at work here was perhaps less a passive decline than active discouragement by the powers-that-be. And not only on the part of government officials but by the party power brokers as well: "For different reasons, neither the political elite nor the bureaucracy encouraged the revival of old, or the emergence of new, local voluntary associations in response to local needs . . . . [T]he spirit of voluntarism that had characterized the Jewish community in Palestine almost disappeared during the 1950s and 1960s."[30] The bureaucracy quite "naturally" viewed any such movement as an impingement on its newfound sphere of authority; the politicians and parties viewed any such development with great wariness as a possible independent threat to whatever party power and authority they still retained.

As a result, when voluntary interest-group activity did finally emerge in the seventies it was to be found in the "curious" guise of extraparliamentary behavior. The Black Panthers, the Young Couples, the *Shinui* and *Gush Emunim* protest movements were all grassroots groups which could not find their place within the Establishment-- whether governmental or political party. Realizing their earlier mistake, many of Israel's parties made strong attempts to woo these autonomous movements back into the party fold, with not much success. Once again, the political parties' shortsighted and narrow-interest policy in the early post-State years ended up turning away precisely those potential party activists who constituted the new blood which the parties were eventually so desperately to seek.

(D) *Ideology*--One of the distinguishing characteristics of Israeli politics (perhaps to the greatest extent even before the State's establishment) was its intensive ideological belief system. Given that Zionism stood not only for the setting up of a state, but for a state with a specific purpose, even mission, it is not surprising that ideology should have played such a central role in its politics. As a result of their strongly held ideological belief, party leaders viewed the role of their organization as much more than mere mobilization of electoral support. Rather, a critical function was ideological education: the molding of the thought pattern and lifestyle of the public along the "desired" lines.[31] With missionary zeal, then, the parties went about the task of mobilizing as many adherents to the cause as they could--a task made all the easier by the public's enthusiasm for joining in the great Zionist project of building the State in each citizen's respective ideological image.

Over time, however, ideological fervor began to wane among the public at large.[32] Such a trend had an impact as well on the amount and type of members who were mobilized by, or who voluntarily joined, the party in the later post-State period. The traditional party leadership, still hewing to an ideological line, was not interested in "nonbelievers," but found it increasingly difficult to socialize such ideological agnostics into the true path. Rather than dilute the ideological purity of their party (a situation which would also ultimately threaten their personal status and power within the party), such leaders restricted (or at least did not actively seek) new members of questionable ideological pedigree. Once more, party renewal was blunted.

INTERNAL FACTORS: (A) *Party Size*--While we have already hinted at a general decline in party membership over the past few decades (more on which in a short while), one must realize that simultaneously there may be an increase in the *absolute* number of members and a percentage decrease in their *proportion* relative to the general population. This is especially possible in a situation of a sharp population rise, as was the case in post-1948 Israel.

Unfortunately, from an internal communications standpoint size can be said to be a natural, negative factor. Medding illustrates this point well regarding Israel's dominant party:

> After 1948 Mapai's local branch organization found it easier to attract members than to give them a sense of participation in party affairs. This situation contrasted markedly with conditions between 1930 and 1948. Prior to 1948 the party developed a highly participant ethos in theory, and a marked sense of participation in practice, facilitated by its small size . . . . With the establishment of the state this situation altered appreciably . . . . The numerical increase . . . destroyed much of the sense of intimacy and personal contact with leaders that had characterised the party previously. Party leaders were often too busy to concern themselves with the kind of widespread informal contact that they had undertaken before, and what direct contact they did have reached few of the party's 100,000 members. This was particularly true of the party's top leaders who were charged with ministerial and parliamentary responsibilities and with a widely increased domain of decisions.[33]

Thus, by the very nature of the country's demographic enlargement Israel's party leaders and party members found themselves unable to communicate as in the past. For the former, this was not felt to be any major problem as they had "more important" things with which to deal. The latter, however, saddled with a highly participatory party ethos but suddenly finding themselves without the means of its fruition, became disenchanted and slowly left the fold or turned inactive. Instead of developing new organizational means for overcoming this "natural" distancing, Israel's parties let matters go from bad to worse[34]--with serious repercussions over the long term for both themselves and the polity as a whole.

(B) *Bureaucratization*--Concomitant with the growing size of the parties was the equally natural tendency toward establishing a permanent bureaucratic apparatus to maintain the increasingly unwieldy organization. This was especially true given the party leadership's need to focus on extraparty (i.e., governmental) matters. As a result, a layer of "communication intermediaries" began to evolve, further exacerbating the distance between rank and file and the leadership.[35]

Indeed, in the case of *Mapai* such a layer of apparatchiks (the *Gush*) actually compounded the political-communication problem, for they perceived their role as being one-sided and unidirectional: "The *Gush* was quite prepared to leave important matters of policy to Ben-Gurion and the Ministry [the Cabinet], and believed that its task was constantly to give him majority support for what he wanted in order to make it easier for him to govern. Its function, as it saw it, was to keep the party in order and leave the governing to those who knew best."[36]

Nor was this merely a matter of serving as a communications buffer (i.e., "allow the Old Man to rule in peace"). As we shall now see, the *Gush* (and party bureaucrats in many of the other major parties) was a central force in the two other internal factors influencing party petrification in Israel.

(C) *Oligarchy*--Once systemic bureaucratization set in, the "iron law of oligarchy" within the party could not be far behind. And indeed, the party bureaucrats made sure that the procedures for nomination and election of Knesset candidates and party officials would not threaten their standing.

Speaking of virtually all the important parties in Israel, Yanai notes the following, first regarding parliamentary candidates and then regarding party officials:

> Members of Israeli parties participate directly only in the election of delegates for the party convention, and . . . their local district council . . . . The scope and significance of the elections for the party convention have generally been limited by their infrequency, various inhibiting rules and practices, and lack of meaningful competition. Party conventions were held in most parties after irregular and sometimes long intervals and in some cases without any form of election.
>
> Israeli parties selected their permanent bodies without direct participation of party members. In an overwhelming number of cases, these bodies were selected by a nominating committee or its equivalent body . . . . In other words, members of the permanent party bodies were not generally selected by secret ballot in a wider party body, but were nominated by a small group representing the leadership of the inner party.[37]

Among other things, this tends to explain (at least in part) the constant sunderings and subsequent reagglomerations of party factions in Israel, as real opportunities for self-expression and influence on the part of internal party "oppositions" were rare if not nonexistent. One can view this organizational schismatism as a form of internal party protest on the part of the activists; how much more difficult any attempt at political communication to the party (and government) elite on the part of the common citizen who was not an official member of the party structure.[38] In short, not only did the general electoral system prevent direct communication with the country's leaders, but so did the internal party election processes as well.

(D) *The Next Generation*--The party bureaucracy and leadership saw to it not only that no policy "surprises" would occur from the bottom up, but that the party "bottom" would stay put for as long as the party elders remained alive and functioning. Indeed, it is here that we can see the systemic blockage within the party in all its "glory"--with obvious effect on the political system as a whole. Part of the problem may have been the "founding father" nature of the party elders, coupled with the element of ideological intensity mentioned above. As Yanai notes of *all* the major parties:

> Because of their charismatic self-image the veteran leaders had but limited tolerance of demands for leadership circulation and competitive nominating practices . . . . For the party leaders, the party was not a routine institution existing merely to ensure the smooth political functioning of a given democratic society, but rather an extraordinary political organization for the realization of a national and social utopia . . . . [At best] the founders' approach instituted a system of party democracy which may be termed a system of democratic approval in contrast to a system of democratic choice.[39]

Whereas the party founders' high self-regard led them to view the next generation warily, the approach of the party bureaucrats could only be termed antagonistic: "If the Gush was the party then all who were not part of it were some kind of 'foreign invader' to be fought at all costs and against whom all methods might be used to ensure their exclusion."[40]

The battles between the "young guard" and the elders in both Mapai and (twenty years later) in the Likud were vicious. Ben-Gurion (*the* Elder) ultimately left his party to set up a new one (*Rafi*) in part because of the refusal by the *Gush* to let its younger members advance; sometime after Menachem Begin retired, his party's nominating convention broke up in a paroxysm of smashed tables, flying chairs, etc., as a result of the old guard's attempts to stymie the rise of David Levy, the next generation's "heir apparent."[41] Given such examples of old-line recalcitrance, only the most ambitious and patient of potential party activists would continue joining, and working through, the party apparatus. For the vast majority of citizens who did not view the party as a full-time career, there was little reason to join and/or work in this normally critical institution for political communication and influence.

More broadly, as Eisenstadt concluded, "the combination of these sundry trends within the structure of the various public apparatuses, the elite-to-citizen relationships, and the parties' structure . . . --all these have led to very strong tendencies towards general bureaucratization. In other words, palpable feelings of superiority on the part of those within the system toward the citizen."[42] Slowly but surely, the Israeli public found themselves shut out of precisely those channels which were meant to transmit their thoughts, wishes, and demands to the governing elite. The actual results were eventually clear for all to see.

The Decline of Party Membership and Parliamentary Activism

Given this wide-ranging list of factors, it will come as no surprise to find that party membership in Israel has declined dramatically over the past twenty-five years. On the face of it, the situation seemed to be actually improving in the first decade and a half after the State's establishment. For example, *Mapai*'s official membership figures went from 41,000 in 1948 to 196,000 in 1964--an almost fivefold increase![43] However, the real picture was far less sanguine.

To begin with, the country's general population had by then increased more than threefold. Second, "official" party membership tallies are not very reliable, as the party itself conceded on at least one occasion.[44] Third, a very large proportion of the new members were new immigrants who had to take out membership in order to get a job through the party spoils system. Most of these were either apolitical or at best completely at a loss as to the inner workings of their party (and if they did manage to learn, the center/periphery problem came into play).

Fourth, and perhaps most significant, the quality of party membership and activism suffered a real decline from precisely those sectors which had been *Mapai*'s populist core in the past. Medding notes, for instance, "the development among the younger kibbutz members of marked demonstrative apathy towards the party . . . . Thus by the mid-1950s only about 43 percent of kibbutz adults were party members (as compared with over 75 percent in the early 1940s)."[45]

The general party membership situation in Israel in the fifties was quite rosy as well. Guttmann notes that in 1952 the parties reported an overall membership total of 300,000--over 20% of the Jewish population--and this increased to between one- third and one-fourth only three years later.[46] As late as the early sixties, he pointed out, "the incidence of party membership among Jews in Israel is certainly one of the highest in the world. At the time of the 1961 election almost one-third of the eligible voters . . . were party members."[47]

Twenty years later the picture had changed drastically, as a steady decline set in. Arian cites the following figures based on several studies over the years: 1969--18%; 1973--16%; 1977--13%.[48] In our 1981 poll, the respondents were asked: "Are you active in any form in Israeli political or public life?" A mere 3.2% answered "active member of a party," with another 8.2% responding "inactive party member." Put simply, in the space of two decades Israeli parties suffered about a *two-thirds* drop in membership! Even more interesting, more Israelis (3.8%) answered that they were "independently active" (e.g., wrote letters to an MK) than those who were active within a party framework. And when one compares the overall party membership tally with our protest-participant results (21.5%), it turns out that by 1981 two and a half times as many Israelis had gone the extraparliamentary route as compared with all those who were active in any "parliamentary" fashion (Appendix B).[49]

Quantity, of course, is not the only measure. When the Israeli public at large was asked throughout the 1980s its opinion of Israeli parties as important institutions within the polity, the results were bleak to say the least. A 1983 poll found that 55% (!) of the public felt that the parties were not critical to Israeli democracy.[50] Even more recently, when asked to express personal trust in Israel's eleven central social, economic, and political institutions, the political parties came in dead last with a combined 56% expressing "almost no trust" (27.3%) and "no trust" (28.7%).[51]

Indeed, so deep is the public perception of party petrification that even some fairly recent attempts at internal reform and membership "outreach" on the part of the parties do not seem to have changed the subjective situation. While each party has different internal elections procedures, the days of backroom candidate appointments by the party elite are waning.[52] Nevertheless, it will most probably take quite a long time before the citizenry begin to return to the fold and start reusing the parties as a central channel of political communication.

There is, of course, another possibility--the development of other public bodies which could take over the "political communication" functions which the party system once held. The most accepted such substitute is "public-interest (pressure) groups." Recent research in Israel has found that Israeli society does not suffer from a dearth of such mediating organizations. However, as Galnoor suggests, many such groups cannot adequately serve as transmitters of anti-Establishment messages: "On the one hand, a survey of membership in organized bodies would find that [in Israel] we are talking about a highly organized society with a high rate of membership in such bodies . . . . On the other hand, the same survey would find that the number of such independent [from the State's various authorities] organizations . . . is very small."[53]

Such a comprehensive study appeared very recently. Surveying 151 interest groups in the mid-1980s, Yishai discovered some things which relate to our analysis here. While a large number of such organizations were established by their members, usually such founders were also part of the country's political leadership! Indeed, "what distinguishes Israel from other Western countries is that a significant part of its 'quality of life' groups were founded . . . by members of the political authority."[54] Furthermore, almost a quarter of all such groups are supported financially by the government (here too a figure which, the author admits, is higher than the situation in the West), while a quarter of the leaders are political party activists. In short, "the State's hold over its interest groups has weakened but slightly."[55]

From a "political communication" standpoint, this is both advantageous and problematic. It does afford relatively easy access (at least for the groups' leaders) to the powers-that-be, so that messages are conveyed relatively efficiently. On the other hand, it tends to somewhat sharply curtail the type, and extent, of non- (and especially anti-) Establishment demands which the public may want to transmit.[56]

We now can understand more clearly the reason that "ad hoc" protest constituted the majority of such events in Israel over the entire period. True, ad hoc protest declined from 72.4% in the first early period to around 55% for the last three decades, an indication of the growth of interest-group pressure over time (12.3% in the first period; 38.1% in the fourth). But Israeli interest groups never manage to even approach ad hoc protest in frequency owing to their establishmentarian nature. Even less surprising, in light of this chapter's analysis, is the fact that political party-initiated protest has declined significantly over the years--from 15.3% in the first period (more than interest-group protest!) to 6.6% in the most recent period.

In summation, one cannot as yet argue that the Israeli system suffers from complete systemic blockage--at least not for those whose demands are economically distributive and/or ideologically supportive of (or at least do not contradict) the accepted order. The petrification of the party system has resulted in some compensatory developments such as the growth of interest-group pressure. Nevertheless, this latter "solution" does not at the present constitute an adequate substitute for the traditional central channel which has undergone serious erosion and enervation.[57]

Indeed, even if an American-style interest-group system were to develop, by itself it could not resolve the "problem" of protest entirely, for as we mentioned at the start of this chapter it is not only the parties but the general political system itself which has ossified over time. Without fundamental change in the election system and other important areas of the polity, protest will most probably continue to be perceived as one of the most efficient means of communicating with the powers-that-be, especially for those lacking the personal resources to go through more formal, but presently also far more complicated, channels. We shall devote some space to the question of specific proposals for change in the concluding chapter; first, however, it must be proven that the link between systemic petrification and blocked communication on the one hand, and between public protest on the other, indeed exists.

Chapter 8

Bypassing the Ossified System: The Protest Phenomena

While the last chapter showed quite clearly the problem of political systemic petrification in Israel, especially regarding the all-important party system, so far we have only assumed that the high levels of protest in the country are (at least in part) a function of such blockage and decay. The present chapter will attempt to *empirically* show the connection between the polity's ossification and extraparliamentary activity.

As noted, however, this is not an easy task--for the simple reason that direct statistical proof is hard to come by regarding such a nexus. We shall, therefore, have to use various indirect methods; in a few cases, viewing from a slightly different perspective some of the data presented in earlier chapters. Alone, each of these is not adequate "proof." Together, however, they constitute strong evidence that the lack of systemic communication channels explains a good portion of Israeli public protest.

Local Reform, Central Protest

As we saw in chapter 4, over the four major periods protest against Israel's central authorities rose somewhat, that against the local authorities declined, and that against foreign bodies was inconsistent. We shall remove the latter from our consideration at this point for the sake of clarity and simplicity (it is also not relevant to our argument).[1]

Table 8.1 presents a seemingly clear picture. Not only has there been a steady rise in public protest directed against the central government and its associated institutions, with a concomitant decline on the local level, but the gap between the two has evolved from a modest 9.2% in the first period to a huge 45.4% in the fourth!

Table 8.1:
Absolute and Relative Protest against
Central/Local Authorities

	1949-1954	1955-1970	1971-1978	1979-1986	Total
Central	166	301	557	1,114	2,138
	54.6%	56.5%	64.5%	72.7%	66.2%
Local	138	230	306	419	1,093
	45.4%	43.5%	35.5%	27.3%	33.8%
Total	304	531	863	1,533	3,231
(Gap)	(9.2%)	(13.0%)	(29.0%)	(45.4%)	(32.4%)

On the face of it, this trend is somewhat surprising in light of the fact that there has been a slow but gradual transfer of authority from the central government to the localities over these four decades.[2] If such is the case, why would we find proportionally less protest addressed to those with more responsibility?

The answer: if protest is a result of systemic dysfunction, then a decrease in protest leveled at local government might be a sign of the latter's greater power being used in relatively satisfactory fashion. And, if our analysis of political petrification is correct, the reason for improved functioning and lower protest should lie in the ability of the specific system to reform itself and/or develop multiple channels of formal political communictaion.

That such systemic innovation and internal development has occurred within the municipalities is by now a truism in Israel. As Elazar notes, it is "at the local level that the most innovative developments are taking place and local governments are far more advanced than the government of the state in institutionalizing the new democratic republicanism."[3] For our purposes we need only broadly outline the parameters of this reform.

One of the first innovations was the "local committee" which originated in the *polis*-like moshavim and kibbutzim, eventually extending to unincorporated urban settlements within the more densely populated regional councils--"the Israeli version of the town meeting principle [projected] in new directions."[4] In the larger cities, the route was somewhat different, as Weiss points out:

> The municipal committees have their own uniqueness. The very opportunity to send to most of these committees "public representatives" who aren't counted among the elected ostensibly opens it up to superior talent . . . outside the narrow group of active apparatchiks . . . . There is no doubt that there exist quality people, skilled and trained in the realm of municipal activity . . . outside of the "internal" political party group. From this perspective, the structure of the municipal committees is preferable to the structure of the Knesset committees. The possibility of establishing committees for every field and to fill them partly with people outside of the ranks of the elected, in theory affords it the ability to set up committees on the right issue, at the right time, with the right people.[5]

Still more recently, Israel's massive cooperative program with the Jewish Diaspora--Project Renewal--focused on dozens of the most underprivileged neighborhoods. While the general public's attention was centered on the improvement of the physical environment, much was going on behind the scenes from a socio-political standpoint as well. As one newspaper report explained: "Three additional neighborhoods have been ushered into the Jerusalem Project, an experimental 'citizen-participation' programme . . . . The heart of the project is the neighborhood council formed in each area composed of residents and representatives of municipal and public agencies providing services there. The council's job is to serve as a channel of communication between the neighborhood and the city."[6]

At least as important a development, starting from 1978, has been the direct election of the mayor--the only direct elections in effect in Israel today at any political level--cementing a link which had been growing for some time between the local administrations and their respective constituencies. This is but the natural continuation of several electoral trends already evident in the sixties and early seventies.

For one, voter ticket-splitting between the central and local parties became an accepted and fairly widespread phenomenon.[7] This is a mark of the voters' greater sophistication and concern about local matters. Indeed, quite a number of localities have gone so far in this central/local separation that they have voted into office *independent* local party (nonaffiliated) lists--a minor revolution of sorts in highly party-politicized Israel. Even Jerusalem's politically invincible mayor Teddy Kollek cut the umbilical cord (from Labor) in the 1978 municipal elections, handily defeating the *Likud* as an independent.[8] In fact, after those elections local (independent)-list candidates throughout Israel ruled over a population sector larger than that of the *Li-kud* itself, a mere year after that party had won a decisive victory in the national polls![9]

All these phenomena, then--transferral of authority, new representative and participatory institutions, direct mayoral elections, ticket-splitting, independent local lists, and the increasing independence of local luminaries still attached to the central parties--point in the same direction. Local government which used to be the stepchild of Israeli politics[10] has come of age, and with the rise of political power has taken great strides in forging closer links with its local constituency. Even this may be somewhat understating the case; in many respects the local citizens have taken over their government--they now not only hold their local officials accountable for nitty-gritty performance, but have also involved themselves (through various local councils and committees) in the actual decision-making and governing processes.

In such a situation--where ideology no longer holds sway, where formerly excluded groups are now recruited or even force themselves into the system, and where political responsiveness is expedited as a result of rulers and ruled understanding and communicating with each other as a matter of course--it is little wonder that political protest against local authorities should decline relative to the unreformed central system.[11]

Election Periods

In chapter 5 we attempted to find a correlation between election periods and public protest. None was found, but as noted, this may have been a consequence of the grossness of the scoring system--annualization of protest events.

Table 8.2:
Pre- & Post-Election Protest in Israel--1951-1984

Year	E - 2M	Elec. Day	E + 2M	Gov't Formed	G + 2M
1951	4	30 July	10 (+)	9 Oct.	17 (+)
1955	2	26 July	4 (+)	3 Nov.	4 (+)
1959	5	3 Nov.	1 (-)	16 Dec.	4 (-)
1961	3	8 Aug.	7 (+)	2 Nov.	4 (+)
1965	8	2 Nov.	12 (+)	12 Jan. ('66)	8 (=)
1969	13	28 Oct.	9 (-)	15 Dec.	6 (-)
1973	11	30 Dec.	16 (+)	10 Mar. ('74)	21 (+)
1977	11	17 May	17 (+)	20 June	15 (+)
1981	29	30 June	32 (+)	5 Aug.	40 (+)
1984	33	23 July	39 (+)	13 Sep.	31 (-)
Pre- to Post- Change			8(+) : 2(-)		6(+) : 3(-) : 1(=)

Code: + (increase from preelection period)
          - (decrease from preelection period)
          = (no change)

In order to overcome this difficulty, Table 8.2 sets out more simply but accurately the protest data for the two-month[12] election campaign before the actual election date (E - 2M), and the two-month period after both that date (E + 2M) and the date on which the new government was formed (G + 2M), for each relevant year.[13] The reason the latter was included is that before a government is formed there is no real address against which to demonstrate (on the national level), although Israelis are not averse to occasionally using "street pressure" to nudge the coalition bargaining process in a specific direction.

The differential between pre- and postelection protest was apparent virtually from the start and has held relatively constant over the entire period. In eight of the ten periods, protest immediately after the elections were over increased as compared to the campaign period itself. The same held true, albeit less pronounced, after the government was formed.

The economic-cycle explanation (mentioned in chapter 5) is not at all sufficient to account for such short-term fluctuations, as any postelection increases in inflation and/or unemployment would take far longer to manifest themselves in significant fashion; indeed, before the government is formed there is no new economic policy being implemented.[14] A more time specific argument is necessary, and political communication fits the bill.

First, on the "output" side, during election campaigns most Israeli citizens feel far less need to communicate their antagonism to any specific policy or problem because someone within the system is already doing it for them. Virtually all voters are hearing from some source the things that they wish to hear--especially in a multi-party system such as Israel's where the array of promises and policies runs the gamut. Moreover, because one party never receives an outright majority, the chances of each voter's preferred party becoming a member of the upcoming governing coalition are quite high, further affording a sense of "my message will be addressed from within"--lessening the need for extraparliamentary activity to ensure that the authorities will deal with that citizen's concerns.

Such an eventuality may not even need to be objectively possible or even probable. Even when the campaign "output" does not truly match a voter's expectations, the subjective interpretation of such oratory may provide the same sense of substantive adequacy. As Edelman argues, "people read their own meanings into situations that are unclear or provocative of emotion."[15] And given some of the internally contradictory ideological approaches within each of the major parties (especially over the last two decades),[16] the citizenry has increasingly been fed "interpretable" oratory. This only adds to the potential voter's feeling of well-being regarding message content, for the less clearly defined the verbal output the greater will be the "contribution" of the receiver. In such a situation there is little felt, and perhaps no actual, need for extraordinary communication measures in the other direction.

The problem, of course, begins after the elections are over. On the one hand there are clear losers, and their supporters now see that their messages will not be readily transmitted within the formal system. On the other hand, whatever the winning parties' ambiguities and/or two-faced promises, the voter has understood the oratory to mean that something concrete will be done along the lines of the received/reinterpreted promises. Unfortunately, given the exigencies of coalition bargaining in Israel, it is rare that most winning voters will get precisely what they wished for on the policy front--and even if the winning parties from their own perspective do not go back on their promises, they are still caught in the vise of their supporters' subjective understanding of what was promised. Once the government is formed and its basic principles are simultaneously declared, many of its erstwhile supporters may find it necessary to use extraparliamentary pressure, as the Establishment (from their perspective) "can't be trusted to keep even its own promises"--so how can one transmit messages through the formal apparatus which it controls?

This brings us to the "input" side of the matter. The election campaign (not to mention the act of voting) seems to have an effect on the voters' perception of input potential. As Edelman points out, "election campaigns . . . give people a chance to express discontents and enthusiasms, to enjoy a sense of involvement . . . . [But while] voting may be the most fundamental of all devices for reassuring masses that they are participants in the making of public policy . . . this is participation in a ritual act . . . ; only in a minor degree is it participation in policy formation."[17]

There is, therefore, a modicum of self-delusion occurring here regarding the opportunities to communicate with, and the ability to influence, the government as a whole.[18] During the election campaign, the politicians' seem eager to listen; anyone wishing to ask a question, get an answer, or otherwise transmit messages probably can in one way or another. The system, in short, at least seems to be open, with a lot of "hot air" emerging from the masses; once the elections are over the channels close up-- and the communication pot begins to boil instead with protest.

In sum, the relative ease of political communication, coupled with a lower felt need to transmit messages during the election campaign, inevitably results in reduced levels of public protest at such times. The converse just as inevitably leads to a marked increase after the election results are in. Paradoxically, the Israeli public's high level of political interest and relatively high rate of voter participation only reinforce this dual tendency, for virtually all of the citizenry is caught up in the intoxication of the campaign (reducing protest), and virtually all are frustrated and feel "blocked" after the elections (thereby increasing protest). As a result, in Israel at least, elections can be seen as a reinforcement of the parliamentary process, as well as a facilitator of extraparliamentary activity--both owing to the element of political communication in its various guises.

The Advent of Television

If our hypothesis regarding the linkage between protest and political communication is correct, then one would expect to find that a significant change in one realm is influential in changing the other. We turn, then, to the only significant communications change during Israel's first forty years--the advent of television in the late sixties.

Protest, as public as it might be, is not very effective without a public channel which can heighten and transmit the message to the powers-that-be and/or the citizenry at large. Other than enabling the discontented to let off steam, is there much purpose in protest which does not reach the eyes and ears of its intended target? Whether there would objectively be any protest in a country devoid of mass media is an unanswerable question; what is fairly certain is that when such media are expanded, then protest tends to increase in their wake.

While altogether logical, even to the point of being self-evident, this contention need not inevitably be true. If the underlying cause(s) of protest were poverty, inflation, unemployment, modernization, rising expectations, anomie, innate human aggression, political culture, etc., etc., then we would not necessarily expect to find that the expansion of mass media should bring with it a concomitant increase in protest.[19]

The extent to which this does occur is but another indirect indication of the link between the two.

Television news broadcasts commenced in 1968 in Israel. As we saw in chapter 3, a veritable explosion in protest frequency occurred in 1971, continuing unabated to this very day. The three-year time lag can be explained in a number of ways: it took awhile until a significant part of the population purchased TV sets; it takes at least as much time until the public and the newscasters acclimatize themselves to this new medium; 1968-1970 was marked by the War of Attrition, dampening protest for unrelated (to TV) reasons; those same three years were led by a National Unity Government, also lowering the internal political heat.

More to the point is the fact that the Black Panther eruptions--despite lacking broad popular support--seemed to set off waves of protests by other population groups on wildly dissimilar issues. Here lies the dual crux of the matter. On the one hand, television enables all population sectors to learn from each other: "if the unschooled Black Panthers can demonstrate," many Israelis probably said to themselves, "why can't or shouldn't more sophisticated people like me do the same?" And if this new medium of television seems to actually get the message across to the usually deaf authorities, all the more reason to hop on the bandwagon.

To be sure, this nexus is not exclusive to Israel. Commenting on the American scene, Etzioni noted: "The number of demonstrations in the pre-mass television decade (1948-58) was much smaller than the first television decade (1958-68) . . . . [T]elevision has played a key role in the evolution of this particular form of political expression and in the increasing frequency with which this form is applied, in effect, in creating demonstration democracy."[20]

More specifically, Singer's study of the 1967 Detroit riots illustrated how television can serve as the chief learning vehicle regarding violent protest--by providing information on the existence of previous riots as well as the riot "rules of the game": "A substantial proportion of [rioting] individuals reported violent aspects of past televised riots . . . ; and it seems likely that this affective aspect, along with routine 'instructions' on how a riot is conducted *when it arrives*, contributed substantially to the riot readiness of a large number of individuals."[21]

Why is the emphasis on television? After all, Israel had quite a thriving newspaper medium from the start, plus a highly professional radio broadcast system. The answer is that television has a few unique qualities which are particularly appropriate for protest as a mode of communication. For one, TV thrives on "action"; public protest events (compared with parliamentary committee work, etc.) promise such "action." In addition, by its very nature--limited time, need to concentrate resources--television seeks out straightforward messages; protests, too, communicate relatively simple ideas and demands. In short, we have here a symbiotic relationship where the two sides feed off each other to their mutual benefit.[22]

We see, therefore, another aspect of the political-communication hypothesis: it is not only the opportunity for protesting (legally established in every democracy), nor the availability of mass media coverage (omnipresent as well in such polities), but equally as important is the relative *efficacy* of such extraparliamentary communication in reaching the proper address. In other words, the average potential protester does a very rough personal cost-benefit analysis before deciding to go the demonstration route. For many, it may pay to protest only if there is almost certain assurance that the message will be transmitted with sufficient force--a situation which seems to be true only in the Age of Television.[23]

Luckily, Israel provided an almost unique opportunity recently to test the specific influence of its television on public protest. For fifty days during October and November 1987, the regular TV station was on total strike (educational TV, which does not broadcast the nightly news program, continued as usual). The respected morning and afternoon newspapers *Ha'aretz* and *Ma'ariv* were surveyed for the fifty days before, during, and after the strike, to ascertain the amount of public protest in those three periods. If the hypothesis about the political-communication functions of Israeli protest is correct, the strike period should have registered a drop in protest frequency relative to the pre- and poststrike periods, as the public was missing its most powerful weapon for transmitting political messages.[24] In the event, that is precisely what was found.

Whereas *Ha'aretz* and *Ma'ariv* reported forty-one and twenty-five protests (respectively) over the first period, with a further twenty-five and sixteen in the third period, the second period (when the TV strike occurred) showed only eleven and one reported protests in these two papers! And this despite the fact that there were slightly more overall daily articles in the papers during the strike than normally in the preceding period.[25] To be sure, one can hardly make any bold statements based on a 150 day survey, but this interesting (and extremely strong) finding does add another brick to our theoretical construct.

In short, Israel's sharp rise in protest frequency in the seventies, coupled with the virtual disappearance of protest during the 1987 TV strike, is a further sign that extraparliamentary behavior is intricately connected to a desire to communicate politically. Systemic blockage may indeed be the necessary condition but it is not by itself sufficient. Only with the development of a powerful and self-interested communications medium will public protest manifest itself in all its "glory."

Outgroup Protest

An additional way of seeing to what extent public protest functions as an alternative channel of political commnunication is to look at the behavior of Israel's "outgroups"--those sectors which for one reason or another cannot or will not utilize the formal system's various processes and institutions. If it turns out that despite several innate group characteristics which would tend to dampen protest, such "outgroup" sectors nevertheless indulge in extraparliamentarism above and beyond other groups similar in character, then we might have yet another indication of the importance of the political-communication factor.

We have already seen that such is the case regarding a number of groups. First, despite having but recently arrived from countries where free political expression (not to mention political criticism) was virtually nonexistent, we found the post-1948 immigrants (especially from the Levant) protesting inordinately frequently. These were obviously people who had no direct voice within the Establishment, and probably had no knowledge of how to transmit messages through the official channels in any case.

A second example (connected to the first) was the Black Panthers, a socio-political "outgroup" par excellence who also had no access to the regular channels;[26] instead, they voiced their protest in the street (despite having low education and low income, characteristics which, as noted in chapter 4, would not make them prime candidates in Israel for protest mobilization). A telling clue that political communication was behind their demonstrations can be seen in the rapid evaporation of their protest once the Black Panther leaders had been coopted into the formal political system, and their messages could be routed in more direct fashion.[27]

These two examples (others such as the Young Couples could be brought as well) are valid, but impressionistic. To strengthen our case, it would be useful to have quantifiable instances of "outgroup" protest activity. These exist as well.

This third example involves the evolution of political party-initiated protest through the years. As seen in chapter 4, such extraparliamentarism by the parliamentarians existed in significant numbers during the early period (over 15% of all events) but declined dramatically over the ensuing decades. Who was in the forefront of such protest in the early fifties? The answer lies in the converse of Ben-Gurion's oft-stated dictum (regarding which parties he saw as potential coalition partners): "everyone, except for *Maki* (the Communists) and *Herut* (Begin's Revisionists)." It was precisely those two parties "written out" of the system which held a virtual monopoly on party-initiated public protest during those years. But as time went on, and especially *Herut* became more "legitimate" (allying with the staid Liberals in 1965; joining the National Unity Government in 1967), the need for back-channel communication through protest waned.[28] By 1978, only 1 of 112 protests was party-initiated![29]

Finally, regarding the "outgroup" approach probably the best example and strongest statistical proof of the "protest as communication" theory can be found among Israel's only Jewish pariah group--the extremist, ultra-religious *Neturei Karta* ("Guardians of the City").[30] This is the only segment of the Jewish population which is avowedly anti-Zionist, to the extent that it does not recognize the State of Israel and refuses to cooperate with the State's duly constituted authorities. And yet, despite the fact that they constitute only a minute segment of the entire Israeli Orthodox population, and even among the ultra-religious they are but a small minority, *the self-ostracized Neturei Karta utilize public protest far more extensively than their counterparts who work within the political system.*

Exact numbers here are virtually impossible to obtain with a high degree of accuracy, mostly because in many newspaper reports it is not made completely clear which type of "ultra-Orthodox" is protesting.[31] After a protest-by-protest examination, though, it can be maintained that roughly 45% of all religious-issue protest in Israel is initiated by the anti-Zionist *Neturei Karta*, another 30% emanates from non-Zionist *Agudah* supporters,[32] about 20% results from those who are identified with the pro-Zionist *Mizrachi* camp, and the rest by miscellaneous other groups.

What is most interesting and relevant to our discussion in these percentages is that an inverse relationship exists between protest frequency and Establishment credentials--and this despite the fact that the smaller the group the more protest it engenders! The explanation lies largely[33] in their respective political communication potential--the anti-Zionists cannot at all use the formal channels, the non-Zionists are not completely within the system, while the Zionists are part and parcel of the system's normal channels of internal political communication and so need much less to go the extraparliamentary route.

In short, public protest is not exclusively the province of Israeli "outgroups." Given the relatively broad socio-political representation found in the Knesset (one of the few advantages of its national proportional electoral system), Israel may even have less of an "outgroup" problem than many other democracies. Nonetheless, in almost every case where such sectors do exist, the level of protest activity is much greater than one would expect (even by Israel's "high" standards). As virtually the only way to get their message across, protest serves a communication function par excellence--something less necessary for those represented within the system as the above numbers attest.

Public Perception of the Causes Underlying Israeli Protest

All of the above methods of addressing our central hypothesis are indirect in nature. In the final analysis, it is always best if a direct way can be found as well. Our 1981 poll enables us to do just that. While such an attitudinal approach (as compared to the empirical methods employed above) also cannot be said to constitute irrefutable proof (as noted at the start of the book, not even the protest participant may always be cognizant of the factors underlying such activity), it can serve as strong corroborating (or contradictory) evidence.

As can be seen below, the factors offered to the respondents represented in a general sort of way the major explanatory theories dealt with in this book.

Answers "a" & "d" represent "political culture"--historical and contemporary.[34] Answer "c" reflects "policy dissatisfaction." Answer "e" relates to difficult "general conditions" (economic, social, security). And answers "b" & "f" involve "political communication"--the former per se, and the latter as an instrumentality.

Table 8.3:
Public Perception of Protest Factors

Question: In Israel, compared to other countries, there are a large number of protest activities. I shall read to you a number of possible reasons for this. Please choose up to three of the reasons which seem to you to be most important in explaining the large number of public protest activities in Israel.

(a)	While in exile the Jews always protested versus the authorities, and continue this tradition also today in Israel	10.7%
(b)	The citizen does not have enough other ways to express himself to the authorities	49.7%
(c)	There is a need to express protest because the authorities do not respond to the will and needs of the public	40.9%
(d)	When the ministers and members of Knesset wish for their opinion to be accepted they shout and do protest activities, and this influences the man in the street	35.1%
(e)	Living conditions in Israel are usually tough and this leads to protest activities against the authorities	39.3%
(f)	Whoever protests publicly in general achieves something. This is one of the only ways to get something	42.2%
(g)	Did not answer	7.7%

We have already discussed some of these answers in earlier chapters. The most preferred responses, however, were both "political communication" in nature, with "the citizen does not have enough other ways to express himself to the authorities" the clear winner (49.7%). When one compares this with some of the other answers, the conclusion is unmistakable (as strange, albeit not necessarily surprising, as it may sound): *insofar as the Israeli public is concerned, harsh environmental conditions, general policy dissatisfaction,*[35] *and Jewish political culture are less salient factors in fomenting protest than the lack of formal opportunities for political communication!*

A demographic breakdown of this question makes this point even more clearly: 53.2% of those who actually participated in protest events chose answer "b," while only 48.6% of the nonparticipants did so.Such a gap is not terribly wide, but it does at least indicate that especially regarding those who should know best (the protesters themselves) the element of "political communication" is paramount in their minds. Perhaps even more interesting, 57.2% of those nonprotesters declaring themselves willing to protest in the future chose "b," as compared to only 44.9% of the "nonpotentials." In short, the self-defined extraparliamentary "activists" (actual or potential) in Israel are of the strongest opinion that systemic blockage is the most important element behind the public protest phenomenon.[36]

Does this mean that the choice is "either/or"--party activity or extraparliamentarism? Not necessarily, for we find that while 21.5% of the entire public admitted to participating in protest activity, a far higher proportion of active party members (42.5%) did so. In essence, in Israel an active member of a political party is twice as likely to indulge in extraparliamentarism as one not active within a party.[37]

On the face of it, this seems to contradict our theory that protest results from lack of alternative communication channels. Logically, we should expect that nonmembers would utilize protest more than those who are within the system. However, there is a simple explanation for this "anomaly." Many citizens who are not members of a party can be defined as "total inactives"--those who for reasons of psychological temperament or personal noninterest do not participate in any public activity of a political nature. These constitute the vast majority in virtually every democracy,[38] and despite the high level of interest in public affairs in Israel the majority here too may be numbered among them.

Thus, the surprising datum which calls for attention in the Israeli context is why 17.1% of the nonaffiliated (with any type of public pressure group) *did* choose to protest in the past. In addition, why do three-eighths of active party members have to protest at all, given their theoretical influence within the system? Part of the answer to both questions lies in the blockage problem: a sixth of the Israeli public is so stymied by systemic petrification that no other mode but protest (i.e., circumvention of institutions) seems to them to be of any use; and such ossification is so advanced that even a significant minority *within* the system find it necessary to employ extraparliamentary means at times to get their message across.[39]

In the final analysis, then, public protest has not become the exclusive substitute for parliamentary behavior. Just because there may be blockage within the system does not mean that it is entirely stopped up. The two modes of political activity can, and obviously do, complement each other. As Marsh argued: "Higher levels of protest potential are not associated with an estrangement from orthodox politics, but are part of a parallel, dualist attitude toward the use of political action."[40] The problem, however, lies in the reason for having to supplement normal parliamentary activity with its more strident partner. The dual use of both modes may be heartening from a civic-democratic perspective; the hardening of the polity's communications arteries most certainly is not.

Conclusion

While the above various indirect approaches to discovering the existence and extent of blocked communication as a key factor underlying Israeli protest are somewhat original, the ultimate finding that the problem involves a systemic factor should not come as any surprise to the student of Israeli politics. For some time now the large gap between Israelis' high "political involvement" and low sense of "political efficacy" has been noted in sundry attitudinal studies.[41] But the explanations or contentions regarding blocked communication have heretofore been mostly surmise or speculation, not based on any (nonattitudinal) empirical analysis.[42]

The same may be said for those few non-Israeli studies which touch on the element of blocked political communication. Etzioni, for example, correctly (but almost entirely intuitively) argued: "When the upward channels of communication are not effective, power relations . . . will tend to grow further apart. The greater the discrepancies between the social and political patterns of a nation, the greater the internal tensions, conflicts, and potential for violence."[43] No factual evidence, though, was presented. Our analysis here suggests that much needs to, and can, be done in other national contexts, to show just how critical (or, alternatively, unimportant) are systemic ossification and its concomitant blocked communication as factors underlying protest.

Which is not to say that reopening such blocked channels will *ipso facto* eliminate protest. As Hall and Hewitt argued: "people will feel that they have communicated when they see the *results* of their verbal exchanges . . . when the course of action they have requested, demanded, or defended is forthcoming."[44] Yet, even they admitted that "[f]or some, . . . and perhaps for many, the ability to talk with a cabinet member or administration aide, or to take part in a mass demonstration close to the White House that is seen on national television, is sufficient to reduce pressure . . . ."[45]

There is little doubt, then, that reforming the system to enable more message transmittal in formal fashion will certainly have some impact. We thus in the next section first turn to an investigation of how much such protest pressure succeeds in achieving "results," and then as part of the concluding chapter to the question of the actual types of systemic reform needed in Israel to reduce public protest.

PART V:

Additional Aspects of Israeli Protest

A few important points remain to be addressed in this final section. Having examined the breadth and depth of public protest in Israel, we must inquire about its efficacy, i.e., to what extent do Israeli protesters achieve their goals? From a methodological standpoint such a question is replete with problems, as is evident in a number of overseas research attempts to grapple with the issue. The approach in chapter 9 is somewhat novel, and leads at first glance to some surprising conclusions.

Our concluding chapter sums up the book's major findings and then looks at what concrete steps the Israeli government, and/or society, could take in order to ameliorate the extent of public protest in Israel. A number of specific recommendations are offered, each derived to some extent from the analyses (contained within the book) of the various significant factors engendering extraparliamentary behavior. While Israeli protest cannot be eradicated in the foreseeable future (especially given the strong cultural factor involved), these prescriptions would go a long way toward relieving the pandemic force of the phenomenon. We then end the study by briefly noting a few aspects of Israeli protest which were not touched upon (or were treated only cursorily) in this book, leaving these neglected (or unanswered) questions for future research and analysis.

Chapter 9

Israeli Protest: Is It Successful?

If Israeli public protest is in large measure a response to a political system incapable or unwilling to transmit messages from the public to its leadership, how successful is such protest in achieving its goals? Unfortunately, there is no current methodology which can answer such a question completely or even satisfactorily. The difficulties are numerous. To begin with, it is not always obvious what the protesters' exact goals are (they may not even be completely clear to the participants themselves). For example, demonstrators calling for reduced inflation may not have any specific policy solution in mind and could be altogether unhappy if their demands were met through an increase in unemployment. As Oscar Wilde once put it: "When the Gods wish to punish us they answer our prayers."

Second, a change in policy (albeit preferred) may not have been the initial goal of a protest. Rather, as we have seen, access to political leadership, i.e., a chance to voice one's concerns before a policy-making body, in many instances is the "real" reason and goal of a protest demonstration. Deciding, then, whether "communication" or "change in policy output" is the goal complicates the matter further.

A third (and somewhat related) problem involves the existence, in sundry types of protest, of several goals--some evident, others less so. A classic example of this could be found in the entire "Stop the Withdrawal from Sinai" protest campaign (1981-1982). The ostensible purpose of the continuing demonstrations was to halt the giveback of the Sinai to Egypt in general, and to save the city of Yamit in particular. Whether the protesters really believed that such a goal could be achieved is somewhat beside the point; at some late stage of the campaign (when it had become clear that the government would not change its policy), another goal--possibly inchoate--emerged: to so traumatize Israeli society and its leadership through the fanatical protest "battles" that no one would ever even consider giving up any other part of the Land of Israel (i.e., the administered territories). And all this is in addition to several other "fallback" subgoals which came to the fore at various stages of their campaign, e.g., higher monetary compensation for the landowners, businessmen, etc., who would suffer economically as a result of the withdrawal.[1]

Add to these some further cogent questions:

> What of the group whose leaders are honored or rewarded while their supposed beneficiaries linger in the same cheerless state as before? Is such a group more or less successful than another challenger whose leaders are vilified and imprisoned even as their program is eagerly implemented by their oppressor? Is a group a failure if it collapses with no legacy save inspiration to a generation that will soon take up the same cause with more tangible results?[2]

Thus, distinguishing between ultimate and subsidiary goals, original and fallback positions, short-term and long-term objectives, ostensible and real beneficiaries, etc., further exacerbates the difficulties for anyone trying to get a handle on the question of protest success. Indeed, in the case of Yamit one could argue that the settlers' "failure" (to prevent the withdrawal) was a "success" of sorts (since future governments might indeed be loath to traverse that same road of fierce opposition)! In such a Kafkaesque situation it is truly a brave or foolhardy researcher who would try to come to any firm conclusions.

As if all this weren't enough, there is a fourth (equally problematical) type of consideration to be taken into account. Even if a certain aim was achieved (e.g., lowered inflation), how are we to ascertain that there is a connection between the specific protest campaign and the ultimate result? In other words, how do we know that it was the series of demonstrations which caused the government to shift policy? There might very well have been other, more influential, factors at work here. Indeed, when one considers the problem of time frame it becomes obvious just how impossible proof of linkage becomes.[3] Change of governmental policy usually takes months, if not years; very few protest campaigns have that kind of staying power. Conversely, on occasion a shift in policy will occur very soon after a protest event, but the political groundwork and factors leading up to that decision may have existed well before the protest itself. Thus, even when a direct causal influence is in evidence, it may be more apparent than real.

Nevertheless, notwithstanding these serious difficulties some interesting attempts have been made in the past to statistically ascertain (not "prove") whether protest does achieve results. Gamson's longitudinal study (employing qualitative criteria) of fifty-three randomly selected American protest movements found that 49% were unqualifiedly successful ("received new advantages") while another 7% had qualified success ("peripheral advantages"). Using the same data, Goldstone found that when one removes those groups which sought to "displace" the ruling establishment, the success of the "nondisplacement" protest groups was an astonishing 100%![4]

A more time-focused study, utilizing quantitative measurement techniques, was undertaken by Welch, who studied the American Black urban riots of the 1960s. Her fascinating conclusion based on public-expenditure allocations: "Cities experiencing riots, more than other cities, increased expenditures in areas assumed to be of concern to those demanding control and punishment of rioters, and to a much lesser extent in areas assumed to be of concern to those rioting."[5] This suggests that the rioters did succeed in gaining some extra resources from the authorities. But this came at a price --even greater amounts of resources being funneled into those institutions (e.g., police) which would deny (or at least hinder) any future use of rioting as a political-communication tactic. For our purposes, however, where the preponderance of Israeli demonstrations are relatively peaceful, Welch's study may not be directly applicable.

Closer to home is the study conducted by Iris, who examined the budgetary responses of the Israeli government to a couple of disruptive protest campaigns (in the early 1970s): the Black Panthers demonstrating against their slum conditions, and the "Young Couples" movement seeking decent housing.[6] Here statistical analysis of time-series budget data did show substantially favorable responses by the public authorities to these two groups' demands. But one can hardly generalize from the specifics of two protest case studies to the phenomenon in general, and certainly nothing can be learned from Iris's (statistically impressive) study regarding protests which have incommensurable goals, i.e., have no financial bottom-line denominator (as in religious or political policy issues).

The most serious attempt to date to understand the extent of Israeli protest success is the work of Wolfsfeld, who used an in-depth interview procedure with the *protesters' leadership* in order to get a closeup view on the matter.[7] We shall shortly return to his results, but for now it can be said that such a strictly attitudinal approach constitutes a great strength and a serious weakness. By turning to those actively organizing protest, the picture can be accepted as quite a knowledgeable one; unfortunately, by the same token, in turning to those with an obvious bias (and perhaps need for self-justification, if not self-interest), the results need to be assessed with a large dose of skepticism.

A more definitive discussion, therefore, of Israeli protest success must of necessity take into account a significant number of protest events or (preferably) campaigns, whose success ought to be evaluated by outside observers--a mixture of Wolfsfeld's broad range with Iris's objective assessment. In drawing up a comprehensive list, however, one must avoid the natural tendency to remember and highlight the resounding protest successes while forgetting and/or discounting the failures. The media, for one, hardly ever return with a nonstory of a protest group's failure to achieve its goals; far more "newsworthy" is the item regarding the authorities' capitulation in the face of a protest onslaught. This aspect by itself is enough to leave the public and the researcher with a distorted impression of the extent of protest success.

Having said that, one must also note a certain paradox here. Such cognitive distortion of the situation is important in its own right and must be taken into account as well. In simple language, at times the *perception* of reality is as important as the reality itself. If Israelis believe (even mistakenly) that their protests' chances of achieving something are high, then that (mis)perception will undoubtedly influence the extent of their extraparliamentary behavior. More to our point, if the country's leadership shares that (mis)perception, then there may be a greater willingness to bend or even give in to what may be felt as a political force of nature. In short, if success breeds success, no less so may the perception of success lead to more future protest events and perhaps even (from the government's standpoint) to concessions based on the belief of the "inevitability" of those protests' success.

What, then, is the Israeli public's perception on the matter? Two related questions in our public opinion poll were asked in order to determine the cognitive perception of Israeli protest success: "In your opinion, do legal (illegal) public protest activities succeed in achieving their aims?" The answers are both interesting and relatively unambiguous as can be seen from Table 9.1.

Table 9.1:
Israeli Public Opinion on Protest Success

Answer	Legal Protest	Illegal Protest
Yes, always successful	5.8%	3.9%
Yes, usually	19.1%	12.3%
Sometimes	40.2%	33.3%
Infrequently	15.6%	20.3%
Never successful	17.1%	28.1%
Did not answer	1.6%	2.1%

If we take the first three answers ("always," "usually," and "sometimes") as an indication that the respondents believed that the chances of success were reasonably good, we find that two-thirds of the Israeli population (among those answering the question) were of the opinion that a connection does exist between protesting and achieving one's goals. Interestingly, though, there is some difference between the perception of success on the part of Israelis who have actually participated in a protest and those who have been passive in this regard. Whereas only 61.6% of the nonprotesters believed that success is sometimes achieved, fully 77.7% of the protesters answered in a like affirmative.[8]

As noted above, one can read this specific statistical difference in two opposing ways. On the one hand, it could be an indication that those with "experience" personally gained from their extraparliamentary endeavors, and thus are indicating more than merely a belief in protest success. On the other hand, and just as plausibly, these protesters might be merely justifying to themselves their protest actions, magnifying the "success" and attributing causality where none in fact may exist. In any case, there is little doubt that Israelis generally perceive success to be a reasonably likely outcome of peaceful protest.

Perhaps even more remarkable, over half (of those responding to the question of success) felt the same way with regard to *illegal* protests--as much a reflection of the accepted (if not acceptable) political culture of "illegalism" which has evolved over the years among the Israeli Establishment (and the public)[9] as it is of the "street's" cynical belief that in extraparliamentary behavior the ends justify the means.

These results of *perceived* success are close to, albeit below, the percentages which Wolfsfeld found in his study. When the question was addressed only to the political protest leaders, fully 87% answered that their protest involved either a "great deal" or "partial" "general success,"[10] an extremely high level by any standard.

The perception, then, certainly exists among Israelis that it pays to protest. One should note, however, that the further removed from the protest cauldron one is, the lower the perception of protest success. The protest organizers see the most success, their supporting participants somewhat less so, and the general public even less, although still at a high level. In addition, despite some variation regarding protest intensity, the level of perceived success remains high whether one plays by the official rules of the game or not. This is not to say that Israeli protest can take any form; as in Welch's study, there seems to be an intensity point past which public backing turns negative.[11] In fact, Wolfsfeld found a curvilinear relationship: taking the above two success categories together, legal protest scored 62%, disorderly protest 88%, and violent protest 67%.[12]

All in all, it is little wonder that so many Israelis have participated in protest events. By virtually any private political cost-benefit analysis--especially in light of the low efficacy of going the "normal" parliamentary route--protesting is perceived to be worth the effort.

But is it *really* as successful as the public's perception indicates? In order to more rigorously determine the answer (with due acknowledgment to all the aforementioned methodological difficulties), and given the need for a broad-based analysis beyond Welch's couple of case studies, a list of twenty-eight protest campaigns for the fourth period (1979-1986) was drawn up--representing all the significant sustained extraparliamentary campaigns of that period. In order to minimize the problem of evaluation subjectivity, this list was given to ten experts on Israeli politics who were asked to score each protest campaign for its success/failure on a scale of 1 (total failure) to 5 (total success).[13]

The overall average for these protests was a "success score" of 2.5--well below partial-success/partial-failure.[14] *This finding does not substantiate the majority impression in Israel that protest is quite successful.*

Were there any specific protest categories which could be said to characterize the more successful and/or unsuccessful protests? A review of the intensity, size, organization, and issue categories is only partly productive (the other categories were not relevant, e.g., reaction, or authority addressed, etc., did not have a large enough category frequency to allow for any conclusions).

Table 9.2:
Average Success Score per Protest Category

Intensity:	Peaceful		Disruptive		Violent	
Avg. Score:	2.68 (N = 10)		2.50 (N = 11)		2.47 (N = 7)	

Size:	Small	Medium	Large	Huge
Avg. Score:	1.67 (N = 3)	2.52 (N = 17)	2.79 (N = 5)	3.27 (N = 3)

Organization:	Ad Hoc	Pressure Group	Political Party
Avg. Score:	2.79 (N = 3)	2.55 (N = 24)	2.11 (N = 1)

Issue:	Political	Economic	Religious	Social
Avg. Score:	2.51 (N = 9)	2.65 (N = 6)	2.63 (N = 10)	2.29 (N = 3)

As can be seen from Table 9.2, the only variable exhibiting a noticeable simple correlation is "size" of protest, i.e., the average number of participants. The larger the protest group, the greater the chance of the protest being successful--an eminently reasonable finding. Yet even here one must be careful not to come to any hard and fast conclusions, given the low number of "small" and "huge" protest campaigns which were scored (only three for each of these categories respectively).[15]

The same caveat holds doubly for the "organization" variable which at first glance seems to show (unreasonable) differences between ad hoc, organized group, and political party protest success (there was only one case of the latter and merely three of the former). And as for the "intensity" and "issue" categories the differences are too small to be meaningful, although there is a slight indication that peaceful protest campaigns tend to be more successful than disruptive and/or violent ones,[16] a contradiction of Wolfsfeld's finding.

We are left, then, with the unanswered question regarding the possible reasons for protest success in general, and/or the relative lack of success in the Israeli case in particular. But if the general question of whether protests succeed was methodologically difficult, the concomitant question regarding the reasons for success/failure involves an even higher degree of research complexity and ambiguity!

The list of possible factors is almost endless. Some of the intuitively more logical and/or previously empirically tested ones:

(A)   The sundry strategies and tactics of the protesting groups.
(B)   The relative political/economic/social power of the protesters.
(C)   The willingness and ability to form alliances with other groups.
(D)   The timing of the protest, i.e., during times of crisis or quiet, war or peace.
(E)   As noted above, the size of the protest demonstrations and/or the number of citizens which the protest group represents.
(F)   The organizational characteristics of the group (level of institutionalization, flexibility, financial backing, unity or factionalism, etc.).

(G)   The nature of the demands, i.e., radical or moderate, displacement of the ruling elite or resource redistribution, expanded "rights" or material benefits.

(H)   The protesting group's willingness to use violence.

         And on the other side of the protest fence:

(I)   The degree to which the protesters have support within the ruling establishment.

(J)   The environment of social support, i.e., whether a significant proportion of the general population sympathizes.

(K)   The power, cohesiveness, strength of purpose, etc., of the challenged group(s)-- especially the Government.[17]

Unfortunately, all of the studies which were conducted to answer the question of why protest succeeds/fails have one or more methodological flaws or weaknesses (almost inevitably, given the problems). Even worse, as noted in the previous footnote, their results are contradictory. As Gurr sums up: "there is no cumulativeness or generalizability to these studies. They examine protests in diverse political and cultural circumstances, any combination of which may have contributed to their generally favorable outcomes."[18]

What we can offer at this stage, then, is only an intuitive answer regarding the central factor behind Israeli protesters' relative lack of success. And it should come as no surprise to find that it is indirectly connected with the analysis outlined in the previous two chapters.

One of the central factors underlying protest in Israel is the lack of adequate formal channels of political communication. As we have seen, the party system has become ossified, party membership has plummeted over the years, the central government's institutional framework has undergone virtually no change or reform, and no specifically geographical representation exists on the Knesset level. All this has in a sense forced the Israeli public to bypass the system by taking to the streets, in order to continue sending messages to the powers-that-be.

But this is precisely the factor behind those same protests' relative lack of success. Because the present Israeli system is not designed to heighten representative accountability (as a result of the election system of national proportional representation), and considering that no government in Israel has ever been composed exclusively of a single majority party, public pressure must usually be generalized, scattershot. There is no specific Knesset representative, no one party, which the public can hold accountable if the protest demands are not met.

An indication that the public has come to realize this inherent "flaw" in the system is the fact that over the past several years more and more demonstrations have been held at the offices of specific ministries, and even on numerous occasions in front of the prime minister's (or treasury minister's) home! But even when a specific personage or government ministry is straightforwardly addressed by a group of protesters, such an addressee can always governmentally "hide" in the bosom of cabinet "collective responsibility" in general, and politically within the ranks of the party list in particular.[19]

In short, Israeli protesters are usually shooting at a moving, and occasionally ambiguous, political target. Ringing bull's-eyes are not that uncommon, but the shots wide of the mark are greater in overall number. To the above long list of factors behind protest success/failure, then, we may add another: the institutional democratic relationship between the governors and the governed. In Israel's case, it is precisely those systemic factors that cause a high level of protest in the first place which also undermine the efficacy of alternatively taking the extraparliamentary route. There are in essence two messages here: one for the protesters, the other for the governmental authorities.

In a relatively tolerant democracy such as Israel there is little "cost" for citizen groups (or individuals) to protest (other than the expenditure of personal time and some minimal sums of money). On the plus side, some protest campaigns actually do ultimately succeed in achieving at least part of their goals. Thus, as noted earlier there is little need for such groups to think twice about demonstrating. While the odds of succeeding are not particularly high, the costs of failure are next to nil. For any group feeling strongly about a public issue, the protest route in Israel is certainly worth a try.

On the other side of the fence, however, the message for the government is quite different. Contrary to Israeli conventional wisdom, the authorities do not as a rule kowtow in the face of even sustained protest. Therefore, there is no general rule, no overall precedential norm "forcing" them to accede to such demands (especially in light of the fact that escalation into serious violence is not very likely in the Israeli milieu).

This is not to say that there is necessarily anything positive in their showing spine. If, as we have suggested throughout, much of Israeli protest is due to the public's inability to communicate through more normal channels of political communication, the authorities' ignoring of such extraparliamentary demands may just be a continuation of their serious divorce from Israeli society at large. But it must be cautioned that no self-respecting government can continually give in to the "street" without seriously undermining the stability of the nation's representative democracy. Just as each pressure group must decide for itself whether to go the protest route based on its own needs and resources, so too the ruling authorities must decide how to react on the basis of the inherent merits and pressures of each individual case. The most one can say pertaining to the last several years is that Israel's authorities have not caved in as a matter of course, but neither have they been completely deaf or unresponsive to the extraparliamentary pressure from below.

Chapter 10

Conclusions: Findings, Prescriptions, New Directions

As noted in the introduction, this book has two central purposes: first, to test and advance some of the traditional theories of protest through the use of a national case study for the first time; and second, to understand in depth the nature and roots of the phenomenon within the Israeli context. Given the necessary heavy emphasis on the specific Israeli data and phenomena, the former goal at times may have been obscured. These concluding remarks, therefore, will be devoted largely to placing our specific Israeli case study within the relevant cross-comparative and theoretical framework.

Our first--and from an aggregate data research standpoint, most important--finding was that the contemporary anarchy regarding theories of conflict (i.e., the factors underlying the phenomenon) is most probably due more than anything else to the poverty of the data bases upon which such research projects rely. We found that the number of protest events scored by previous cross-comparative studies (which use far less exact sources than those employed here in the Israeli context) is undercounted by an order of magnitude between eight and fifty times!

This raises extremely serious questions as to the usefulness of employing international and/or regional newspaper sources in such types of research, and an equally profound question regarding any conclusions which are based upon such data (ergo, the present theory confusion). Such doubts are especially germane to any cross-comparative study which includes relatively low-level (nonviolent) protest, but studies of "turmoil" (e.g., riots) also rest on somewhat shaky quantitative foundations.

Having said that, we must note that the above does not prove in any way that such theories of conflict are wrong. Rather, it merely states that given the results of this study's Israeli protest event frequency totals, such theories are left hanging without much of an empirical base to support them. Nevertheless, almost all of these theories are sensible (indeed, many are quite logically persuasive), and therefore can serve as the starting point for any local/national study on the subject. The theories tested and/or analyzed in this book were felt to be either the most convincing in past studies (despite the remarks above) or the most relevant to the Israeli case. This in no way suggests that these are the only theories which should be tested in future local/national studies. Quite the opposite, each country has its own specific elements which may call for other theories being put to the statistical and analytical test. I have attempted to highlight some, though not all, of the ways in which this can be done.

The various explanatory theories, divided into two general parts, quantitatively addressed "standard" empirical factors that have been traditionally put through the statistical mill, and qualitatively analyzed in comprehensive fashion two theories which have been relatively neglected in the professional literature.

The results of our regression analysis raise some serious questions regarding several previous theories. On the economic front, most devastating are the findings related to objective relative deprivation, as this factor refused to appear in any of our results. Similarly, theories which highlight rising consumption (whether from a national or individual perspective) also find very little support in the Israeli case. On the other hand, such palpably onerous factors as high taxation, unemployment, and to a lesser extent inflation were found to be relatively significantly correlated to protest, suggesting that a specific class of economic variables, and related theories, are germane to extraparliamentarism.

What distinguishes these three variables from others such as relative deprivation, consumption, GNP, and the like is the fact that the taxation/unemployment/inflation trio is much more easily tied to government policy. The citizen understands that it is the government which can lower the rate of taxation, it is the government which can (largely) control inflation, and it is the government which can resolve problems of unemployment in relatively easy or direct fashion (whether such policies are objectively advisable is another matter entirely). The same cannot be said for rising consumption, GNP growth, and relative deprivation. Such a new approach to theorizing about the impact of economic factors on protest at least has the advantage of being highly reasonable, while also giving the protesting populace credit for some intelligence. Be that as it may, this hypothesis needs far more testing before it can enter the ranks of accepted conflict theory.[1]

On the social front, it is clear at least from the Israeli case that sharply rising population (e.g., mass immigration) does not affect protest frequency over time, although in very specific circumstances it may have some role to play. On the other hand, the gross level of population is correlated with protest--even when controlling for population growth! This factor is too often neglected in the literature, as in, for example, Taylor and Jodice's *World Handbook of Political and Social Indicators* which constitutes one of the central sources for protest data. They present only the absolute protest figures (in volume 2), while listing population elsewhere (in volume 1). More problematic is the fact that the latter data are given only in gross form for two periods, thus making it impossible for any researcher to combine the two factors on an annualized (or any other) basis.

An even more interesting finding is that periodicity may be a significant factor in its own right, i.e., the dynamics and norms of certain time periods may have characteristics all their own which influence the level of protest during that period. In a sense, this is a refinement of some previous theories which posit a "culture of conflict" based on previous levels of conflict. The findings here suggest that this may be true, but only for a certain time frame, until some "break point" changes the protest environment, with subsequent protest basing itself on the "culture" of that period alone and not necessarily events which may have happened before the "break point."

The most general finding--and from a research and methodological standpoint, by far the most important one--is the erroneousness of testing any theory on the basis of a general dependent variable called "protest." As people protest on specific issues, it makes far more sense to divide the protest-frequency figures among a number of issues, and test each theory relative to each (broad) issue category.

Our four issue-discrete regression models show clearly that this is the only way to come to any sort of real understanding as to the significant factors underlying "protest" in all its variegation, for in most cases the significant factors underlying one issue area were different from all the others. *No previous protest study has approached the phenomenon from this perspective, and here we may have still another reason for the jumble of contradictory evidence produced by earlier studies.* If one country has mostly economic-issue protest (but all the events are scored as general "protest"), while another has social-issue conflict (but the same general classification is in force), etc., there should be little surprise that the factors found to be significant among those nations differ greatly.

Another reason for the present state of conflict theory confusion was addressed subsequently: political-culture and political-communication factors are less amenable to quantification, and thus are not very widely addressed by previous studies. Here a more analytical and qualitative approach was employed.

Regarding the first factor, it was briefly argued that given the peculiar past of the Jewish people, a political culture of "oppositionism" evolved over the millennia which was expressed historically, theologically/philosophically, and legally/institutionally. This oppositionist heritage manifested itself in several ways--argumentativeness, protest, disobedience, and rebellion--and may be a core cultural factor underlying Israelis' willingness (or at least lack of aversion) to protest.[2]

Much more work has been done in the professional literature regarding the political culture of protest during the contemporary period. Yet here too there is a paucity of approaches, with the overwhelming emphasis on attitudinal surveys and the virtual avoidance of all other "softer" means of analyzing the subject. There is no doubt that many of these public opinion survey works are first-rate (e.g., Barnes and Kaase; Wolfsfeld), and significantly add to our understanding of protest as seen from the perspective of the public at large and the protesters specifically. This, however, is not enough for the development of a full-blown theory of the political culture of protest, for the protesters, and certainly the public, are not always aware of the "cultural" factors underlying their thoughts and behavior.

As a result, we took here a more comprehensive approach, focusing on certain socio-behavioral manifestations which highlight the existence and nature of such a protest culture. To begin with, if an oppositionist culture did exist in a country's past, to what extent does the present society still identify with it? Second, in areas other than the purely political, are there signs of citizen willingness to act against (or circumvent) the norms, institutions, and even the law (e.g., an underground economy)? And third, even if this is not generally the case, assuming that official and institutional avenues of protest exist (e.g., ombudsman, civilian review boards, etc.), to what extent are they utilized by the public?[3]

There is one extremely important aspect of political culture which should be noted here as well, usually referred to as the "frequency fallacy." Not only is culture usually not taken into account as a factor underlying protest (this is especially true for statistically based studies), but virtually all cross-comparative studies implicitly take it for granted that any given level of protest frequency will have somewhat the same impact on the nations surveyed. However, above and beyond objective/institutional differences regarding the addressee (the authorities) in each country--e.g. breadth of the government's popular support, electoral accountability (if any), etc.--the matter of a protest cultural norm might be quite central: "The 'destabilizing' impact of any particular political event, X, is determined by the extent to which that event constitutes an 'abnormal' *deviation* from the previous pattern of X's which is evident within that system in the previous time period."[4] In other words, a protest wave or outbreak might have a very different impact in a country without a significant protest tradition as compared to a country already inured to endemic protest.

Indeed, much the same could be said for the same country at different time periods. An example of this in the Israeli case would be the eruption of the Black Panther protest, which caused an almost immediate reaction on the part of the government, coming as it did after almost fifteen years of relative quiet. In the eighties, on the other hand, there were numerous protest campaigns of equal intensity with far less impact--coming as they did during a period of protest plenitude, with the authorities being "accustomed" to protest attacks. If this is true, then our conclusion regarding the degree of protest success in Israel can be said to be true only for the specific period covered (1979-1986), and not necessarily the case for any "protest campaigns" from 1955 through 1970 when Israeli protest in general was far less frequent.

When we turn to the final major factor underlying protest which we studied--blocked political communication--we find that the possibilities of investigating this aspect are, albeit indirectly, even more numerous. One important point, regarding which Israel may constitute somewhat of an exceptional case, must be stated at the outset: it is not so much how many channels are petrified or blocked that is critical in explaining the degree of extraparliamentary protest, but rather how many formal channels are open and relatively easy to access. The reason we have focused on the "blockage" side in the case of Israel is twofold: first, because the importance of this factor and the ways in which it can be investigated needs emphasis, and second, because in Israel open institutional channels of political communication (from the public to the authorities) virtually do not exist!

In brief, the elements we found relevant for any single- (or even multiple-) country study are: (1) the frequency of voting opportunities; (2) the system of elections, i.e., proportional or district, which affects (to some extent) the level of political accountability and openness to public input; (3) the organizational size, membership, structure, and functioning of the political parties (i.e., large and cumbersome vs. small and efficient; mass mobilizing vs. elite; complex vs. simple hierarchy; and ideological/lifestyle-influencing vs. instrumental/vote-gathering).

In addition, we analyzed a number of other party-related elements which have broader research application to the entire political system: (4) center-periphery (social, economic, and political) relationships; (5) the level of and opportunities for "voluntarism" (self-initiated public activity); (6) bureaucratization; and (7) openness to generational change. All these can serve as useful indicators of the reasons underlying blocked political communication in any society.

The question of whether, and to what extent, actual blocked communication that exists in a country can be addressed through an investigation of some of the phenomena was reviewed next. First, a comparison between various levels of government regarding the frequency of protest over time can be very useful, especially in those countries where significant electoral or institutional change has occurred on at least one of the governmental levels. Second, despite quite a lot of work which has already been done regarding protest and the electoral cycle, no one has attempted to hold the economic variables constant in order to ascertain if a residue of protest remains which might be explained by political-communication theory. As the data presented in our analysis suggest, economic explanations for the decline of protest during election periods are not sufficient to account for the entire phenomenon.

Third, the (un)availability of mass media (especially television) in Israel seems to be strongly connected to protest frequency. Studies of other countries could certainly use this as a springboard for more refined research not possible in the Israeli case. For example, in those countries with strong local TV coverage one might be able to discover whether the number of local stations is correlated in any way to the degree of local protest (the same, of course, could be done with newspapers)--other factors being held constant. Fourth, virtually every nation-state has its outgroups on the margins of society. The degree to which they avail themselves of protest (especially relative to other "ingroup" population sectors with many of the same socio-demographic characteristics) can also serve as an indication of the extent of blocked channels of political communication.

The last area of general research interest with which we attempted to come to grips was the question of protest success. Our approach can best be defined as "subjective-professional-empirical," i.e., asking political scientists with extensive knowledge of the local situation to evaluate the measure of achievement of all protest campaigns found to exist over a specific time frame. Such an approach (as opposed to other more rigorously statistical methodologies employed by previous researchers) was chosen because many of the protest campaigns in Israel are over relatively incommensurable issues not readily quantifiable. The same probably holds true at least to a certain extent in all other countries. Thus, such an approach is meant not to take the place of, but rather to supplement, previous methodologies.

The Israeli results suggest that success is somewhat limited. Whether this is universally true can be determined only by future research employing a similar methodology in other national contexts. To be sure, there is room for improvement and refinement. For example, one might disseminate a questionnaire among the protest-group leadership as well as the political decision-makers (bureaucratic and political), as Wolfsfeld has done in the Israeli case. The possible gap between their respective perceptions might explain the persistence of protest on the one hand, and its relatively limited success on the other.

Insofar as Israel specifically is concerned, our general conclusions are clear. First, during the last two decades the protest phenomenon has been growing fairly steadily to the point where it now constitutes and is accepted as a "normal" part of the general political process. Second, despite the very high level of protest participation, Israeli public protest until now has been fairly nonthreatening to the social and political order. The degree of protest violence is fairly low, and the vast majority of demands are of the "low-level" variety: changes in governmental policy, legislation, or resource distribution--not threats to the government or regime.

Third, the reasons for such protest are numerous, but three general factors seem to be at work as we noted above: (1) some traditional economic and social factors; (2) a Jewish cultural tendency to be "stiff-necked" and oppositionist; (3) a serious ongoing process of systemic political petrification (on the level of central government) which has made political communication from bottom to top increasingly difficult.

As noted from the outset of this study, any attempt to rigorously quantify the relative importance of these factors (and others as well) is doomed to failure, primarily because the latter two do not lend themselves to easy statistical manipulation (if they are quantifiable at all). Based on the findings of this study it is possible to suggest only in gross terms the relative importance of the three.

The element of discrete economic, political, and social variables, in quite varying strengths, is obviously important in explaining the short-term ups and downs of protest frequency. Given that protest variations do exist on an annualized basis, it would be foolish to try to tie these variations to such relatively constant factors as culture and institutional (dys)functioning.

On the other hand, even in the quietest of social, economic, and political times (the late fifties and most of the sixties, notwithstanding a few notorious episodes), political protest existed in Israel--suggesting that as a constant "background" factor Jewish (and Israeli) political culture is of some, and perhaps even great, importance. To be sure, the Israeli accretions to the hoary Jewish political culture have been changeable, and in some ways have even developed subsequent to (and not before) changes in Israeli protest behavior. Nevertheless, there are too many stereotypical (justifiably so) traits of the Sabra--not to mention a number of macro-social behavior patterns which we outlined in chapter 6--which tie in very neatly with the notion of a cultural predisposition on the part of the average Israeli to verbally attack, generally complain, and politically protest.

Our third central factor--blocked political communication--seems to be the most important one of all, especially over the past two decades. Almost all of the socio-economic variables have remained fairly constant during this period compared to the first twenty or so years; it would be even harder to suggest that Israeli political culture *per se* has shifted dramatically since the early seventies (although as we have shown, over time protest tends to legitimize future protest, so that a slow cultural shift has taken place). The major independent variable that has changed significantly over the years (for the worse) is formal citizen political communication, and obversely (for the better) informal means of communication, specifically television. The overlapping fit between these two elements on the one hand, and the continuing surge of public protest on the other hand, indicates quite clearly that systemic petrification constitutes an overriding long-term factor underlying Israeli extraparliamentarism.

The final analysis, then, is both positive and negative. Israelis continue to be very interested and involved in their country's political life, but are being forced to utilize modes of political expression which are potentially socially disruptive and in practice relatively inefficient. While their cultural mindset may predispose them to being contentious in any situation, they have shown that given the opportunity they would prefer to channel such protest through formal or official routes.

Thus, the question facing the Israeli leadership is not how to lower the public's political input. Rather, the challenge facing the authorities is how to routinize such input in a general "parliamentary" fashion by establishing institutions and processes that would enable protest transmission in fairly orderly fashion. Above and beyond the serious security, economic, and social difficulties the country continues to harbor, the problem of systemic political reform stands as the overriding challenge facing Israel today.

What are the political and policy reforms that could be instituted in order to ameliorate much of Israeli extraparliamentarism? While a comprehensive survey and analysis of all the possibilities would lead us too far afield at this point, several of the more significant options can be briefly highlighted.

(A) *Electoral Reform*: Israel is the only country in the Western world with a national proportional election system whereby one's vote is cast for a political party list exclusively, with the entire country constituting one gigantic "district." Put another way, no citizen in Israel has a geographic representative; no Knesset member represents a geographic constituency. The result is a divorce between ruler and ruled, as the Israeli voter has no means of holding specific representatives accountable for their (mis)deeds, no way of ensuring even that such elected officials will listen to the concerns of their "constituents"--other than voting for an entirely different party (with the same impotence the next time around), a matter of some overkill.[5]

The choice currently under serious consideration is the multi-candidate regional district system--coupled with national proportional representation (similar to that found in West Germany). This is the "official" version recommended by a special bipartisan Knesset Committee (in early 1989), after an initial push by Israel's academic community.[6]

This proposed type of system would seem to resolve the fundamental problem of the present divorce between the representative and the constituent in a more complete manner, as it places three representatives in each of twenty regional districts, with the other sixty MKs being elected nationally. However, it is not ideal because each individual voter still has no single representative to hold accountable, while each MK can "foist" blame on his/her regional colleagues. Still, it has the potential of significantly improving political communication and accountability, rendering extraparliamentary activity mostly unnecessary except as a last resort.[7]

In any case, few would deny that such a system is superior to the present one which has no features encouraging such orderly political dialogue. Changing the election system (in whatever fashion) will almost certainly lead to some diminution in the extent of Israeli extraparliamentary activity.

(B) *Internal Party Reform*: As noted earlier in the book, from the establishment of most of Israel's significant parties in the 1920s and 1930s until at least the mid- to late 1970s the parties' internal political structure and processes were marked by a high degree of centralization and "democratic authoritarianism" bordering on the oligarchical.[8] This was especially true regarding the nominations process which constituted the central control mechanism of the party leadership--for decades taking place in the proverbial "smoke-filled room" of what was called the *va'adat minuyyim* (nominating committee). As a result, there was little incentive for the MK to be close to the public, and the quality of the Israeli MK tended to suffer.

While it is true that some changes have been made in the past decade,[9] and that these reforms undoubtedly have broadened the socio-demographic base of the Knesset candidate lists, it is doubtful whether they in any manner have succeeded in loosening the link between MK and party to the benefit of the broader citizen constituency.[10] One could even make the argument that the reverse is the case, as now each potential Knesset candidate must spend a lot more time in rounding up Central Committee delegate support than in the past, ultimately also leaving the MK with many more political obligations than heretofore.

In short, the great divide between voter and MK continues to exist despite some democratization of the internal party nominations process. Direct primary elections would be a much more significant solution; but even if this is deemed too unpalatable or radical a step for the dominant parties to accept, then at the least they should try indirect primaries whereby the competing candidates for delegates to the party convention (i.e., Central Committee) expressly declare whom they support within the party for Knesset membership. The ensuing political obligation of the Knesset party-list winners to their supporting delegates will be no less, but at least these delegates would then be somewhat responsible (and held accountable by the rank and file) for the respective MKs' parliamentary behavior.

(C) *Political Decentralization*: One of the more obvious prescriptions which emerges from our earlier analysis is the need for greater decentralized decision-making in Israel. It should be stated at the outset that few would suggest a constitutional transformation into a federal-type system with some rough equality between central and local authorities. Yet there exist many intermediate possibilities which would enable local government to perform to its maximal ability, thereby reducing the pressure on the overburdened (and unadaptive) central system.

Perhaps the single most important reform in this sphere would be the granting of full revenue-raising authority (local income tax, etc.) to the municipalities and regional councils. As presently constituted, the Interior Ministry provides approximately half of the localities' annual budget through mandated apportionments and grants,[11] while strictly limiting the ways in which they can raise money through taxation. The result is worse than outright central control since neither level of government has sole responsibility or accountability. Mayors who are directly elected by their local constituents are held accountable for poor performance, but may not necessarily be responsible (in the sense of lack of sufficient legislative or taxing authority to ameliorate the problem). Central government functionaries (including the ministers themselves) may be ultimately responsible, but within the present electoral system cannot be held politically accountable (in the sense of suffering personal electoral punishment). Thus, whatever amount of power is to be delegated to the local leadership, it must be relatively whole and clearcut.

If the protest data are any indication, one can generally suggest that the more autonomy given the localities the better the Israeli public would be served--and the less need for them to protest. Even more interestingly, these localities could well serve as the political laboratories for some of the electoral and systemic reforms mentioned above. Indeed, the first such experiment has proved to be a rousing success. Direct election of the mayor, a heretofore revolutionary step within the Israeli context, was met with the greatest aplomb by the electorate which, despite some decline in voter participation, showed a relatively high level of sophistication through ticket-splitting and the election of independent (ideologically unaffiliated) candidates as well as local party lists. Surprisingly, given Israeli politicians' penchant for mudslinging, the system has in general worked quite peacefully as the local leaders have come to realize that they are being judged on the basis of performance and not ideological rhetoric or superficial personality. With greater freedom over their local political system, the localities might even venture to usher in some types of primary elections and other forms of electoral democratization--thereby serving as models for the central government to emulate after due testing in the local arenas. In short, one of the easiest and successfully proven ways for the central government to reduce protest is to transfer important functions, along with the concomitant full budgetary and operative powers, to those who more closely understand--and are already being held accountable by--the service constituency.[12]

(D) *Mass Media Development*: The emergence of television in Israel in the late sixties roughly coincided with the dramatic increase in public protest, as we saw earlier in the book. Indeed, it was even noted that a good case can be made for the assertion that this mass medium in no small measure *caused* such an increase. Wouldn't, then, the projected development of television and related media (a second TV channel, satellite pay TV, cable TV, teletext, additional radio stations, etc.--all in various stages of legislative consideration and/or bureaucratic implementation as of this writing) only further strengthen the protest phenomenon?

Not necessarily. It all depends on what use will be made of these additional media, by both the government and the public at large. We may begin here by noting a puzzling irony. If one compares the American and Israeli respective interrelationships between their electronic media and the government's use of such media, one discovers that while government legal control is far more pronounced in Israel, the constructive political use of television (especially) is more advanced in the U.S. For example, very rarely does one find the prime minister or any minister holding an open press conference as is *de rigueur* periodically in the American context. In general, governmentally initiated use of formalized media avenues in order to explain official policy is almost non-existent in Israel. This is all the more paradoxical given Israel's comprehensive and sophisticated *hasbarah* ("public relations") network around the globe--almost as if the Israeli government is more worried about what Jew and Gentile is thinking overseas than the local constituency back home!

Greater governmental use of the media's "open" channel of communication to the Israeli public would be no small step in reducing certain kinds of protest. While it is true that most protest results from disagreement with policy and/or the inability to more formally express such discontent, other times it emanates from a lack of understanding of the reasons and necessity for difficult measures. Were the Israeli authorities to treat the population as mature citizens and publicly reason with them-- especially when the going gets rough--the public might even surprise them on occasion[13] and not take to the streets in angry protest.

(E) *Governmental Withdrawal from the Market Economy*: Much has been written about the government's overwhelming dominance of Israel's quasi-market economy, especially regarding the deleterious economic effects of exaggerated control, intervention, and supervision. In simple terms, the main argument is that the less public bureaucratic control over the market, the healthier the economy. To this we can add, the healthier the economy, the less public protest which might ensue.

But there is an equally important additional aspect here, albeit far more subtle in nature. It has to do with the Israeli public's economic psychology, i.e., its culture and mentality of governmental paternalism. Since the start of the Zionist enterprise early in the twentieth century, the economic development of the *yishuv* and later of the State itself has been based primarily on channeling resources through the central institutions downwards, and not on the free-choice initiatives and efforts of the pioneers and (later) citizens themselves. As a result, the Israeli public is predisposed not only to turning to its government for help in times of economic distress but also to reflexively turning *against* its government in protest for causing such travail.

More recently, however, a noticeable shift in macro-economic policy can be discerned as the Israeli government (whether led by the Likud or Labor) is less willing, and certainly less able, to bail out each failing company or economic enterprise. In the short run, such a policy about-face is sure to engender even more protest over economic and social issues. However, over the long run steady and consistent governmental withdrawal from the market is bound to change the public's traditional attitude regarding Israeli economic paternalism. With their expectations of governmental involvement lowered, economic pressure--in the guise of protest demonstrations--should subside (or at least be deflected to the local, private source of the specific problem).

(F) *Ministerial and Bureaucratic Efficiency*: As noted in several places in this book, Israel's bureaucracy is unwieldy and inefficient, with an increasing measure of corruption in evidence as well. There can be little doubt that part of the reason Israelis need to protest is the relatively low quality of governmental service, especially in light of the high levels of taxation which they must bear. Among other things, this can be seen in the high number of annual complaints to the state ombudsman (who finds roughly half to be justified). Thus, while the "big"-issue protests capture the headlines (national security, religious legislation, etc.), many Israeli protests address themselves not to policy but to *implementation*.

It is at this point that we need to return to our finding regarding the relationship between cabinet size and public protest. There seemed to be some evidence that as the number of ministers increases, the activist citizens who wish to communicate politically have more (and better-defined) addresses to turn to, especially for social protest over the post-1967 decades. We can add here that while the ratio of ministers to parliamentarians in 1986, for example, was probably the highest in the world--25 of 120, or over 20%--this absolute number of governmental portfolios was smaller than that found in many other democracies (e.g., Great Britain, France, etc.). The "problem" of "bloated" government is obviously a relative one, but it seems to offer a number of advantages impinging on protest. The most direct one, of course, is the enriched "nerves of government" phenomenon just mentioned.

Beyond that, however, may lie a more indirect connection, for as the purview of any particular minister narrows (as a function of there being more portfolios to hand out), the better the job such a minister can perform in supervising, understanding, and controlling that specific bureaucratic bailiwick. The "waste" of paying for another ministerial Volvo, chauffeur, and secretary may in the final analysis more than pay its way in improved bureaucratic functioning--and subsequent reduced public pressure and protest against the ministry's inefficiency.[14]

The prescription here, then, goes counter to Israeli conventional wisdom: certainly from the standpoint of reducing public protest, Israel would do well to institutionalize within its ministerial/bureaucratic structure a relatively high number of departments, each with its own minister.

(G) *The Arab-Israeli Conflict*: This subject has been left for last, not because it is relatively unimportant (exactly the opposite), but because it is not one readily amenable to any hard and fast prescriptive solutions. Any such offering would be extremely presumptuous, not to mention that it would lead us very far afield. We shall merely schematically outline how the conflict impinges in many different ways on Israeli protest, thereby indirectly illustrating the extremely positive effect the resolution of the conflict would have on Israeli extraparliamentarism.

First and foremost, the majority of political-issue protest in Israel is tied to the conflict: territories, settlements, peace negotiations, etc. In addition, the majority of all Israeli-Arab protest is conflict-related. Complete peace would directly remove at a single stroke about 25% of all Israeli protest.

Second, the economic cost of keeping up a huge army (relatively speaking) seriously distorts the Israeli economy, with effects felt on inflation and especially high taxation. Additionally, the reserve duty required of most males every year (from thirty to sixty days, above and beyond the three years of initial service) is a severe drag on the efficient functioning of the society, not to mention a psychological element which does nothing to improve the mood of the conscripted/mobilized populace. Here too, a significant decrease in military expenditures and service would bring a sharp decline in protest.

Third and finally, the amount of mental and political energy which the Israeli authorities must devote to the conflict is enormous, severely undermining the political system's ability to respond adequately to other, no less pressing (and for many citizens, more immediate) concerns. With the yoke of the conflict lifted, Israel's politicians could devote much more time and thought to solving these nonsecurity problems, many of which have been held in abeyance for almost forty years (the decrepit educational system; the collapsing health system; the overwhelmed transport system; etc.).

In summation, it should be obvious that this wide array of prescriptive proposals involves both technical and fundamental reforms, short- and long-term changes, political as well as socio-economic developments, plus protest-specific and generalized structural revisions in the Israeli body politic. Some are already underway, others in the pipeline, most still in the discussion stage, if that. The whole package of these proposals need not be implemented, however, in order to reduce Israeli protest; as already stated, introduction of a few would go far toward accomplishing that goal.

The interesting thing is that it is not merely the Israeli general public which seems to be demanding reform of the system. So are Israel's opinion leaders. In a poll conducted during the winter of 1987 encompassing over 250 of Israel's political, social, and economic elite, one of the questions referred to the possible need of fixing the political system. As Table 10.1 makes clear, very few felt that there was no need for systemic change.

Table 10.1:
Israel's Opinion Leaders' Responses to Systemic Political Reform

Answer		1st Preference	2d Preference
(1)	Change the election system	50.4% (N = 127)	14.3% (N = 36)
(2)	Transfer to a Presidential system	13.5% (N = 34)	13.1% (N = 33)
(3)	Develop more means of citizen participation in decisionmaking	9.9% (N = 25)	11.5% (N = 20)
(4)	Restrict number of parties	9.5% (N = 24)	15.9% (N = 40)
(5)	Strengthen Prime Minister's authority	5.9% (N = 15)	9.5% (N = 24)
(6)	Strengthen Knesset's authority	4.0% (N = 10)	11.9% (N = 30)
(7)	No need to change much in the present political system	4.0% (N = 10)	1.6% (N = 4)
(8)	Do not know	1.6% (N = 4)	0.0% (N = 0)
(9)	Did not answer	1.2% (N = 3)	22.2% (N = 56)
Total		100.0% (N = 252)	100.0% (N = 252)

For their first preference, over half chose changing the election system--as was recommended and analyzed above. The third most preferred course of action is also in line with our analysis here: to develop more ways in which the people can participate in decisionmaking. And even the second most acceptable option--to switch over to a presidential system--is connected to the need for more direct political accountability and links with the people. In short, those within the "system" are no less aware of the problematics of the current situation.

When a different poll (Table 10.2) queried the general Israeli population--"Here are suggestions for change; which seems to you to be the most important?"--the results were somewhat different (so were the options presented), but still illustrate the "blocked political communication" problem.[16]

Table 10.2:
Israeli Public's Response to Systemic Reform

Answer
(1)	Preferably there should be fewer parties in Israel in order to lessen the political pressures	45%
(2)	It would be best to give greater and clearer legal powers to the Prime Minister, but with adequate checks on him	13%
(3)	It is worthwhile to devolve political authority to the local governments	5%
(4)	It would pay to change the election system so that the public would have direct influence on who their representatives to the Knesset would be	19%
(5)	It is advisable that with critical issues the government turns to the public for a referendum as is the case in other countries	17%

N = 1,079

As can be seen here, fully 41% (numbers 3 through 5) picked as their highest priority one of the recommendations outlined in this chapter. This is not nearly as strong a perception of seriously blocked communication as is found among the opinion leaders, but it is indicative nonetheless that a considerable part of the general public is thinking along those lines as well.

In short, upon nearing forty years of protest--modern Israel's equivalent of sojourning in the political wilderness--the time has come for change, as even Israel's political and social leadership acknowledges. Today's "children of Israel" have paid their dues, have shown that they have the political maturity--and certainly the willingness--to more actively participate in the Promised Land. The age of the contemporary elders has passed, with all the political paternalism of the rulers and consequent protest rebelliousness of the ruled which such a system necessarily engendered. In order to prevent Israeli protest from deteriorating into anarchic political pressure and anomic socially dysfunctional behavior, significant steps must be taken to open up the Israeli system from virtually every perspective: governmental, electoral, political party, mass media, and economic, among others. As Israeli colloquial parlance might put it, the time is ripe for both Israel's stiff-necked citizenry and their stiff-necked representatives to stick their respective necks out and begin making strides toward uncorking their mutual bottle-necked system.

We have traversed quite a distance in this book, with the problems and issues addressed being many and varied. Nonetheless, despite our attempts at digging deeper and throwing our research net wider than is usually the case, some things remain unresolved while others were virtually not touched upon at all. It is incumbent upon us to at least mention these in final passing, leaving for the future the task of coming to grips with the difficult elements involved--in the Israeli case specifically, and around the democratic world in general. We shall do so in the form of questions, without undue elaboration of all the elements involved, or the methodological difficulties which they entail.

(1) *Internal Group Dynamics*: How do ad hoc protest groups get started? Are the underlying factors social in nature (i.e., do the leaders know each other from previous experience, not necessarily extraparliamentary; have they higher educational attainments)?[17] Or perhaps the factors explaining such ad hoc protest initiative are socio-psychological: politically activist types who are personally affected by an issue?

Indeed, do we find the same activists over time constantly initiating and organizing ad hoc group protest, or is such extraparliamentarism a product of "randomly" self-selected leadership?

With regard to institutional group protest, how is the organization set up for such activity? What is the general strategy, i.e., main and subsidiary goals? Who decides this, when, and how often? How are the operational tactics decided upon, and what are they as a general rule? To what extent are they actually implemented, and what, if any, are the difficulties in such tactical implementation? Indeed, what types of financial (and other) resources are needed in "protest campaigns" over a period of time?

Linked with this, of course, is the relationship of the protest group with the mass media: what type of permanent communications setup is there for notifying the press and encouraging wide coverage? To what extent is the media aspect taken into account in developing a protest strategy in the field? Conversely, to what extent do the media "incite" the protest organization generally, and the protesters in the street, to higher levels of intensity?

On the other side of the fence, what precisely goes on in the give and take between the protest leadership and the police in setting the protest conditions? What are the usual points of contention at this stage, and when are there misunderstandings at the actual protest site?

This brings us back to the subject of internal dynamics: how well does the protest leadership control the group at the protest site? What are the internal "political" constraints within the group from the standpoint of determining moderation as opposed to violent protest behavior? Is there a higher level of leadership turnover in such groups as opposed to other political organizations with more "normal" approaches to influencing the political system?

(2) *Extraparliamentarism and the Political System*: To what extent is there concrete financial and logistical support provided by the political party to the protest movement? How is it accomplished without undermining the "independence" of the protest group?

Such questions open up a wholly different line of investigation--the use by parliamentary opposition groups of *extra*parliamentary modes of activity: under what set of circumstances will such nonruling parties turn to nonformal means of political oppositionism? Is this a matter of national political culture, or does the phenomenon exist (perhaps in several variations) in most democratic systems?

Conversely, not enough has been done regarding the parliamentary/extraparliamentary crossover from the other direction: how widespread a phenomenon is cooptation of the protest leadership by the "Establishment"? What are the tactics employed by the latter to attract the former "into the fold"? If such occurs, does it necessarily entail the demise of the protest movement or will a new generation of protest leaders emerge to carry on the fight? In such an eventuality, what (if anything) is the relationship between the new protest leaders and their predecessors who have now crossed the political Rubicon? One might even speculate that this is the best of all worlds for the protest movement, having supporters both within and outside of the formal political system; indeed, might not this be a "Trojan horse" exercise by the protesters to penetrate the Establishment, rather than a successful "raid" by the latter of the protesters' leadership--as has been thought until now?

Which leads to another, albeit related, line of inquiry: to what extent do extraparliamentary groups or movements use parliamentary modes of political activity as well? We have noted on a number of occasions in the book that protest usually supplements normal political activity, but which of the two approaches is most used by such groups? Are the two meshed or integrated in any way, or do they move on parallel tracks unconnected to each other?[18]

(3) *Protest from the Politicians' Perspective*: How do the politicians perceive protest pressure? What are the criteria by which protests are assessed for their political impact? Size? Intensity? Staying power? Public backing? Media support? Is such protest pressure overtly considered when decisions are made, or is it more a matter of an additional "background" variable to be subconsciously taken into account?

Second, how do Israeli leaders perceive the general success rate of protest in their country? We have already mentioned the possible ramifications of misperception on this score, but does such misperception actually occur as is the case with the general public? Is such (mis)perception a function of the specific governmental role, or personal party prominence, of the politician?

(4) *Public Protest and Systemic Change*: In other democratic countries which (unlike Israel) *have already undergone significant systemic reform*, are there any indications (based on a comparison of prereform and postreform periodic protest) that a correlation exists between "opening the political-communication channels" and the level of extraparliamentarism?

Similar cross-comparative efforts could be made from the quite opposite direction: are there other democratic systems which have suffered "political decay" similar to that of Israel in the form of blocked political communication? If so, would a longitudinal analysis of protest frequency over time reinforce, or contradict, the hypothesis presented here? In addition, can we replicate in other democracies some of the indirect "proofs" (e.g., election-period protest, locally/centrally addressed protest, etc.) as outlined in our study?

(5) *The Culture of Oppositionism*: Is there attitudinal proof (not just culturally extrinsic) of any existing connection between a tendency to protest (in all its elemental components) and Jewish cultural identity? In addition, while a few cross-national studies have tested for protest activity on the part of Protestants as compared to Catholics, what would the inclusion of Jews, or Moslems in such countries as France and West Germany, show us? Alternatively, what would happen if we polled Christians, Moslems, and Druze in Israel, compared to Israeli *Jewish* responses?

Furthermore, a number of questions come to mind with regard to Israeli Jewry: does "degree of religiosity" have a reinforcing influence in the direction of protest activity? While the "religiosity" variable in our poll indicated no such correlation (with protest participation), perhaps this was a result of the standard underrepresentation of ultra-Orthodox Israeli Jews? Or maybe the intervening (and critical) variable is Jewish education, i.e., familiarity with the "oppositionist" historical heritage and/or intensity of biblical/talmudic study?

(6) *The Problem of Data-Source Sufficiency Revisited*: To what extent is protest not reported in the daily press? Could we perhaps get a more exact picture of this by "tagging along" with several established protest groups over a relatively lengthy period of time, to see whether and how their protest activity is covered by the media? (This would also aid in addressing some of the aforementioned suggestions relating to protest group/police relations, as well as the internal decisionmaking process regarding the strategy and tactics of the group, especially its need for continuous media coverage.)

Alternatively, might it not be very useful for a researcher (or team) to be stationed outside the Knesset and/or prime minister's office (similarly, the U.S. Congress and/or the White House, etc.) for a month or two in order to quantitatively tally and qualitatively score the protest events which occur there, and compare these with the papers' subsequent reports?

And what about the *electronic media* as a resource for fact-gathering? Given the far larger impact that television (especially compared to the press) has on the public as well as its elected representatives, hasn't the time come for more systematic use and study of this medium both as a source for protest data and as a facilitating factor in the entire process of protest generation?[20]

(7) *Other Forms of Public Protest*: Beyond public group demonstrations, are there other significant forms of extraparliamentarism which might shed additional light on the phenomenon in general? For example, what is the significance of "poster protest," which has been found to be widely employed in Israel among the ultra-Orthodox (not only externally against the secular government but also internally between various factions within this "closed" socio-religious community)? As "poster protest" seems to be of great importance in some other cultural settings as well (e.g., China), is this the preferred mode of extraparliamentary expression in traditional societies? How widespread is such protest around the world? What are its "rules of the game" and dynamics?

Second, as the "public petition" has had a long and illustrious history, shouldn't some attention be given to it? What types of groups are generally behind such petitions? What are their goals, and the reasons for choosing this (seemingly more tortuous) route instead of a protest demonstration? Conversely, one might investigate the socio-demographics of the petition signers: what is their political typology (e.g., activist, mildly participatory, generally apathetic, etc.)?[21]

Third, what of the press as a venue for protest expression? One can begin with letters to the editor critical of government policy, advance to freelance articles attacking such policy (or laws), and graduate to a content analysis (quantitative and qualitative) of in-house press commentaries (whether by-lined or editorial column) protesting against the way things are being done within the polity as a whole: of these three general journalistic forms of critical expression, which is generally most frequent? Which tends to spearhead (or initiate) protest campaigns? Which carries the most weight for the Establishment as well as the public?

More generally, does "protest journalism" (in all its variegated manifestations) precede or postdate the rise of street protest? If a cursory study of the post-Yom Kippur War and the anti-War in Lebanon protest phenomena is any indication, media protest tends to lag behind the public's own protest, but is this generally the case in Israel and/or around the world?

Fourth and finally, what role do cultural media (i.e., the arts) play in the protest milieu? In Israel, for example, during the late seventies and eighties almost all "serious" films produced locally were protest-oriented (above and beyond high culture's normal role of social criticism); much of the country's theater is highly politicized, with several plays causing national scandals because of their "unwanted" protest message; more recently still, some Israeli pop music and photography/art have begun to include overt protest messages--do any of these influence the general public, potential protest activists, and/or the government? The anti-Vietnam War movement and that decade's revolutionary culture suggest that a strong link may indeed exist in certain circumstances, but what precisely is the connection, and under what conditions?

This book concludes, then, on both a depressing and an exciting note--depressing because of the huge gaps that remain in our knowledge regarding public protest; exciting because of the challenges which still lie ahead. If this book has succeeded in illuminating significant portions of Israeli protest specifically, and the overall phenomenon in general, then this final concluding section provides an antidote to any illusions of fully understanding extraparliamentarism. Like the success ratio of public protest in Israel, we (hopefully) have succeeded in achieving some of our goals. Complete success on this score will have to await much further work addressing some of the same aspects covered in this book, and most of the additional elements merely mentioned above.

Appendix A:
Biblical List of Oppositionism to Authority

CODE: *   = Non-Jewish
        A   = Argumentativeness
        P   = Protest
        D   = Disobedience
        R   = Rebellion
        O   = (general) Opposition

(1)*   Gen. III, 10-24: Adam and Eve eating of the Tree of Knowledge   [D]

(2)*   ---- IV, 9: Cain's response to God: "Am I my brother's keeper?"   [A]

(3)   ---- XVIII, 23-33: Abraham arguing with God over the number of wise men sufficient to save Sodom and Amorah   [A]

(4)   ---- XXXII, 25-32: Jacob "struggles" with a "man" (angel of God) and wins; he is renamed as a result   [O]

(5)*   Exod. I, 17: The Egyptian midwives not heeding Pharaoh's order to kill all the Hebrew male babies   [D]

(6)   ---- V, 21: The Children of Israel protest to Moses and Aaron because the "intercession" of the two with Pharaoh has caused their work to become even harder   [P]

(7)   ---- XIV, 10-13: The Israelites protest to Moses over being brought out of Egypt only to be pursued by their former taskmasters   [P]

(8)   ---- XV, 24: "The people murmured against Moses" because of the lack of drinking water   [P]

(9)   ---- XVI, 2-3: Again the Israelites complain about the lack of food   [P]

(10)   ---- XVII, 1-3: Once again complaints over the lack of water   [P]

(11)   ---- XXXII, 1-6: Making the Golden Calf, a serious transgression against the word of God   [D]

(12)   ---- XXXII, 7-14: God announces his intention to destroy Israel; Moses forcefully reminds God of the divine promises to Israel; God relents   [A]

(13)   Numb. XI, 11-17: Moses complains to God about the Israelites' demands for meat   [P]

(14)   ---- XII, 1-15: Conflict over authority between Miriam and Aaron versus Moses as seen in the claim "Hath He [God] not spoken also with us?"   [P]

(15)   ---- XIV, 1-4: After receiving a negative report from ten of the twelve spies sent to Canaan, the Israelites murmur against Moses and talk of selecting a new leader to return them to Egypt   [P]

(16)   ---- XVI, 1-14: Rebellion of Korah against the authority of Moses and Aaron   [R]

(17)   ---- XX, 1-5: Once again the Israelites protest to Moses and Aaron for bringing them into the wilderness   [P]

(18)   ---- XXI, 5: Again complaints about the wilderness, lack of water, and monotonous bread   [P]

(19)*   ---- XXIII-XXIV: Balaam blesses the Children of Israel instead of cursing them as King Balak wanted   [D]

(20)   ---- XXV, 1-9: The Israelites consort with the Midianite women and
        bow to their gods   [D]
(21)   Judg. I, 27 to II, 3: Israel transgresses God's prohibition against coming
        to terms with the inhabitants of Canaan   [D]
(22)   ---- II, 11-23: The Israelites continually revert to Ba'al worship, despite
        their Judges warnings (see also IV, 1-3; V, 1-6; VIII, 33-35; X, 6-8; XIII, 1)   [D]
(23)   ---- IX, 6-21: Yotham, son of Gideon, publicly protests the
        anointing of Avimelekh as king   [P]
(24)   I Sam. VIII, 4-7: The Israelites demand the anointing of a king as a temporal
        sovereign against the wishes of the prophet Samuel   [A]
(25)   ---- XIV, 24-33: Jonathan and the rest of Saul's soldiers disobey his
        orders not to eat, even breaking the laws of Kashrut   [D]
(26)   ---- XV, 1-9: Saul disobeys God's command to totally destroy Amalek   [D]
(27)   ---- XV, 10-30: Samuel rebukes Saul, and tells him that the monarchy
        will pass to another   [P]
(28)   ---- XVII, 17: The servants of King Saul refuse to obey his order to
        slay the priests who aided David   [D]
(29)   ---- XXII, 1-8: David in underground opposition to Saul   [O]
(30)   II Sam. XII, 1-14: Nathan rebukes David for taking Uriah's wife   [P]
(31)   ---- XV-XVIII: The revolt of Abshalom against his father, King David   [R]
(32)   ---- XX, 1-22: The revolt of Sheva against David's authority   [R]
(33)   I King. XII, 19: The Israelites rebel against Rehoboam because of
        the heavy load placed upon them   [R]
(34)   ---- XII, 28: Jeroboam fashions two golden calves and sets them up as gods   [D]
(35)   ---- XIII, 19: The prophet sent to warn Jeroboam himself trans-
        gresses God's command not to eat in Shechem; is referred to as "The man
        of God who rebelled against the word of God"   [D]
(36)   ---- XIV, 22-24: The tribe of Judah too commits abominations and idol
        worship (there follows a series of individual kings who transgress against
        God's laws: Nadav, XV, 26; Ba'sha, XVI, 34; Omri, XVI, 25-26; Ahab,
        XVI, 30; Ahaziah, XXII, 52-54; Jehoram, II Kings, III, 1-3; Jehoram, VIII, 18;
        Ahaziah, VIII, 25-27; Jehoazaz, XIII 1-3; Joash, XIII, 9; Amaziah, XIV, 23-24;
        Zechariah, XV, 8-9; Menachem, XV, 17-18; Pekahia, XV, 23-24; Pekah,
        XV, 27-28; Athaz, XVI, 1-4; Hoshea, XVII, 1-2; Menashe, XX, 1-9; Ammon,
        XXI, 19-20; Jehoazaz, XXIII, 31-32; Jehoyakim, XXIII, 36-37. Many of these
        kings were toppled by rebels acting in the name of the Lord, e.g., Jehu,
        II King., IX:14)   [D,R]
(37)   ---- XVIII, 17-21: Elijah opposes the idolatrous practices of King Ahab   [P]
(38)   Isaiah I, 23-27; X, 1-4: Isaiah rails against the corruption of the
        governing elite   [P]
(39)   Jerem. XXII, 1-19: Jeremiah in political and social opposition to the
        ruling government   [P]
(40)   ---- XXXIV, 10-12: After listening to God's command to free their slaves,
        the people cause the slaves to return, thus directly disobeying God   [D]
(41)   ---- XLIII, 1-7: Though commanded not to go to Egypt, the people go
        anyway, in defiance of God   [D]

(42)   ---- XLIV, 15-19: In defiance of Jeremiah's admonition, the Jews in
       Egypt declare their intention to pursue a course of idolatry   [D]
(43)   Amos II, 6-8: Amos protests against social injustice, greed, and
       sexual promiscuity   [P]
(44)   ---- VII, 7-17: Amos protests against the ways of Jeroboam and argues for
       his right to express oppositionist criticism   [P]
(45)   Jonah I, 1-3: Though commanded by God to prophesy against Nineveh,
       Jonah seeks to escape from God   [D]
(46)* Esther I, 9-12: Queen Vashti publicly refuses King Ahaseurus's request
       to appear before him during a state party   [D]
(47)   ---- III, 2-5: Mordechai refuses to show Haman reverence   [D]
(48)   Daniel III, 13-30: Shadrach, Meshach, and Abednego refuse to bow
       down before Nebuchadnezzar's images   [D]
(49)   ---- VI, 6-23: Daniel publicly transgresses Darius's law of prayer
       only to Darius himself   [D]
(50)   II Chron. XXV, 5-10: An unnamed prophet warns King Amaziah not to
       go to war with a mercenary army   [P]

NOTE: This list is not necessarily complete. Not included are cases in the Bible which
have been interpreted by some as protest and/or disobedience although on the face of
it they are not directly indicated by the Bible's author, e.g., the Tower of Babel story
Nor are instances of disobedience to familial authority included (e.g., Tamar vs.
Judah) except where a public authority element exists as well. Finally, this list does not
take into account the important examples of civil disobedience found in the
Apocrypha, most notably the Books of the Maccabees, as well as Judith, etc.

Appendix B:
Public Opinion Survey on Israeli Public Protest

QUESTION 1: Here is a list of various public protest activities. With regard to each one please say whether in your opinion such an activity is justified in order to influence decisions affecting the whole public. [Note: The percentages are given for the "strongest" level that each respondent indicated, unless otherwise noted.]

Type of Activity	Justifying
Nonviolent, licensed demonstration	45.9%
Nonviolent, unlicensed demonstration	21.8%
Obstruction of traffic/invading government office	3.6%
Property damage: breaking windows/office equipment	0.2%
Violence against people/personal injury	3.6%
Only traffic obstruction/gov't office invasion	0.2%
Nonviolent, licensed demonstrations or traffic obstruction/ gov't office invasion	1.0%
Did not answer	1.4%
Do not justify any of the above activities	22.5%

QUESTION 2: Have you ever participated in a public protest activity (e.g., demonstrations--peaceful or non-peaceful; political strikes; invasion of government office; obstruction of public traffic, etc.)? If so, how many times?

Never participated	77.9%
Participated once	10.2%
Yes, twice	5.4%
Yes, three times	2.5%
Yes, four times	0.8%
Yes, five or more times	2.6%
Did not answer	0.6%

Of the respondents who indicated that they had not participated in public protest events (N = 974) the following question was asked:

QUESTION 3: Do you think that in the future you will participate in protest activities with regard to issues that are important to you?

	% of Whole Sample	% of "Never Participated"
Yes	25.8%	33.1%
No	51.8%	66.4%
Did not answer	22.4% (weren't asked)	0.5%

QUESTION 4: In your opinion, do legal public protests in Israel achieve their objectives?

Yes, always	5.8%
Yes, usually	19.1%
Sometimes	40.2%
Infrequently	15.6%
Never	17.7%
Did not answer	1.6%

QUESTION 5: In your opinion, do illegal public protests in Israel achieve their objectives?

Yes, always	3.9%
Yes, usually	12.3%
Sometimes	33.3%
Infrequently	20.3%
Never	28.1%
Did not answer	2.1%

QUESTION 6: In your opinion, do nonviolent public protests strengthen or weaken Israeli democracy?

Strengthen and weaken	11.2%
Strengthen	42.5%
Don't strengthen/don't weaken	29.2%
Weaken	13.7%
Did not answer	3.4%

QUESTION 7: In your opinion, are demonstrations of unemployed people justified or unjustified?

Justified	61.4%
Unjustified	34.1%
Did not answer	4.5%

QUESTION 8: In your opinion, how do the police handle demonstrations--too strongly, too weakly, or as they should?

Much too weakly	6.7%
A bit too weakly	15.5%
As they should	51.7%
A bit too strongly	14.0%
Much too strongly	4.7%
Did not answer	7.4%

QUESTION 9: In Israel, compared to other countries, there are a large number of protest activities. I shall read to you a number of possible reasons for this. Please choose up to three of the reasons which seem to you to be most important in explaining the large number of public protest activities in Israel. [The total percentage is well over 100% as the respondents could choose more than one reason.]

(a)	While in exile the Jews always protested versus the authorities, and continue this tradition also today in Israel.	10.7%
(b)	The citizen does not have enough other ways to express himself to the authorities.	49.7%
(c)	There is a need to express protest because the authorities do not respond to the will and needs of the public.	40.9%
(d)	When the ministers and members of Knesset wish for their opinion to be accepted they shout and do protest activities and this influences the man in the street.	35.1%
(e)	Living conditions in Israel are usually tough and this leads to protest activities against the authorities.	39.3%
(f)	Whoever protests publicly in general achieves something. This is one of the only ways to get something.	42.2%
(g)	Did not answer	7.7%

QUESTION 10: Are you active in any form in Israeli political or public life?

Active member of a party	3.2%
Active member of a pressure group, i.e., a nonparty group which attempts to influence issues of public interest	1.9%
Independently active (e.g. writes letters to the editor, to members of Knesset, involved in community affairs, etc.)	3.8%
Inactive party member	8.2%
Not involved in any way	82.4%
Did not answer	0.6%

QUESTION 11: The political parties in Israel differ one from the other in their ideas and their values (from right to left). Where would you place yourself on the political map, i.e., who is closer to your own ideas--the left, moderate left, moderate right, or right?

Left	6.8%
Moderate left	22.9%
Moderate right	33.8%
Right	19.8%
Did not answer	16.7%

QUESTION 12: Is your personal economic situation average for people with your education, talents, and amount of work, or is your economic situation above average or below average?

Above the average	7.7%
Like the average	76.0%
Below the average	12.1%
Did not answer	4.2%

Appendix C:
Success/Failure Scores of Twenty-eight
Protest Campaigns (1979-1986)

Protest   Avg. Score

(1) Demonstrations, rock throwings by ultra-Orthodox over Ramot Road--
trying to stop its use on the Sabbath (1979-1983)   3.38

(2) Demonstrations by ultra-Orthodox vs. plans to build sports stadium in
Shuafat, Jerusalem (1979-1982)   4.25

(3) Protests by veteran Israeli Ethiopian Jews to pressure the Israeli government
into making greater efforts to bring the rest of their brethren to Israel
(1979-1982)   2.44

4) Demonstrations and "pseudo"-settlements by Gush Emunim in order to
advance and speed up settlement of the administered territories
(1979-1986)   3.13

(5) Demonstrations by ultra-Orthodox vs. the City of David archeological
digs (1979-1983)   2.94

(6) Outdoor prayer meetings and demonstrative "tours" by the Temple
Mount Faithful--to transfer sovereign control of the Temple Mount from the
Arabs to the Jews (1979-1986)   1.28

(7) Demonstrations against the peace process with Egypt and vs. conceding
Sinai (1979-1982)   1.56

(8) Protests and riots by Israeli Arabs on "Land Day" vs. land expropriation,
etc. (1979-1986)   2.11

(9) Demonstrations of groups such as *Yesh Ge'vul* vs. forcing reservists to
serve in the territories (1979-1986)   1.28

(10) Demonstrations, roadblocks, etc., of settlers vs. the "weak security
policies" of the Israeli army in the territories vis-a-vis local Arab terrorists,
inciters, etc. (1979-1986)   2.69

(11) Demonstrations by the ultra-Orthodox vs. autopsies (1980-1983)   3.00

(12) General strikes and demonstrations by Israeli Arab local authorities to
equalize government grants with those of Jewish localities (1980-1986) 2.00

(13) Demonstrations and class boycotts of teachers vs. nonimplementation
of "Etzioni Committee" recommendations (1981-1986)   2.81

(14) Demonstrations and "city closure" by Yamit (and other Sinai) residents for increasing their withdrawal compensation payments (1981-1983) 3.83

(15) Demonstrations by policemen's wives for a raise in their husbands' salaries,
plus parity with regular army soldier grades (1982-1986)   2.50

(16) Demonstrations by El Al and Histadrut workers vs. closure of El Al
on the Sabbath (1982)   1.00

(17) Demonstrations by the Orthodox for passage of the "Who Is a Jew?" bill
(1982-1986)   1.75

(18) Protests by "Peace Now," "Parents Against Silence," etc., vs. the Lebanon
War, and for the return of the army to Israel as soon as possible
(1982-1985)   2.94

(19) Mass demonstrations after the Sabra and Shatilla camp massacres for
Ariel Sharon's dismissal and establishment of an official commission of
inquiry (1982)   4.28
(20) Demonstrations by the ultra-Orthodox vs. building a new hotel wing in
Tiberias on top of a "Jewish cemetery" (1983-1985)   4.20
(21) Violent demonstrations by Druze in the Golan Heights vs. getting
Israeli ID cards and vs. the region's annexation (1983-1986)   2.20
(22) Demonstrations and class boycotts by university students vs. large increases in tuition (twice, from $700 up to $1,150) (1984-1985)   3.43
(23) Demonstrations by the Orthodox vs. opening a cinema on the Sabbath in
Petach Tikva (1984-1986)   1.67
(24) Demonstrations by ATA Textile workers vs. the company's closing
(1984-1985)   1.33
(25) Protests in favor of legislation prohibiting racism and preventing parties
such as Kach from running for election (1984-1986)   2.33
(26) Demonstrations, hunger strikes, etc., by Ethiopian immigrants vs. the
Chief Rabbinate's demand for their mass conversion (1984-1986)   2.33
(27) Demonstrations and vigils in favor of presidential pardons for
"Jewish Underground" convicts (1985-1986)   3.25
(28) Demonstrations by the Orthodox vs. building a "Mormon University" on
Mount Scopus (1985-1986)   1.75

NOTE: Scale of 1.00 to 5.00, with 1.00 = total failure, 3.00 = partial success/partial
failure, 5.00 = total success.

Appendix D:
Israeli Protest: Categories and Variables

At the start of the study it was decided to score each protest event along twelve different categories. At a relatively early point it became apparent that two of these categories--legality of the protest, and ideological vs. utilitarian nature of the protest-- were extremely problematic from the scoring point of view. On the one hand, the newspaper reports hardly ever mentioned whether a demonstration had received a license. On the other, scoring for ideological or utilitarian content proved to be too subjective a task. For example, should a protest in favor of settlements in the administered territories be considered ideological or utilitarian? Some settlers couch their fervor in distinctly national/theological/ideological terms, e.g., *Eretz Yisrael Ha'shlayma* (The Greater Land of Israel). Others view the need for settlement in purely utilitarian terms: security and (more recently) relatively inexpensive housing. It was thus decided to drop these two categories from the study, and focus on the following ten.

Categories of Protest Variables

(A) Intensity
1 - Peaceful
2 - Obstructive/Disruptive
3 - Violence vs. property
4 - Violence vs. people
5 - General riot

(B) Reaction of the Authorities
6 - No reaction
7 - Noncoercive reaction
8 - Arrests
9 - Physical force
10 - Firearms

(C) Size
11 - Small (10-99)
12 - Medium (100-999)
13 - Large (1,000-9,999)
14 - Huge (10,000+)

(D) Organization Initiating
15 - Ad hoc
16 - Organization/Pressure group
17 - Political party

(E) Issue
18 - Political
19 - Economic
20 - Social
21 - Religious

(F) Level of Authority Addressed
22 - Central government
23 - Local government
24 - Other (foreign)

(G) Duration
25 - Short (under 3 hours)
26 - Medium (3 to 24 hours)
27 - Long (over 24 hours)
28 - Not available
29 - Dispersed by police

(H) Type
30 - Outdoor rally
31 - Indoor meeting
32 - Strike (hunger, political)
33- Other

(I)   <u>Location</u>
     34 - Central city
     35 - Peripheral city/town
     36 - Rural/uninhabited

(J)   <u>Nationality</u>
     37 - Jewish
     38 - Moslem-Arab
     39 - Combined Jewish/Arab
     40 - Other (Christian, Druze)

Appendix E:
Regression Analysis Variables[1]

ECONOMIC: Nine economic variables were included in the regression, the first five of which could be considered "negative" factors, the rest "positive" in their impact, although even this is not as simple as one might suppose.

(1) *Annual rate of inflation* (INF)--Price inflation affects all citizens, albeit not necessarily equally. Israel has suffered quite severely from wild fluctuations throughout the years, with a minimum rate of 1.6% (1967) and a maximum rate (in 1984) of 373.8%! The inflation rate used here is on a calendar year (and not fiscal year) basis.

(2) *Unemployment* (UNMP)--The figure used here is not the annual average percentage, but rather the average number of mandays (due to the fact that during the earlier years, only this figure was reported). Unemployment is a narrower but more intense indicator, as far fewer suffer from it, but those who do are affected quite severely. Israel has suffered far less unemployment than most other developing countries, except during the earliest mass immigration period.

(3) *Unemployment (average mandays) per capita* (UNPC)--In order to neutralize the effect of a five-fold population increase over the years, this variable was included as well.

(4) *Income tax (maximum bracket)* (INTX)--Through most of Israel's history, the country has been among the world's leaders in high level of taxation (maximum bracket of 80% in the early fifties, and still 60% by 1986).[2] Here too we have a broad indicator of the economic burden which almost all Israelis must bear, as the lower tax brackets have generally moved in consonance with the top bracket.

(5) *Income tax revenue as a % of national income* (INTXNI)--This is a related, but somewhat different, indicator which tests for the burden which the citizenry as private individuals must bear relative to other sources of national income (corporate taxes, overseas grants, etc.). In fact, the variance in Israel has been quite dramatic: from a mere 4.8% in 1950 to 34.6% in 1986!

(6) *Private consumption increase* (PCON)--In real (inflation-controlled) terms, this variable indicates the annual rise in standard of living for the citizenry as a whole.

(7) *Private consumption increase per capita* (PCONPC)--Again in real terms, this measures improvement in standard of living, but taking into account population increases from year to year (occasionally quite substantial, due to immigration). Variations for both these indicators have been wide over the years (although usually on the high side, relative to most other developing countries), ranging from + 12.4% to - 5.2% in the PCONPC case. Overall, however, there has been a dramatic rise in private consumption, with Israel starting out as a distinctly underdeveloped and poor country, but ending up as an almost fully developed, high consumption society, by the eighties.

(8) *Gross National Product Increase* (GNP)--This variable is somewhat different from the previous two in that it represents national wealth instead of private standard of living. It measures real percentage growth in the country's GNP from year to year.

(9) *GNP Growth Per Capita* (GNPPC)--This is the same indicator, but controlled for population growth. Once again, both GNP variables have exhibited sharp

fluctuations over time (GNPPC, from + 17.0% to - 4.5%), but overall the trend has been quite strongly positive.

In the case of the latter four positive indicators, one cannot necessarily assume that as the numbers go up protest will decline. Such an outcome may seem eminently logical, but two other factors (noted in chapter 3) may be at work here: in times of rapid growth, especially, different sectors of the population may benefit disproportionately, leading to turmoil; and/or the process of rapid modernization could undercut traditional institutions and the cultural basis of society, thereby becoming a destabilizing factor as well.[3] Of interest, therefore, will be not only whether any of these variables make it into the regression equation, but what sign they have.

SOCIO-POLITICAL: An additional six variables of social or political nature were included in the initial regression run.

(10) *Cabinet size* (CABSZ)--This indicator represents the number of ministers in each government. As a result of coalition considerations the number of governmental departments almost never stays the same, and even wider variations are to be found regarding the actual number of ministers (some of whom have no portfolio at all), with a range of twelve to twenty-five over this entire period. Here again, two opposing relationships are theoretically possible: a negative correlation could indicate that smaller cabinets are not capable of handling all the public pressure input which might be addressed to them, and thus protest rises; a positive correlation might be an indication that coalition weakness (the more political parties in the coalition, usually a result of electoral fragmentation in Israel, the weaker or less unified the government) leads to increased protest pressure.

(11) *Gini Index* (GINI)--This is a social indicator which measures the relative gap between the lower and upper income deciles (it has ranged in curvilinear fashion over the past twenty years from .3590 to .2418 and back up to .3152). As such, it constitutes a fairly good test for the "relative deprivation" theory. Unfortunately, this index has been available in Israel only from 1967 onward, and so could not be included in the general regression run (otherwise, the missing observations would have forced the run to ignore all the other data for the first eighteen years). It was decided, therefore, to make a separate regression run which did include GINI. The results of that regression must be considered to be less convincing given the low number of observations.

(12) *Population* (POP)--Despite the fact that a decision was made to score the dependent variables on a per capita basis, there may still have been a residual factor of population size. This can be considered either a "social" variable or an "environmental" one.

(13) *Population increase* (POPIN)--Due to occasional sharp growth spurts in population (as a result of massive immigration in the early fifties, and to a lesser extent in the seventies), this variable was included to account for such absolute annual changes and their possible effect on protest.

(14) *Population increase percentage* (POPIPC)--This is a variation of the previous variable, which takes into account the relative annual increase of population. Simply put, an annual increase of 100,000 people when the entire country has only 1,000,000 residents might be an entirely different affair than a similar annual increase of 100,000 when there are 4,000,000 residents (the impact of the latter being far smaller).

(15) *Period* (PER)--The POP variable repeatedly entered the regression analysis--despite the decision to score the protest variables relative to population size. As Israel's population grew continuously from the start, while the protest frequency figures did not move in linear fashion throughout the whole period under review, it was suspected that the POP variable may actually represent a varying pattern of protest related only indirectly to population size (or growth).

A scatter diagram of PROT was drawn, and four different periodic levels of public protest appeared (along the lines of the four protest periods used in chapter 3). Consequently, four different periods were defined and statistically tested through an Analysis of Variance and then a Multiple Range Analysis, and in both cases the four periods were found to be significantly different in their general level of protest (p < .0000).[4] This indicated that such a PER variable was indeed justified, with the underlying assumption that there may be some nonquantifiable factors indigenous to each period for which our regression could not otherwise account. One possible example of this is the eventual breakdown of national consensus on the issue of security after the 1967 conquest of the territories. If it were a truly significant factor, we would find that PER would enter at least the POLPROT regression model, if not the overall PROT model as well. Other possibilities are analyzed in the discussion of the findings.

Notes

Introduction

1. Ehud Sprinzak, *Nitzanei Politikah Shel De'legitimiut Be'Yisrael, 1967-1972* (Jerusalem: Levi Eshkol Institute, 1972).
2. Ehud Sprinzak, *"Gush Emunim: Model Ha'karkhon Shel Ha'kitzoniyyut Ha'politit,: Medinah, Memshal, Ve'yakhasim Bain-Le'umiyyim,* No. 17 (Spring, 1981), pp. 22-49.
3. *"Politikah Khutz-Parlamentarit Be'Yisrael,"* in *Skirah Khodshit* (August-September, 1984), pp. 35-45.
4. Eva Etzioni-Halevy, "Protest Politics in the Israeli Democracy," *Political Science Quarterly,* vol. 90, #3 (Fall, 1975), pp. 497-520.
5. Ibid., p. 519.
6. For an interesting case study of a protest campaign, see Gadi Wolfsfeld, *"Pe'ilut Politit Be'Yisrael: Ha'mikreh Shel Yamit,"* *Medinah, Memshal, Ve'yakhasim Bain-Le'umiyyim,* No. 22 (Winter, 1984), pp. 39-50. Most important is his recent book *The Politics of Provocation: Participation and Protest in Israel* (Albany, N.Y.: SUNY Press, 1988). In a sense it very neatly complements my book here. Wolfsfeld's work is based almost exclusively on a very comprehensive and in-depth self-initiated public opinion survey (conducted in April, 1982), in addition to previous survey research work done in Israel and abroad, and some aggregate protest data for the years 1979-1984. Its great strength lies in analyzing the personal-psychological factors underlying Israeli political protest (and conventional) behavior and attitudes circa the 1980s (and to a lesser extent the 1970s). While my present study includes a (less comprehensive) poll from around the same period, it concentrates on aggregate protest data over the *entire* period since the establishment of the State of Israel.
   Thus, this book goes well beyond Wolfsfeld's study from a number of important (and original for Israel) substantive perspectives, as I have included a wide-ranging and detailed historical analysis of Israeli protest; an in-depth breakdown and discussion of the protest events' internal characteristics; statistical analysis of empirically measurable economic, social, and political factors influencing protest; a description of Jewish, and especially Israeli, protest culture; the use of extensive aggregate protest data to support the hypothesis of blocked political communication; and an investigation, based on non-self-interested assessments (i.e., data and evaluations external to the protest participants themselves), of protest success. There are, to be sure, a few important areas of agreement between us--especially regarding some of the central conclusions (not regarding protest success, though). In short, Wolfsfeld's book is primarily an attitudinal, time-specific analysis from the *micro* perspective, whereas my book is primarily an empirical, longitudinal analysis from the *macro* perspective. As such, I shall not relate to his work on an ongoing basis (merely where some of his data or points are specifically relevant to mine), but do recommend that his book be read for its own particular strengths.
7. He devotes a chapter to a schematic overview of Israeli protest from the beginning, but not being based on any empirical evidence his conclusions regarding the earlier period are greatly flawed. In any case, virtually the entire focus of his study is contemporary (where his analysis is truly excellent), but the lack of longitudinal aggregate protest data does not enable him to make any historical comparisons or reach any overall historical conclusions.
8. Sprinzak, *"Nitzanei,"* op. cit., p. 3.
9. Mordechai Bar-On, *Shalom Akhshav: Le'diyuknah Shel Tenuah* (Tel Aviv: Hakibbutz Hameukhad, 1985).
10. Zvi Ra'anan, *Gush Emunim* (Tel Aviv: Sifriat Poalim, 1981).

Chapter 1

1. An in-depth survey of this vast research is completely beyond the capabilities and purpose of this chapter. For the interested student, the best introductory work that can be recommended is Ted. R. Gurr, ed., *Handbook of Political Conflict: Theory and Research* (New York: The Free Press, 1980). This anthology not only surveys just about every aspect of political protest and turmoil, but has a bibliography running well over fifty pages. No attempt will be made here to "summarize" this vast corpus; rather, in the next several pages we shall discuss some of the more important considerations underlying the methodological and theoretical thrust of this study, leaving to specific future chapters a more detailed analysis of the discrete methodologies (but not the great array of theories) used and tested.

2. Arend Lijphart, "The Comparable-Cases Strategy in Comparative Research," *Comparative Political Studies*, vol. 8, #2 (July, 1975), pp. 158-177. There are a few other worthwhile accompanying articles included in that issue's focus on "Comparative Methodology."

3. Howard A. Scarrow, *Comparative Political Analysis: An Introduction* (New York: Harper and Row, 1969), p. 7.

4. Donald T. Campbell, "'Degrees of Freedom' and the Case Study," *Comparative Political Studies*, vol. 8, #2 (July, 1975), pp. 178-193.

5. Heinz Eulau, "Comparative Political Analysis: A Methodological Note," *Midwest Journal of Political Science*, vol. 6, #4 (November, 1962), p. 397.

6. Bruce Bueno de Mesquita, "Theories of International Conflict: An Analysis and Appraisal," in *Handbook of Political Conflict: Theory and Research*, ed. Ted Robert Gurr (New York: The Free Press, 1980), p. 364.

7. Op. cit., p. 14.

8. See, for instance, Eckstein's essay (chapter 4), especially regarding findings on the relationship between socio-economic change and political violence (p. 156). Different studies found different results not only across different continents but for different levels of political violence!

9. David Sanders, *Patterns of Political Instability* (London: The Macmillan Press Ltd., 1981), p. xvi.

10. Ibid., p. xvii.

11. David Snyder, "Collective Violence: Research Agenda and Some Strategic Considerations," *Journal of Conflict Resolution*, vol. 22, #3 (September, 1978), p. 516.

12. Carl J. Friedrich, "Some Methodological Reflections on the Problems of Political Data," in *Comparing Nations: The Use of Quantitative Data in Cross-National Research*, ed. Richard L. Merritt and Stein Rokkan (New Haven: Yale University Press, 1966), pp. 62; 66.

13. For a solid review of the work done in this area see Edward N. Muller, "The Psychology of Political Protest and Violence," in Gurr's *Handbook*, op. cit., pp. 69-99. His summation is quite clear: "The findings from micro-level research on psychological antecedents of political protest and violence indicate that the frustration-aggression hypothesis has only weak explanatory power when applied to politically aggressive behavior. Most kinds of frustration, not to mention sheer deprivation, are at best weakly associated with individual differences in potential or actual participation in aggressive action. The exception is frustration arising from the belief that one's just desserts are unfulfilled. . . called relative deprivation by Gurr. . . but the evidence is by no means decisive even on this point" (pp. 96-97). Similar, or even more damaging, conclusions are reached by others. Based on ten research reports of five different American riots in the sixties, Clark McPhail in his "Civil Disorder Participation: A Critical Examination of Recent Research," *American Sociological Review*, vol. 36, #6 (December, 1971) found: "Of the total 173

associations bearing on the DFA [deprivation-frustration-aggression] explanation,
32% were not significant, 61% were of low magnitude, 7% were of moderate
magnitude and less than 1% were of high magnitude . . . . [Thus] there is
considerable reason for rejecting the sociological and popular cliche that absolute
or relative deprivation and the ensuing frustration or discontent or despair is the
root cause of rebellion" (p. 163). See too Anthony Oberschall, "Theories of Social
Conflict," *Annual Review of Sociology*, vol. 4 (1978), especially pp. 299-306 for a
strong critique of the RD theory.

There is one narrow sense of frustration-aggression (not generally employed by
the theorists) which this book does address: frustration at not being able to
politically communicate which leads to protest (chapters 7 and 8). Muller also
includes "protest justification" and "belief in success" among the psychological
variables which he reviews, and these will be discussed at the appropriate points
later on in the book.

14. For details, see chapter 2, and Appendix B.
15. A further attempt was made to measure RD indirectly by including the Gini Index
    in our regression analysis (chapter 5). The results tended to generally support our
    other evidence that economic relative deprivation is not a very significant factor in
    the Israeli milieu.
16. See for example Ted R. Gurr, "A Causal Model of Civil Strife: A Comparative
    Analysis Using New Indices," *American Political Science Review*, vol. 62, #4
    (December, 1968), pp. 1104-1124; Douglas Bwy, "Political Instability in Latin
    America: The Cross-Cultural Test of a Causal Model," *Latin American Research
    Review*, vol. 3 (Spring, 1968), pp. 17-66; David Snyder and Charles Tilly, "Hardship
    and Collective Violence in France, 1830 to 1960," *American Sociological Review*, vol.
    37, #5 (October, 1972), pp. 520-532.
17. For a good summation of these problems see David Snyder, "Theoretical and
    Methodological Problems in the Analysis of Government Coercion and Collective
    Violence," *Journal of Political and Military Sociology*, vol. 4, #2 (Fall, 1976), pp. 277-
    293.
18. Eva Etzioni-Halevy with Rina Shapira, *Political Culture in Israel* (New York:
    Praeger Publishers, 1977).
19. Eva Etzioni-Halevy, "Protest Politics in the Israeli Democracy," *Political Science
    Quarterly*, vol. 90, #3 (Fall, 1975), pp. 497-520; Alan Arian, *The Choosing People*
    (Cleveland: Case Western Reserve University Press, 1973). More recently Gadi
    Wolfsfeld has done intensive work regarding this theory. A measure of the lack of
    connection made among most Israeli scholars can be gleaned from a work such as
    Yitzchak Galnoor's *Steering the Polity: Communication and Politics in Israel* (Beverly
    Hills: Sage Publications, 1982). it is an extremely comprehensive and thorough
    account of such elements as access, efficacy, channels, participation, etc., but
    nothing in his (altogether correct, as far as it goes) analysis is tied into protest
    (which does not even appear in the index as an item)!
20. Gurr, "A Causal Analysis," op. cit., p. 1121. The analysis is more finely delineated
    in his article (coauthored with Raymond Duvall) "Civil Conflict in the 1960s: A
    Reciprocal Theoretical System with Parameter Estimates," *Comparative Political
    Studies*, vol. 6, #2 (July, 1973), pp. 135-170, where previous magnitudes of conflict
    (especially turmoil and man-days, less so historical rebellion) are found to be
    positively related to subsequent similar phenomena. See too M.N. Cooper, "A
    Reinterpretation of the Causes of Turmoil: The Effect of Culture and Modernity,"
    Comparative Political Studies, vol. 7, #3 (October, 1974), pp. 267-291.
21. Samuel H. Barnes and Max Kaase, *Political Action: Mass Participation in Five Western
    Democracies* (Beverly Hills: Sage, 1979), pp. 31; 59.
22. For an almost exhaustive--but still very small--list of these studies, see Harry
    Eckstein, "Theoretical Approaches to Explaining Collective Political Violence," in
    Handbook, op. cit., p. 160; and Ekkart Zimmerman, "Macro-Comparative Research
    on Political Protest," ibid., pp. 202-203.

23. Robert J. Jackson and Michael B. Stein, "The Issue of Political Protest," in *Issues in Comparative Politics*, edited by them (New York: St. Martin's Press, 1971), pp. 265-284.

24. For a short review of the literature see Eckstein, "Theoretical Approaches," *Handbook*, op. cit., p. 146. See too p. 157 where he brings several studies which empirically refute this general line of approach. The *Handbook*'s subsequent essay by Zimmerman, "Macro-comparative Research," op. cit., also reviews this line of approach (pp. 188-190), concluding that the "conceptualization of political instability or political decay that arises from several structural imbalances merits continued attention" (p.190).

25. Snyder, "Collective Violence," op. cit., p. 516.

26. Of course, there have been numerous books and articles written about conflict within individual nations, from a qualitative-analytical perspective--many of which are both thought-provoking and useful from the standpoint of theory. Without some sort of empirical grounding, however, they remain just that: thought-provoking, and not conclusion-generating.

27. These three countries come under quite in-depth historical and statistical scrutiny in Charles Tilly et al., *The Rebellious Century, 1830-1930* (Cambridge, Mass: Harvard University Press, 1975). David Snyder and Charles Tilly extend the analysis of France another thirty years in their article "Hardship and Collective Violence," op. cit.

28. S.G. Levy, "A 150-Year Study of Political Violence in the United States," in *Violence in America: Historical and Comparative Perspectives*, ed. Hugh D. Graham and Ted. R. Gurr (New York: Signet, 1969), pp. 81-91.

29. Alan March, *Protest and Political Consciousness* (London: Sage Publications, 1977).

30. Barnes and Kaase, *Political Action*, op. cit., covers all five of these countries.

31. Again, as will be explained later on, there is a technical exception to this statement in Wolfsfeld's work.

32. Ted Robert Gurr and Raymond Duvall, "Introduction to a Formal Theory of Political Conflict," in *The Uses of Controversy in Sociology*, ed. Lewis A. Coser and Otto N. Larsen (New York: The Free Press, 1976), p. 147. Another part of their "manifesto" has been largely followed in our book as well: "Virtually all contemporary writers acknowledge that 'other conditions' than their chosen explanation may have some bearing on the outcome, but they usually add, 'only a little.' None that we know of has been willing to base theory on the premise that conditions at all levels of social analysis--psychological, structural, cultural and political--are of interdependent importance for comprehensive explanation of the phenomenon of group conflict . . . . Any general explanation which neglects any of these levels of analysis is seriously incomplete as a theory of the magnitude of manifest conflict" (ibid.).

Chapter 2

1. Charles Lewis Taylor and David A. Jodice, *World Handbook of Political and Social Indicators*, vol. 2 (New Haven: Yale University Press, 1983, 3d edition). This is a continuation of a series which constitutes the data base for many cross-comparative studies over the past two decades. Some of the more famous studies using their (or similar) data bases: Ivo K. and Rosalind L. Feierabend, "Aggressive Behaviors within Polities, 1948-1962: A Cross National Study," *Journal of Conflict Resolution*, vol. 10, #3 (September, 1966), pp. 249-271; Ted R. Gurr, "A Causal Model of Civil Strife: A Comparative Analysis Using New Indices," *American Political Science Review*, vol. 62, #4 (December, 1968), pp. 1104-1124; Michael C. Hudson, *Conditions of Political Violence and Instability: A Preliminary Test of Three Hypotheses* (Beverly Hills: Sage Comparative Politics Series--#01-005, 1970); and Douglas A. Hibbs, Jr., *Mass Political Violence: A Cross-National Causal Analysis* (New York: John Wiley, 1973).

2. Taylor and Jodice, p. 185, for a control comparison between scoring by reading through the paper and relying on the *Times* Index. For the randomly selected month (January 1970) a total of 897 events were scored from a daily reading of the *New York Times* whereas a mere 262 events were found in the Index--a 342% difference! And yet due to cost considerations the latter is used throughout, and it is this dataset upon which most cross-national studies are based. Additionally, the authors are quite forthright about listing several of the deficiencies of an "international source" such as the *New York Times*: overemphasis on the spectacular; sporadic (in)sensitivity over time to events in various regions of the world; the need to primarily publish news of interest to its local readers; concentration of reporters in certain countries; etc. They also are courageous enough to present the amount of skew due to the use of the *Times* Index and not a thorough daily reading of the paper's contents. Randomly selecting control months they found (among others who scored somewhat better) that South Vietnam scored 91 events instead of 195, the U.S. scored 4 events instead of 318, and Israel scored but 1 event instead of 36! It is quite a strong self-indictment regarding the accuracy of the protest data appearing in their book. For an expansion of the above list regarding the problems of using the *New York Times*, see Joseph M. Scolnick, Jr., "An Appraisal of Studies of the Linkage between Domestic and International Conflict," *Comparative Political Studies*, vol. 6, #4 (January, 1974), pp. 486-488.

3. Robert Burrowes, "Theory Si, Data No! A Decade of Cross-National Political Research," *World Politics*, vol. 25, #1 (October, 1972), p. 133; Andrew Mack, "Numbers Are Not Enough: A Critique of Internal/External Conflict Behavior Research," *Comparative Politics*, vol. 7, #4 (July, 1975), pp. 597-618.

4. Robert W. Jackman and William A. Boyd, "Multiple Sources in the Collection of Data on Political Conflict," *American Journal of Political Science*, vol. 23, #2 (May, 1979), pp. 434-458.

5. Leo A. Hazlewood and Gerald West, "Bivariate Associations, Factor Structures, and Substantive Impact: The Source Coverage Problem Revisited," *International Studies Quarterly*, vol. 18, #3 (September, 1974), p. 324.

6. Ibid., pp. 329; 335.

7. Charles F. Doran et al., "A Test of Cross-National Event Reliability: Global versus Regional Data Sources," *International Studies Quarterly*, vol. 17, #2 (June, 1973), pp. 175-203. This came as a response to the suggestion by the Feierabends and Betty Nesvold that there is "evidence that our data provide a representative picture of the comparative levels of instability and violence of the nations in the sample, although the bank undoubtedly does not include every single relevant event." [In Hugh D. Graham and Ted R. Gurr, *Violence in America: Historical and Comparative Perspectives* (Washington, D.C.: U.S. Government Printing Office, 1969), p. 628]. See too Edward E. Azar et al., "A Quantitative Comparison of Source Coverage for Event Data," *International Studies Quarterly*, vol. 16, #3 (September, 1972), pp. 373-388.

8. M. Herbert Danzger does address the question of the validity of using local newspapers as sources for data on conflict events (using America as a case study). He argues that these too are poor sources for cross-comparative purposes, because the coverage of local protest is a function of whether a city has a local wire service office within its confines (AP or UPI). See his "Validating Conflict Data," *American Sociological Review*, vol. 40, #5 (October, 1975), pp. 570-584. However, David Snyder and William R. Kelly disagree in a following article, "Conflict Intensity, Media Sensitivity, and the Validity of Newspaper Data," *American Sociological Review*, vol. 42, #1 (February, 1977), pp. 105-123. Their study shows no geographical news wire bias; rather, the protest coverage differential is a function of the events' *intensity*. We shall touch upon this element late in the chapter.

9. See, for example, David Snyder and Charles Tilly, "Hardship and Collective Violence in France, 1830 to 1960," *American Sociological Review*, vol. 37, #5

(October, 1972), pp. 520-532. For that study, two national newspapers were read on a daily basis from 1830 to 1960 (for a three-month period each year from 1861 to 1929). The latter researcher then went on to author a much larger study with Louise Tilly and Richard Tilly--*The Rebellious Century, 1830-1930* (Cambridge, Mass.: Harvard University Press, 1975), which included Germany and Italy as well, all based on *national* newspaper sources in addition to archival and other historical material. It is worth noting here what their experience taught (especially conclusion #4), given the very similar methodology employed in our present study:

(1) Every source omits some of the events we are interested in and some crucial details of other events; the smaller the event, the greater the omission. (2) All the comprehensive sources pay disproportionate attention to those events which occur in central locations or have wide political impact. (3) Published sources are less reliable for details of the events than for the fact that an event of a certain kind took place. (4) For the two purposes combined, a continuous run of a national newspaper is a somewhat more reliable source (and a more practical one) than any major archival series we have encountered, a much more reliable source than any combination of standard historical works, and superior to any other continuous source it would be practical to use (p. 16).

See too their Appendix D (pp. 313-322) for a discussion of the methodology employed in gathering data from the sundry national sources.

10. Ekkart Zimmerman, "Macro-comparative Research on Political Protest," in Ted R. Gurr, *Handbook of Political Conflict: Theory and Research* (New York: The Free Press, 1980), p. 225. Emphasis mine.

11. Taylor and Jodice, op. cit., p. 181.

12. There is another, somewhat secondary, reason for concentrating on local sources: they are the media reports (and not the *New York Times*, etc.) which influence future protest behavior within each respective country. We shall have more to say on this score in chapter 8.

13. For reasons of time and budget, the study had to be limited to a complete review of only one newspaper. While I started out using several assistants to do the initial reading and scoring, it quickly became apparent that the lack of clarity in many newspaper accounts (and the scorers' various and different ways of scoring the variables) left me little choice but to do the entire work myself--the equivalent of about one-half year's full-time work! As a result, this study at least does not suffer from any lack of scoring consistency.

14. They found a gap of 1:7 for "demonstrations." There was no comparison made for riots. Op. cit., p. 184.

15. This is arrived at by multiplying their 1:7 ratio (international to regional) by our 1:8 ratio (local to regional/international). To be sure, the Doran et al. study looked at Latin America whereas ours deals with Israel, so that such a statement is by no means definitive at this stage. Our next comparison, however, compares apples with apples.

16. Jonathan Wilkenfeld, Virginia Lee Lussier, and Dale Tahtinen, "Conflict Interactions in the Middle East, 1949-1967," *The Journal of Conflict Resolution*, vol. 16 #2 (June, 1972), pp. 135-154).

The Doran et al. study looked more intensively at some *inner* disparities between the totals of the international and regional sources. For one, they found that the disparity was *not* consistent over the years, ranging (regarding all their data) between 1:7 to 1:2 at different times (p. 178). A similar comparison between our (local-source) totals and those (I/R source) of Taylor and Jodice finds that for demonstrations the proportional error ratios ranged from 1:57 (excluding those years when they scored zero events) in 1949 down to 1:5 in 1970, and for "riots" from 1:16 in 1949 down to a reverse 2:1 in 1959 (the only year when their total was higher than our study's). This is especially important when one wishes (as we shall in chapter 5) to run regression analyses over the entire period. The above huge disparities, especially regarding nonviolent demonstrations, suggest that the I/R sources are far more "sporadically sensitive" (to use the phrase of Doran et al.), and thus far less reliable for such time-sensitive analyses. Second, when one compares the rate of annual extremes *within* each source (i.e., lowest annual to highest annual over the whole period), Doran et al. found the international source ratio to be 1:9 whereas the regional source ratio was only 1:4 (pp. 179-181). Comparing the Taylor and Jodice totals from this perspective to our study's we find the former to be 1:15 for demonstrations and 1:12 for riots, compared to our 1:8 and 1:18 respective ratios. Once again, all this suggests that regarding lower-level protest events there exist very serious problems regarding the accuracy of I/R sources, whereas the picture is somewhat better (but by no means satisfactory) when one turns to violent events exclusively.

17. One good example of this is Bayley's analysis of Indian protest and his reaction to Raymond Tanter's famous study ["Dimensions of Conflict Behavior within and between Nations, 1958-1960," *Journal of Conflict Resolution*, vol. 10, #1 (March, 1966), pp. 41-64]; "To anyone familiar with demonstrations in India the figure of thirty per year is ridiculously low. Such a figure clearly indicates the extent of underreporting in the international news sources commonly used in studies of this kind"--in David H. Bayley, "Public Protest and the Political Process in India," in *Issues in Comparative Politics*, ed. Robert J. Jackson and Michael B. Stein (New York: St. Martin's Press, 1971), p. 332.

18. *World Handbook*, op. cit., p. 176.

19. There are a number of other problems which I will not touch upon as they are relevant to cross-comparative studies only. For example, Merritt and Rokkan raise the issue of "comparability of measurements for aggregates." If various countries have different criteria upon which their data are formulated, then cross-comparisons are rendered problematic, if not meaningless. See Richard L. Merritt and Stein Rokkan, *Comparing Nations: The Use of Quantitative Data in Cross-national Research* (New Haven: Yale University Press, 1966). While their focus is on such "official" data as unemployment, welfare disbursements, security forces budgets, etc., in the final analysis this specific issue will have to be dealt with by any researcher attempting to perform cross-comparative analyses using national protest data accumulated from different newspaper sources among the several nations.

20. Some general assessments will be offered in the book's final chapter.

21. John V. Gillespie and Betty A. Nesvold, *Macro-quantitative Analysis: Conflict, Development, and Democratization* (Beverly Hills: Sage Publications, 1971), p. 20.

22. Raoul Naroll, *Data Quality Control: A New Research Technique* (Glencoe, Ill.: The Free Press, 1962), p. 10.

23. My thanks to Mr. Aryeh Bendel for the data in Table 2.2, work done for a Master's seminar paper under my direction. He surveyed the Hebrew newspapers for one month each during the years 1950, 1966, 1975, 1985, and 1986 (based on the very strict and detailed criteria regarding each variable as outlined in chapters 3 and 4). I have included the *Jerusalem Post* results (from the same months) derived from my own project.

24. This survey was carried out by my students in a seminar entitled "Israeli Extraparliamentarism." Each student was given one source to intensively survey over the entire period. The students were thoroughly briefed as to the criteria for event inclusion and scoring, with a followup review on my part for incorrect inclusions. There remains the possibility that a few protest events were missed by some students, but given the results such minor omissions could hardly change the general picture. The *Jerusalem Post* was surveyed by me. My thanks especially to Mr. Zvi Granot for the difficult and complicated computer work involved in making order out of the large pile of information.

25. Why this paper should score so much better than the others is a matter of speculation, and would take us very far afield. One guess (only that) might be its Anglo-Saxon heritage and readership being more "attuned" to protest than the Israelis.

26. The technical problems in doing this on a wider scale, and over a longer period, proved to be insurmountable: not only are such licenses granted and stored locally by each police precinct, but they are destroyed after approximately three years! In addition, these would include only legally licensed protests; it is my estimation that a significant number of all protest-event organizers do not request a license (whether out of ignorance, fear of rejection, or principle).

27. This does not mean that internal police archival material cannot be of great utility in other respects. For one, it did provide invaluable information with regard to the strategic and tactical policy of the Israeli police in the "control" of public protest. See chapter 4 for a discussion of this protest aspect.

28. My thanks to Mr. Daniel Berdugo who chose to undertake his Master's Thesis under my supervision in furtherance of my overall protest-research project. Its official (translated) title is "The Police Reaction to Demonstrations in Israel and Subsequent Press Coverage" (Ramat Gan: Bar-Ilan University, 1988; unpublished), with a significant part being devoted to a comparison between his analysis from the field and the subsequent newspaper coverage. The following statistics are taken from his study.

29. Both afternoon papers are far larger than their morning counterparts. However, newspaper size is not perfectly correlated with protest-reporting completeness or accuracy--*Ha'tzofe* is the smallest of the group but still ranked above *Ha'aretz* in most categories. In addition, there were significant differences between the papers depending on the protest issue involved. In brief, for economic protest *Ma'ariv* scored highest and *Davar* lowest; for political protest, *Ma'ariv* and *Yediot Akhronot* highest, with *Ha'tzofe* and *Ha'aretz* lowest; social protest--*Yediot* highest, while again *Ha'tzofe* and *Ha'aretz* were lowest; and finally, for religious-issue protest *Davar* scored best, while *Ha'aretz* was the worst (Berdugo, ibid., p. 135).

30. Indeed, the whole problem of number of protest participants itself became a political issue in the early eighties--especially after it was reported in almost all the media that 400,000 protesters showed up at the huge 1982 demonstration in Tel Aviv after the Sabra and Shatilla refugee camp massacres in Lebanon (perpetrated by the Christian Phalangists in Israeli-held territory). For a critique of the 400,000 estimate and a general analysis of the head-count difficulty see Macabee Dean, The Numbers Game," *The Jerusalem Post* (October 1, 1982), p. 18. For a followup on the media's performance see Shulamith Marcus Gunders, "Head Hunting," *The Jerusalem Post* (June 28, 1985), p. 18. Her schematic analysis bears out the findings in Berdugo's study.

 Much the same conclusions are arrived at overseas. See Herbert A. Jacobs, "To count a crowd," *Columbia Journalism Review*, vol. 6, #1 (Spring, 1967), pp. 37-38. Jacobs developed a formula for counting crowd numbers which the Israeli media might do well to take to heart: pace off the length and the width of the crowd, multiply the two numbers, and divide by seven (an average of seven square feet per person in a moderately densely packed crowd). This should give a number with a maximum 25% deviation from an actual head count.

31. As a result, these most probably were the types of protest events to also most readily come to the attention of the newspapers. If that is so, then we have a possible explanation of the apparent disparity between the Bendel and Berdugo studies: Israel's afternoon newspapers do a somewhat better job of covering the larger and more visible protest events, while the *Jerusalem Post* does a far better job in its coverage of the "lesser" protests.

32. The term "unusual" is extremely relative, and entails two further methodological complications. First, during a period of few public protests the papers might tend to report a higher percentage of such events than when public protest has become

almost *de rigeuer*. This would mean, paradoxically, that a lower annual number of reported protests reflects that year's reality better than a higher annual number. Put another way, a logical initial hypothesis would be that the more events reported in the press, the greater the number of events not reported in that same time period! My general impression was that this holds true in the Israeli case from the late 1970s onwards (when protest events were reported on average every second day), and not in the early 1950s when there were a surprisingly high number of such events, but the phenomenon was still considered to be "aberrational." However, I was only half correct.

First, this was not the case in the 1950s for quite a different reason. Virtually all the daily print media in Israel tended back then to support the government line or at least tried to avoid direct criticism of the authorities (probably because of a fear of undermining the authority of the regime which might lead to political instability, something the embattled fledgling State could ill afford). As a result, protest events were not highlighted in the press, and might even have been partly avoided during the first decade or two. Nevertheless, as we shall see in chapter 3, the phenomenon still received substantial coverage by the *Jerusalem Post*. Second, as a result of stiffer competition between different protest groups for the media's attention during high-protest periods, it is probably true that such groups will "increase" the intensity level of their demonstration (usually "artificially) and/or the papers will tend to proportionally overreport those protests which are larger and more action-filled. For confirmation of this see David Snyder and William R. Kelly, "Conflict Intensity, Media Sensitivity, and the Validity of Newspaper Data," *American Sociological Review*, vol. 42, #1 (February, 1977), pp. 105-123. In our Israeli case, however, as we shall see, protest intensity (of those events reported) was not higher (during 1971-1978, actually lower) than in the previous, low-protest periods; there is no significant increase in the size of the protests over the years (chapter 4).

33.   For the classic analysis of article selection see David M. White, "'The Gatekeeper': A Case Study in the Selection of News," *Journalism Quarterly*, vol. 27, #4 (Summer, 1950), pp. 383-390.

34.   Warren Breed, "Social Control in the Newsroom: A Functional Analysis," *Social Forces*, vol. 33, #4 (May, 1955), pp. 326-335; Ben H. Bagdikian, "The Politics of American Newspapers," *Columbia Journalism Review*, vol. 10, #6 (March-April, 1972), pp. 8-13; Gaye Tuchman, "Objectivity as a Strategic Ritual: An Examination of Newsman's Notion of Objectivity," *American Journal of Sociology*, vol. 77, #4 (January, 1972), pp. 660-670, and his "Making News by Doing Work: Routinizing the Unexpected," ibid., vol. 79, #1 (July, 1973), pp. 110-131; Lee Sigelman, "Reporting the News: An Organizational Analysis," ibid.,pp. 132-151.

35.   The interview was conducted by me on October 10, 1987 in the editorial head office of the *Jerusalem Post*. It included general policy questions of the paper with regard to "public protest" items, as well as the opinion of Mr. Rath regarding several issues of Israeli protest which will be discussed in subsequent chapters.

36.   As far as he could recall, the only time when a "political decision" was made not to cover a protest event was in the case of Rabbi Meir Kahane whose anti-Arab (arguably overtly racist) propaganda was considered by the paper as constituting incitement, and thus not worthy of coverage. Most of the Israeli press seemed to have made much the same policy decision after his election to the Knesset in 1984. The Israeli Supreme Court subsequently banned his election list in October 1988.

37.   Parenthetically, it should be noted that this would tend to overexaggerate the extent of protest "violence," very low in any case in the Israeli context, as we shall see in chapter 3.

38.   In order to more concretely understand the paper's editorial policy regarding protest reportage, a small exercise was undertaken with Mr. Rath. Four headlines were presented to him, with the explanation that these had arrived at the editorial desk a mere half-hour before deadline. There was room in the paper to include

only two. As can be seen from the following list, two dealt with "extraparliamentary" events and two with "parliamentary" items:

(1) *Knesset Labor Committee Approves Flextime Legislation for Second Hearing on Knesset Floor*

(2) *10,000 Social Workers Demonstrate All Day versus Government Economic Policy; Catcalls but No Violence in Front of Treasury Ministry*

(3) *Peres Shouted Down at Central Committee Meetings: Scuffles between Labor Doves and Hawks during Speech*

(4) *Police and Slum Dwellers Clash during Protest in South Tel Aviv--All 25 Demonstrators Arrested after Rock-throwing Incident*

The articles which the *Jerusalem Post* would choose for inclusion are first #4 and second #2, with an attempt being made to also place a small box for #3. Put simply, the two extraparliamentary events take precedence over the parliamentary ones, despite the "violence" in one of the latter (#3) and the peacefulness of one of the former (#2). Here is the first indication that extraparliamentary behavior in Israel has come to be considered as legitimate, important, and/or normative as its alter-ego parliamentary activity; we shall return to this point at length in chapter 6.

39. For my earlier attempts at coming to grips with this element, see my "Public Protest and Systemic Stability in Israel: 1960-1979," in *Comparative Jewish Politics: Public Life in Israel and the Diaspora*, ed. Sam Lehman-Wilzig and Bernard Susser (Ramat Gan: Bar-Ilan University Press, 1981), pp. 171-210; and Sam Lehman-Wilzig and Meyer Unger, "The Economic and Political Determinants of Public Protest Frequency and Magnitude: The Israeli Experience," *International Review of Modern Sociology*, vol. 15 (Spring/Autumn, 1985), pp. 63-80. These studies included only the protest data for the years 1960-1979 and 1950-1979 respectively.

40. The disparity between this figure and the totals in Table 2.4 is probably a pretty good indication of the extent to which many protest groups take out licenses but in the end do not actually demonstrate.

41. The only other involvement I was able to track down from the myriad public opinion polls conducted over the years was one (!) question asked in a survey conducted in January 1950 by the Israel Institute for Social Research. We shall be referring to it in chapter 6. As noted earlier, a more extensive poll was conducted subsequent to mine by Dr. Gadi Wolfsfeld of the Hebrew University. Our two polls should serve as a solid base line for similar future surveys which would enable us to develop a longitudinal picture of Israeli protest attitudes post-1980.

42. The program used was STATGRAPHICS (STSC, Inc.), version 2.6. The process of discarding the variables was done automatically by the program, but checked manually after each regression round. This afforded us the opportunity to see whether the program was not blindly discarding variables which might have been very close to the level needed for inclusion, and thus possibly still worthy of retesting in the subsequent round.

43. As this study covered thirty-eight years, there should have been that number of observations. However, three years had to be dropped from the regression analysis. Regarding 1949 and 1950, data for several independent variables do not exist, and so had to be deleted; 1979 was dropped for a more complex methodological reason, which demands a brief explanation. In statistical analyses, all observations are scored under similarly representative conditions. However, it may happen that some of the observations represent a pattern of relationship between the dependent variable and the independent variables which is at variance from that of the other observations. One way to detect such "outliers" is to observe the residuals from the regression analysis. When these residuals are expressed in terms of their standard deviation, residuals larger than, say, + or -3 are very improbable, and their occurrence testifies to the existence of an "outlier" (which could seriously distort the regression results). The residual of the 1979 protest-data observation was repeatedly found to have exceptionally high values, and thus that observation was omitted. The deviance of 1979 can be explained by two different and

extraordinary phenomena occurring that year. First, the peace treaty negotiations with Egypt were in full gear, causing a leap in political protest. Second, and even more critical (as we shall see in the following chapter), by the end of that year inflation had pushed into the triple digits (annualized basis), causing social protest to skyrocket (almost triple the previous year).

44. The methodological problems, specific alternative techniques, and general findings for the variables "elections" and "wars" are respectively described, explained, and analyzed in chapters 5 and 8.

45. For example, number and size of ethnic groups.

Chapter 3

1. This variable was divided into four groups: political-, economic-, social-, and religious-issue protest.

    Political: This includes such topics as foreign policy, settlement in the territories, political personalities, war policy, election violence, etc. It was not always easy to decide if a protest belonged here or elsewhere (a recurring problem in many variables). For example, were *Gush Emunim* protests "political" or "religious"? I decided to score such problematic events on the basis of how the general society, and especially the authorities, view the issue; in the case of *Gush Emunim*, "political." Approximately 10% of "political" protests scored had a measure of such ambiguity.

    Economic: This does not include "normal" economic strike activity (but did include hunger strikes, general strikes, etc.). An economic strike to protest the government's "mishandling" of the economy, etc., or even versus the authorities who refuse to save a failing company, was included. The usual topics were unemployment, inflation, high taxation, welfare, etc.

    Social: Included here are such topics as housing, education, discrimination, health, culture, sports, transportation, immigrant absorption, *ad* (almost) *infinitum*. Once again, there was occasional "overlap": e.g., housing could certainly have been scored as "economic" too. The criterion was whether the issue was purely financial or had significant other nonmonetary elements (e.g., land ownership, apartment purchase credits, etc.).

    Religious: Autopsies, archeological digs, Sabbath observance, religious legislation, public (im)modesty, religious identity, Gentile missionary activity, etc., were included. While the vast majority of such protest is initiated by the religious section, religious-issue demonstrations by secular groups against "religious coercion" were scored here as well. See Sam Lehman-Wilzig and Giora Goldberg, "Religious Protest and Police Reaction in a Theo-democracy: Israel, 1950-1979," *Journal of Church and State*, vol. 25, #3 (Autumn, 1983), pp. 491-505.

2. An ordinal scale of five subvariables was devised: (a) *Peaceful:* No significant disruption of public order; (b) *Obstructive/Disruptive:* Significant, intentional blockage of pedestrian or vehicular traffic; blocking passage to, or invading, public buildings/offices; burning tires, etc.; (c) *Violence against Property:* Smashing windows/windshields; desecration of public places; large-scale vandalism; uprooting trees/orchards, etc.; (d) *Violence against People:* Fighting with police; throwing rocks at drivers; attacking government workers, etc.; (e) *General Riot:* Uncontrolled looting; indiscriminate violence, etc. This was scored only when the security authorities were not around or lost control over the proceedings for more than a few minutes.

    A problem arose regarding how to score a protest event with one intensity level overall, when a few protesters behaved in worse fashion. The most dominant intensity was usually scored, unless the deviation became significant whereupon either the higher intensity level was registered, or (if the small group broke away) two different events were scored, each with its respective intensity.

3. Such a division has already been attempted by Sprinzak whose chronology involves five distinct time periods: (a) 1948-1957: The decline of pre-State extremist groups; (b) 1957-1967: The "Golden Era" of Israeli parliamentarism; (c) 1967-1973: The unsuccessful first rebellion of the periphery; (d) 1973-1977: The successful second rebellion of the periphery; (e) 1977-1984: The institutionalization of extraparliamentarism.

   As we shall shortly see, while the general thrust of his periodicization is somewhat correct, it suffers from two flaws. First, the starting and concluding dates of some of these periods are off by several years. Second, by focusing exclusively on *group* protest, Sprinzak's description of some periods are quite misleading.

4. Of course, one could divide the periods by any of the ten categories which will be discussed in this and the next chapter. Indeed, one could even divide the era into more politically "traditional" periodic categories based on Israeli political history external to protest. There is no one "correct" way to doing this. By using protest *frequency* as the determining factor in my periodicization, I am suggesting that it is the most important element, and that more than any other category it reflects the true state of Israeli extraparliamentarism over the entire period of time.

5. *Israel Government Statistical Yearbook, 1956*, p. 33.

6. Dov Levitan, "*Aliyat Marvad Ha'kesamim Ke'hemshaikh Histori Le'aliyot Mi'Taiman May'az TRM"B: Nituakh Socio-Politi Shel Aliyatam U'klitatam Shel Yehudai Teiman Be'Yisrael Be'ait Ha'khadasha*" (Ramat Gan: Master's Thesis presented to the Department of Political Studies, Bar-Ilan University, 1983; unpublished), p. 196 (translation mine).

7. In dozens of additional cases it was impossible to determine whether the protest involved recent immigrants or Israelis of long standing, especially with regard to demonstrations by the unemployed away from the transit camps (e.g., in front of a local employment office).

8. One contemporary analysis by the director of the Jewish Agency's Department of Absorption, Giora Josepthal, should suffice to suggest the depth of the problem and the potential powder keg inherent in the situation: "The camps must be seen when fifty men and women, elderly and children are in a single dormitory. It is quite inevitable that an impossible situation should develop . . . . We need the Government to know that forty-seven souls [in one dormitory] in camps represent explosive material." Quoted in Dvorah Hacohen, "Mass Immigration and the Israeli Political System, 1948-1953," *Studies in Zionism*, vol. 8, #1 (spring, 1987), p. 109.

9. From the very start, *Herut* was far more interested in political issues, tending to relegate social and economic problems and concerns to the back burner. To a great extent this continued to be true even after the party took power in 1977, as most of the key economic ministries were given to *Herut*'s sister partner within the *Likud*-- the Liberal Party.

10. Eliezer Don-Yehiya, *Shituf Ve-konflikt Bain Makhanot Politiyyim: Ha'makhaneh Ha'dati U'tnuat Ha'avodah U'mashbair Ha'khinukh Be'Yisrael* (Jerusalem: Doctoral Dissertation presented to the Department of Political Science, Hebrew University, 1977; unpublished), pp. 535-537.

11. Don-Yehiya argues that the "modernization" policy is only a partial explanation for such official strategy by those running the transit camps and later the more permanent *ma'abarot*. He points out that there were in addition strong party-interest considerations here, as the large number of religious immigrants potentially threatened to undermine the Labor camp's political preeminence (ibid., pp. 495-505; 541-545). However, while such considerations were undoubtedly at work here as well, he himself notes that the Investigative Commission concuded otherwise: "The bureaucracy saw as its primary function the adaptation of the [immigrant] child into the Israeli experience, as it existed in

society . . . and the error . . . was that [the bureaucracy] measured each adaptation by its own lights . . . " (p. 540; translation mine). Additionally, the individual in charge of the immigrants' education and acculturation expressed himself explicitly in terms of the "modernization" policy, actually working against any attempt to impose a party key in this enterprise (pp. 545-547)--a stragegy which forced some of the religious parties to initiate immigrant protest (Levitan, op. cit., p. 176).

12. As Don-Yehiya notes: "The system was more successful in alienating the immigrants from their traditional culture than in effectively integrating them into the value system of the society which was supposed to absorb them" (op. cit.,page xxxix; my translation).

13. For an interesting description of such early ultra-Orthodox protest see Tom Segev, *1949: Ha'Yisraelim Ha'rishonim* (Jerusalem: The Domino Press, 1984), pp. 219-225. What is most striking about his description is that it portrays a picture which has changed not at all in four decades--the same issues, the same groups, the same police reaction.

14. Don-Yehiya, op. cit., pp. 517-518; 556-559.

15. Most of these events were initiated by the *Neturei Karta*, fanatical anti-Zionists, and not the non-Zionist *Agudath Yisrael* and *Poalei Agudath Yisrael* supporters, the latter two parties being members of the governing coalition from 1948 to 1952. For a more extended analysis of such religious protest, see chapter 8.

16. No attempt will be made in this book to score Arab protest fatalities, in light of the far greater unreliability of the reporting process regarding this population sector. See, however, chapter 4 for a discussion of protest in the Arab-Israeli sector.

17. As a matter of fact, insofar as Jewish protest fatalities are concerned, little more need be said than that over the entire thirty-eight year period there were only *two* reported deaths as a result of protest activity. The first occurred in 1956 (Pinchas Segalov, an ultra-Orthodox demonstrator, was killed by the police during a protest against Sabbath bus transport from Jerusalem to the Tel Aviv beaches) and the second in 1983 (a grenade was lobbed into an anti-Lebanon War demonstration by a sympathizer of the war, killing one Jewish demonstator-Emil Grunzweig).

18. We shall discuss this point, and other related aspects of the authorities' reactions in the field, in chapter 4.

19. It is conventional wisdom in Israel that much of the social protest of the seventies was a result of the discriminatory and heavy-handed modernization policies of the early fifties. I am not suggesting here that this is incorrect, but rather than one can detect already in the sixties the evolution of such a protest reaction.

20. Several hundred children of the new immigrants (from Arab countries) in the early fifties "disappeared" under mysterious circumstances, in most cases listed officially as "natural deaths" occurring in hospital. While never definitively proven, evidence exists that at least in some cases these very children were handed over for adoption to childless native *Ashkanazi* couples. The reasons suggested are: the immigrant families were so large that one child less would make little difference, while that same child would bring great joy to the childless couple; the child would have a much "better" upbringing--materially and culturally--in the adopting economically secure family; such a "transfer" would expedite the modernization efforts of the authorities. See Levitan, *"Aliyat Marvad,"* op. cit., chapter 13 (pp. 254-291).

21. Whatever the reason, in effect it means that the percentage of violent protest from 1955 to 1966 was 21.3%--a bit higher than the first period of 1949-1954. Thus, from the standpoint of protest violence, a proper division into distinct time periods would be pre-1967 and post-1967 (at least until 1979 as we shall see further on).

22. We shall discuss more in depth the relationship between "government size" and public protest in chapter 4.

23. For a concise but excellent historical description of the Black Panthers' political evolution see Yochanan Peres, *Yakhassay Edot Be'Yisrael* (Tel Aviv: Sifriat Poalim,

1976), chapter 7. Peres also advances some reasons for the protests and the movement (pp. 161-164). See also Erik Cohen, "The Black Panthers in Israeli Society," *Jewish Journal of Sociology*, vol. 14, #1 (June, 1972), pp. 93-110; Avraham Shama and Mark Iris, *Immigration without Integration: Third World Jews in Israel* (Cambridge, Mass.: Schenkman Publishing Co., 1977), pp. 141-156; and Gerald Cromer, "The Israeli Black Panthers: Fighting for Credibility and a Cause," *Victimology: An International Journal*, vol. 1, #3 (Fall, 1976), pp. 403-413. The latter analyzes the group from the perspective of the members' criminal background and their attempts to be accorded legitimacy.

24. Ehud Sprinzak, *Nitzanei Politikah Shel De'legitimiut Be'Yisrael, 1967-1972* (Jerusalem: Levi Eshkol Institute, 1973). A number of their leaders went on to successful careers in Israeli national politics, with two--Charlie Biton and Saadia Marciano-- eventually becoming members of Knesset.

25. Moshe Lissak, "Continuity and Change in the Voting Patterns of Oriental Jews," in *The Elections in Israel--1973*, ed. Asher Arian (Jerusalem: Jerusalem Academic Press, 1975), p. 274.

26. Michael Gurevitch, "Television in the Election Campaign: Its Audience and Functions," *The Elections in Israel--1969*, ed. Alan Arian et al. (Jerusalem: Jerusalem Academic Press, 1972), p. 235.

27. Norman Cantor, *The Age of Protest* (London: George Allen and Unwin, Ltd., 1970), p. 326. Similarly on the Israeli scene, for example, the *Jerusalem Post* reported that "Mr. Shmueli [then Deputy Director of the Education Ministry] blames the radio and television . . . for making it too easy for parent groups to gain publicity, thus encouraging unrealistic demands" (Ernie Meyer, "Parents Can Be Unreasonable At Times," Sept. 10, 1975, p. 2). There may be one additional protest connection here: occasionally one can discern the effect of TV crews at the scene in raising the protest event's *intensity* (e.g., the *Jerusalem Post*, May 17, 1976, p. 2; May 20, 1976, p. 2). While the TV camera "redlight" syndrome does in fact exist, the macro-picture in Israel shows no such overall effect. Protest violence decreased in proportional terms during the seventies (to an overall low of 9.4% for the entire third period) relative to the previous two protest periods. For an interesting example of "pseudo-violent" TV-induced Israeli protest see Gadi Wolfsfeld, "Collective Actions and Media Strategy: The Case of Yamit," *The Journal of Conflict Resolution*, vol. 28, #3 (Autumn, 1984), pp. 550-555; 742.

28. Manoucher Parvin, "Economic Determinants of Political Unrest: An Econometric Approach," *Journal of Conflict Resolution*, vol. 17, #2 (June, 1973), p. 293.

29. With regard to the overall statistical evidence in Israel for RD over the years see chapter 5.

30. *Report of the Committee on Income Distribution and Social Inequality* (Tel Aviv: 1971), pp. 4-5. For a more detailed statistical analysis of the narrowing socio-economic gap see Peres, *Yakhassay Edot*, op. cit., pp. 106-112. For example, whereas the Gini Index of socio-economic inequality (based on family income) stood at 61 in 1967, it had risen to 74 by 1971 (quite a significant improvement). indeed, by 1970 the *Edot Ha'mizrakh* had more gas appliances and washing machines per family than their *Ashkenazi* counterparts (p. 112, table 18). A large gap in telephones and private cars did, however, still exist at that date. There is, to be sure, an "objective" RD interpretation possible here as well. Whereas the gap was closing when the family income figures were used, it was widening from the perspective of *income per person* owing to the much larger family size of the *Edot Ha'mizrakh*. Thus, both sides were "right" from their own perspective: the government could justifiably claim that everything was being done to ensure that income disparities disappeared, while the lower-class *Edot Ha'mizrakh* correctly felt that their personal lifestyle was not really getting better.

31. "Perhaps one of the most paradoxical developments in this context was that the very steady economic expansion tended often to worsen the lot of some deprived

lower groups and strata and to minimize their effective accessibility to the new frameworks." These words were written before the seventies without specific reference to the Israeli situation, but were quite prophetic in this regard. S.N. Eisenstadt, *Modernization: Protest and Change* (Englewood Cliffs, N.J.: Prentice Hall, 1966), p. 64.

32. All immigrants from the sixties onwards were given cheap housing loans, tax reductions on large-item purchases, and other benefits to help ease their way into Israeli life. These could save an immigrant family thousands (and at times ten of thousands) of dollars--a princely sum by native Israeli standards.

33. Eva Etzioni-Halevy with Rina Shapira, *Political Culture in Israel* (New York: Praeger Publishers, 1977), p. 116 fn.

34. It must be noted that not every downtrodden neighborhood acted or even felt the same way once the riots broke out. In an in-depth study done (during 1972) of three different underprivileged neighborhoods around the country, it was found that the residents felt less RD than the *Edot Ha'mizrakh* in the country as a whole. Yochanan Peres, *Politikah Ve'adatiut Be'shalosh Sh'khunot Oni* (n.p.: Modi'in Ezrakhi Ltd.--Ha'mercaz Le'mekhkarim Shimushiyyim, October, 1972), pp. 10-11. See too his remarks regarding the Russian immigrants' effect on the Black Panthers (p. 20).

35. Shlomo Avineri, "Israel: Two Nations?" in *Israel: Social Structure and Change*, ed. M.Curtis and M. Chertoff (New Brunswick: Transaction Books, 1973), p. 300.

36. There is always the possibility of another explanation, impossible to verify empirically. The police may react to middle-class demonstrators in a more controlled fashion, thereby not inciting any counter-violence by the protest participants. Such self-control on the part of the police may be due to their perception that middle-class protesters are "decent, law-abiding" citizens, or because such citizens are seen to be less of a potential threat to the public order, or even because of the potentially greater political power which that stratum ostensibly has. But that the police do react to protest intensity based on "extraneous" considerations cannot be denied. See chapter 4 for an interesting statistical analysis of this point with regard to religious-issue protest.

37. In one sense it is not "unusual" at all: conventional wisdom in Israel has it that Israeli citizens are most concerned with "political" issues such as security, foreign policy, war, territories, and the like. However, from the standpoint of public protest (and that should be a very good indication of where the Israeli public's real personal concerns lie), this was not true for most of its history, although proportional to other issues there was a distinct increase of political-issue protest already in the second and third periods (still somewhat below social-issue protest). Thus, contemporary conventional wisdom may well be correct--but only for the most recent historical period!

38. For a description of the protest engendered by the withdrawal, see Gadi Wolfsfeld, *"Pe'ilut Politit Be'Yisrael--Ha'mikreh Shel Yamit,"* Medinah, Memshal, Ve'Yakhasim Bain-Le'umiyyim, no. 22 (Winter, 1984), pp. 39-50. For a lengthier study of the protest groups involved and their tactics plus ideology see Gideon Aran, *Eretz Yisrael Bain Dat U'politikah: Ha'tnuah Le'atzirat Ha'nesigah Be'Sinai U'lekakhehah* (Jerusalem: The Jerusalem Institute for Israeli Studies, 1985).

39. The proportion of protest directed at a "foreign" authority in 1978 was over 15%-- a highwater mark surpassed only during the post-1967 years when there was stiff public resistance in Israel to the American "Rogers Plan" and other forms of pressure by the U.S. government to settle with Israel's neighbors. During 1978 there were several conspicuous and even violent protests in Israel against similar American diplomatic moves to advance the peace protest with the Egyptians. From this perspective, one can say that the Israeli government found itself between the anvil of the hawks who were against a peace treaty (on the terms eventually

settled upon) and the hammer of the doves, coupled with foreign pressure, for an end to its perceived procrastination and recalcitrance.

40. Social-issue protest in 1979 had the same total of 115, but they were spread out over many different subjects. For a good description and analysis of the development, through several stages, of the antiwar protest, see Lilly Weisbrod, "Protest and Dissidence in Israel," in *Cross-Currents in Israeli Culture and Politics*, ed. Myron J. Aronoff (New Brunswick, N.J.: Transaction Books, 1984), pp. 51-68.

41. As we noted in chapter 2, these were most probably exaggerated estimations. Few would argue, though, that they were the largest demonstrations ever seen in Israel.

42. Ze'ev Schiff and Ehud Ya'ari, *Israel's Lebanon War*, ed. and trans. Ina Friedman (New York: Simon and Schuster, 1984), chapters 6 and 7.

43. These two are highly problematic terms in the contemporary Israeli context. If one were to take "dove" to mean a willingness to give back all or most of the territories, then it is an endangered species. If it means that there is a willingness to give back a small part, and/or settle for nonsovereignty over most of the area, then it would seem to be on an equal footing with the "hawks." See Asher Arian and Michal Shamir, "The Primarily Political Functions of the Left-Right Continuum," in *The Elections in Israel--1981*, ed. Asher Arian (Tel Aviv: Ramot Publishing, 1983), pp. 259-279. Our intent here is to suggest that by current Israeli standards Labor is somewhat dovish and the *Likud* hawkish--and their electoral stalemate reflects the rough equivalency in the public between dovishness and hawkishness, as was further evidenced in the virtual-tie election results between the two camps in November 1988.

44. This does not mean that the makeup of the cabinet has no relationship to protest. The extent of such a connection will be discussed in chapter 5.

45. One of the central ironies of the *Likud* administration was that while they were put into office mainly through the support of the lower classes, their "economic liberalization" policy actually caused a significant widening in the gap between rich and poor as measured by the Gini Index. That this did not cause a backlash against the *Likud* by the lower classes can be explained by a number of factors: the Labor-dominated *Histadrut* was blamed for sabotaging the policy; the *Likud* leadership made a concerted 1981 election effort to focus attention on the "rich" kibbutzim and their "swimming-pool lifestyle"--not to mention Finance Minister Aridor's infamous "correct economics" which produced a consumer buying binge (only exacerbating inflation after the elections); many small investors felt richer as a result of the artificially pumped-up stock market (until the bubble burst in 1983); and the continued higher saliency of political issues (security, territories, etc.) over economic ones.

46. At the start, it was not clear to me--or even to the demonstrators themselves--that this would turn into an established protest pattern, so that the first few weeks were each scored as a separate protest event. In addition, infrequently, the venue and/or date would be changed (once, for example, to Sunday morning at city hall), and this was also scored as a separate protest event. Still, such protests are somewhat underrepresented in our totals if we look at the matter purely from the standpoint of how many times they actually appeared and protested at the scene.

47. As mentioned, religious-issue protest is not exclusively the domain of the religious sectors of Israeli society. On occasion, secular Israelis will protest against religious coercion. Such a campaign during our fourth period was the El Al workers' (and other supporters') unsuccessful extraparliamentary attempts at reversing the government's decision to stop all Sabbath flights by the national air carrier. In addition, one other significant protest campaign was the newly arrived Ethiopian Jews' drive to reverse the Chief Rabbinate's decision that they all had to undergo ritual conversion ("to be on the safe side regarding their Jewishness"). Here was a rare case of a largely religious group protesting against the religious Establishment. For a discussion of the success of all religious-issue protest

campaigns see chapter 9 and Appendix C. The following list of demonstrative demands did not always end in success.

48. It is hard to make comparisons between other countries and Israel because of different systems of scoring violence, and because most other studies do not present protest violence percentages. However, to give but one example where a comparison can be made (although admittedly, one can hardly come to any hard and fast conclusion on this basis), Etzioni found that in a one-month period in 1968 in American, almost 35% of the 216 protest events were violent in some measure--fully 20% higher than the (far more complete) Israeli figures. See too David H. Bayley, "Public Protest and the Political Process in India," in *Issues in Comparative Politics*, ed. Robert J. Jackson and Michael B. Stein (New York: St. Martin's Press, 1971), pp. 324-332.

49. That there existed a definite (albeit temporary) problem of political socialization during this early period of mass immigration from the nondemocratic Arabs as well as Communist bloc can be seen from a different perspective too. Of all the national Knesset elections in Israel's history, the one with the highest voter turnout (86.9%) was the first, during January of 1949, right before the immigrants started arriving in significant numbers. On the other hand, the lowest turnout occurred in the very next election campaign of July 1951 (75.1%), after most of these immigrants had already arrived but perhaps had not yet fully acclimatized themselves, at least politically. Subsequent elections saw the turnout percentages move back into the low eighties, a sign that within a short space of time the accepted Israeli parliamentary rules of the game had been fully internalized by the immigrants. It should come as no surprise, then, to find that in the extraparliamentary realm the situation "normalized" around the mid-1950s as well.

50. See, for instance, Simha F. Landau, *"Ha'eem Ha'khevra Ha'Yisraelit Alimah Yoter May'akherot,"* in *Ha'omnam Kasheh Le'hiyyot Yisraeli?*, ed. Alouph Hareven (Jerusalem: Van Leer Foundation, 1983), pp. 171-200. His conclusion is that "in general one can say that the amount of violence in Israeli society, according to the official statistics, is quite moderate in comparison to many countries in the world. Nevertheless, it is higher than a number of Western countries with which we [Israel] usually tend to compare ourselves" (pp. 175-176; my translation). For a more in-depth cross-comparative study (which includes Israel), see his "Trends in Violence and Aggression: A Cross-Cultural Analysis," *International Journal of Comparative Sociology*, vol. 25, #3-4 (1984), pp. 133-158. Not everyone agrees with the general assessment, however. See Gabriel Sheffer, *"Alimut U'politikah,"* *Ha'aretz*, May 8, 1981, p. 14, for a nonstatistical analysis of the centrality of "violence" in Israeli politics.

51. Lynne B. Iglitzin, "Violence and American Democracy," *Journal of Social Issues*, vol. 26, #1 (Winter, 1970), pp. 184-185.

Chapter 4

1. For a list of the ten categories scored for this study, see Appendix D.
2. For a comprehensive discussion of the relationship between this category and the "intensity" one, see Giora Goldberg and Sam Lehman-Wilzig, *"Teguvat Ha'mishtarah Al Mekh'ah Tziburit Be'Yisrael,"* *Megamot*, vol. 29, #2 (August, 1985), pp. 223-229. The five subvariables here are:
   (1) *No reaction*--police presence, but no active involvement.
   (2) *Noncoercive reaction*--specific orders announced to the assembled; placing barriers blocking off the protest processions, etc.
   (3) *Arrests*--this includes temporary administrative detention, without eventual formal indictment.
   (4) *Physical force*--clubbing, punching, use of tear gas, water cannon, and any other physically coercive activity to stop the protest.
   (5) *Firearms*--shooting, even if only into the air.

In general, this is an ascending scale based on the Israeli police's strategy of "measured escalation," but occasionally one may find arrests being made without verbal warning or physical force being used without attempted arrests.

3. See, for example, Herbert M. Kritzer, "Political Protest and Political Violence: A Nonrecursive Causal Model," *Social Forces*, vol. 55, #3 (March, 1977), pp. 630-640. He notes that "the primary determinant of violence by one side is violence by the other side" (p. 638). It should be noted, of course, that this can be a two-way street --police violence may beget protester violence. While this is logically correct and may have been true on some occasions in the Israeli context, an eyewitness study of Israeli protest events found that in only one out of forty events was this the case: Daniel Berdugo, *"Teguvat Ha'mishtarah Le'hafganot Be'Yisrael Ve'hadeevuakh Ha'itoni"* (Ramat Gan: Master's Thesis presented to the Department of Political Studies, Bar-Ilan University, 1988; unpublished). The following data, therefore, are not to be construed as completely accurate, but are most probably a very close approximately of past reality.

4. The data regarding Israeli Arab protest are not too reliable. It is estimated that throughout the whole period over a dozen Israeli Arabs were killed as a result of the actions of the police/border patrol/army in the field. Interestingly, however, when one looks at the "reaction" data according to the indices on the following pages, it appears that in most instances the differences between the handling of Jewish protest compared to Arab protest are not very substantial. For instance, the proportion of "appropriate" reaction regarding the latter is 71.8%--almost exactly that of the former (71.4%)! The police underreacted and overreacted to Arab protests 16.0% and 12.2% of the time respectively, while the figures vis-a-vis Jewish protest are 16.4% and 12.1%. It is only when the intensity of Israeli Arab protest is very high that a reaction differential appears. For example, the police used their guns in 7 of the 12 Arab riots, whereas they did so in only 2 of the 58 Jewish riots.

5. In 16.9% of the events the authorities were verbally or minimally involved (giving orders, placing barricades, etc.). The remaining 65.3% of the protests showed no police intervention whatsoever.

6. Cross-tabulating has the advantage of showing the percentage of cases in which the reaction "matched" the protest intensity, and the percentage of cases in which the reaction deviated from what it should have been. The IR--which matched the two categories in ascending order (i.e., quite protest--no reaction; disruptive protest-- verbal reaction; property violence--arrests; personal violence--physical police force; riot--police guns fired)--presented an overall average of the events running from -4.00 (total underreaction, i.e., a riot where the police did not respond) to +4.00 (total overreaction, i.e., a quiet protest where the police fired weapons), with the intermediate possibilities scored as well (e.g., 0 = appropriate reaction).

7. To be more precise, the following simple table shows the varying degrees of underreaction or overreaction frequency:

Degree of Under-/Overreaction	Frequency	Percent
-4.00	2	0.1
-3.00	24	0.7
-2.00	102	2.9
-1.00	455	12.9
0.00	2,521	71.3
+1.00	330	9.3
+2.00	88	2.5
+3.00	13	0.4

8. The ongoing violent protest disturbance in the administered territories starting in late 1987 were dealt with almost exclusively by the Israeli army, which had very little experience with such a phenomenon (being trained obviously for more purely military campaigns). As a result, hundreds of Palestinian protesters were

killed, and the army's handling of the riots--quite inconsistent in the early stages-- was strongly criticized even within Israel. To be sure, the Israeli police do not usually have to deal with protests of such intensity, but there is little doubt that the Israeli police would have done a better job (as was the case within East Jerusalem where no reported fatalities occurred). By early 1989, more of this work was being handed over to the Border Patrol, a special unit linked to the police.

9. For a comprehensive discussion of these and other elements, see my "Public Demonstrators and the Israeli Police: The Policy and Practice of Successful Protest Control," *Police Studies*, vol. 6, #2 (Summer, 1983), pp. 44-52.

10. Of equal interest is the fact that the standard of deviation for religious protest was higher in every one of these periods. This is in line with what we saw above: there are significantly wider variations in police handling of religious-issue protest than any other. The table here shows that this is true no matter who is in power, although the general underreaction thrust *is* connected to coalitional considerations.

11. William A. Gamson and Ephraim Yuchtman, "Police and Society in Israel," in *Police and Society*, ed. David H. Bayley (Beverly Hills: Sage Publications, 1977), pp. 203-204.

12. Michael Yudelman, "Special police treatment for ultra-orthodox," *The Jerusalem Post*, Friday, May 6, 1983, p. 3.

13. While the criteria used for protest "size" are straighforward, there was a problem in fixing the minimum number of protesters in order for an event to be scored. Israeli law requires fifty or more individuals to request a protest permit (almost always granted). But in somewhat contradictory fashion the law also enables the police to arrest a group of three or more persons for "assembly disturbing the peace." I decided to choose an intermediate number with some Jewish resonance-- ten adults (a *minyan*, the minimum quorum for the Jewish prayer service), male or female.
    (1) Small--10-99 adults   (2) Medium--100-999
    (3) Large--1,000-9,999   (4) Huge--10,000 or more
    One further point: if a number of small protests occurred around the country on the same day, on the same issue, and organized by the same pressure group, then the size was scored as the sum total of all the participants (but as only one event).

14. Actually, there was a significant increase in "large" events from the first years (7.4%) to the second period (15.3%), but thereafter this size category remained steady, even registering a slight drop over the last two periods.

15. The sub-variables are:
    (1) *Ad hoc*--spontaneous demonstration or riot; one-time or one-issue group without a formal organizational apparatus.
    (2) *Organization/Pressure group*--an institutionalized, ongoing framework underlying the protesters.
    (3) *Political party*--either the party initiated the event, or it set up a subsidiary organization under its authority for such a protest purpose.
    Notwithstanding the above, this overall category had a few definitional problems: if an interest group receives money from a political party, how is it to be scored? (My answer: #2.) At what point does a spontaneous group become institutionalized (e.g., the Black Panthers)? Indeed, a few protest groups eventually ran the full gamut of organizational development, and the specific scoring was dependent on my knowledge of their status at respective periods in their history.

16. This split has held remarkably consistent over the years, especially post-1954: 54.1%, 54.0%, and 55.3% over the latter three periods respectively for "ad hoc" protest; 35.3%, 41.9%, and 38.1% for "pressure group" during those years; and 10.6%, 4.1%, and 6.6% for "political party" protest in that span of time.

17. As we shall see, however, those who are so involved in interest-group or even party work do tend to protest more proportionally. However, as they constitute such a

small part of both the general population and all protesters specifically, the above comment stands without contradiction.

18. From the observe side, three-quarters of all political-party protest in Israel has been on a political issue, whereas only 37.6% of pressure-group protest and merely 20.6% of ad hoc protest is on subjects of a "political" nature. Ad hoc "groups" tend far more to social protest (44.4% of all ad hoc events).

19. The size of these various groups' protest is even less surprising: only 6.7% of "ad hoc" protest is either large or huge, compared with 31.3% of "pressure-group" events which were similarly substantial in participation. Political-party protest scored in the middle with 24.7%--higher than "ad hoc" owing to the parties' great organization and resources, but lower than pressure-group due to the fringe nature of these protesting political parties, as we shall presently note.

20. "Level of authority" here pertains to the protest addressee. Here too there were scoring problems. What to do when jurisdiction over a problem was held jointly? I decided this on the basis of the specific grievance and the legally responsible level of government (e.g., flawed curriculum-Education Ministry, lack of classroom space--local authority). How to score protest against public bodies which aren't strictly governmental (e.g., *Histadrut*, Jewish Agency)? As they are inextricably tied to the central government, I scored them accordingly.

    (1) *Central*--Any central government branch, plus national public bodies, including government corporations (e.g., El Al), quasi-governmental institutions (e.g., Social Security), and other bodies under direct governmental regulation (e.g., stock exchange).

    (2) *Local*--Municipal councils, the mayor, regional administrations, as well as officials under their purview (e.g., school principal), unless such people were chosen by the protesters of a symbol of national maladministration, etc.

    (3) *Other*--Protest addressed to foreign powers, such as the U.S.S.R. on Soviet Jewry, or the U.S. on "undue pressure" for peace concessions.

21. This compares with 49.7% of all social-issue protest addressed to the local authorities, 22.8% of all economic protest, and a mere 3.0% of all political-issue protest events. As social protest tends to be somewhat more violent (13.7% overall) than economic and political protest (9.8%), this too adds a bit to the higher violence level of local protest in general.

22. Another possible reason for the very low frequency of violence during such "foreign" demonstrations is that a large number of them are directed against the United States, accepted by almost all Israelis as a true friend of the country and therefore one where violence could only be counterproductive. This is not to mention the fact that the Israeli police do everything within their power to ensure that American sites and visiting dignitaries are fully protected against Israeli protest violence--to the extent that requests for protest permits have been turned down because of the protesters' demands, for instance, that they be allowed to demonstrate in front of the American visitor's hotel.

23. The only significant problem here was what to do with "serial" protest, where the protesters return on a steady basis to the same site over days, weeks, and even months! I decided to score these as one "long" event and not dozens of "short" events.

    (1) *Short*--Under 3 hours

    (2) *Medium*--From 3 to 24 hours

    (3) *Long*--Over a day's duration, or as noted above

    (4) *Not available*--This was the only variable in the entire study where it wasimpossible to gain information for a significant percentage of the events.

    (5) *Dispersed by police*--A protest event ending "before its time" as a result of police intervention.

24. Informed speculation, indeed Israeli conventional wisdom, has it that Begin's resignation in 1983 was due to two central factors: the terrible death toll of that war

and the passing away of his wife. Despite his reputation for toughness, Begin was known to have a soft spot for the Israeli army, and by all accounts he was deeply affected by the almost daily death reports--a feeling which that protest demonstration could only have reinforced with its purposefully grotesque display of the overall body count.

25. The following schema was employed:

(1) *Outdoor rally*--Protest marches, standing demonstrations, prayer vigils, riots, traffic blockages, etc.

(2) *Indoor meeting*--An assembly gathered specifically for a protest purpose. A regularly scheduled group meeting which included some protest verbalization was not included, unless it became the overriding issue of that meeting.

(3) *Strike*--A general strike, or even localized stoppage of work, within the scoring guidelines mentioned in Issue: *Economic*.

(4) *Other*--Miscellaneous forms, such as hunger strikes, sit-ins at government offices, etc. Protest press conferences were also not included unless the ten-adult minimum was in evidence.

This study does not include printed protest--petitions, protest ads, posters, and the like were not scored. In a research seminar paper for my course, Lt. Col. Zvi Shani surveyed *Ha'aretz* and *Ma'ariv* for six months each, every five years from 1950 onwards, focusing on ads for upcoming protest events, announcements of political strikes, and public petitions. Altogether, he found but two cases in the fifties (of those periods checked), two more in the sixties, twenty-six for the seventies, and thirty-four for the eighties--hardly comparable to the protest-event numbers seen in the previous chapter.

26. These percentages have held pretty steady over the four periods, with a small rise in the fourth period for outdoor demonstrations at the expense of "miscellaneous" and the political strike.

27. Protest venue is quite important, for the protest is mostly useless if it occurs where the sound and fury cannot (or is not) ultimately heard by those being addressed. This is also the central justification for using the media as the primary data base, for they "echo" and magnify the protest. If the venue is one where not only the addressees, but the media themselves, are not around, then the message is lost.

(1) *Central city*--Jerusalem, Tel Aviv, and Haifa, exclusively.

(2) *Peripheral cities/townships*--All other medium cities and towns which by Israeli law are considered to be municipalities (approximately above 25,000 population).

(3) *Rural/uninhabited*--Villages, kibbutzim, moshavim, etc., on the one hand; nature preserves, highways, desert, unsettled territories, on the other hand.

Regarding Israel's borders and enlarged territory, the following guidelines were established. First, any territory formally annexed by the Knesset was considered part of Israel from that date onwards, and protest by anyone therein was scored. Second, regarding territory under Israeli military rule (the Golan Heights prior to its annexation of Dec. 15, 1981; the West Bank and Gaza from 1967 onwards), only the protest of Israeli citizens was counted. This means that the present study deals only peripherally with "Palestinian" protest.

28. Given the severe budgetary and manpower limitations of Israeli TV, the chances of attracting a TV crew to one's protest are significantly increased by having the protest take place near the two media centers--Tel Aviv and Jerusalem.

29. Military press censorship and lack of Jewish press interest in the Arab sector render the data here quite problematic. Nevertheless, the trend line of Israeli Arab protest over the years does seem to correspond to political developments, so that our analysis here can shed additional light on the internal Israeli Arab-Jewish situation.

(1) *Jewish*

(2) *Moslem-Arab*

(3) *Combined Jewish/Arab*--An event was scored this way if a significant number of both groups were found participating, regardless of which was predominant.

(4) *Other*--Christian (Arab or other), Druze, Circassian, etc.

30. Only in 1978 with the Egyptian peace negotiations in full swing does Israeli Arab protest return to a modest annual level of six, with the Israeli Arabs probably not wishing to spoil the party.

31. Until 1965 there were few opportunities for Israeli Arabs to mingle with the Jewish population in light of the restrictions of the military government under which they lived. Thus, the story of perceived relative deprivation begins only around 1966, reaching fruition a mere one decade later.

32. Eli Reches, *"Arvi'yei Yisrael Ve'hagadah Ha'maaravit,"* in *Bain Milkhamah Le'hesderim*, ed. Alouph Hareven (Tel Aviv: Makhon Shiloach Le'kheker Hamizrakh Ha'tikhon Ve'Afrikah, 1977), p. 114.

33. For a very comprehensive analysis of the situation of the Israeli Arab sector, and the sundry reasons for their relatively backward state, see Ian Lustick, *Arabs in the Jewish state: Israel's Control of a National Minority* (Austin: University of Texas Press, 1980). As can be seen from the title, his analysis is quite deterministic in nature. For a more organic and cultural approach (albeit published much earlier), see Jacob M.Landau, *The Arabs in Israel: A Political Study* (London: Oxford University Press, 1969).

34. This is not to suggest that "pan-Arabism" does not hold a strong ideological place in Arab politics. The ultimate goal of uniting all the Arab peoples under one political roof continues to be strong, but it is mostly a keenly felt aspiration, with little practical relevance most of the time, especially for Israeli Arabs.

35. The increasing radicalization of Israeli Arabs can also be seen in the votes for the Knesset elections over this time period. The Israeli Communist Party--the only one to seriously represent Arab interests during the sixties--increased its Arab support to 30% in 1969, and then went on to capture around 30% in the 1973 elections and close to 50% in the 1977 elections! In part as a reaction to the *Likud* (with the Arabs' wish to strengthen Labor), this percentage dropped back to 37% in 1981, but with the advent of the Progressive Peace List in 1984, the two non-Zionist parties together went over the Arab 50% mark in that latter election.

36. There are, to be sure, exceptions to this rule, although in almost all cases they involve Arab population groups who found themselves annexed to the State of Israel post-1967, i.e., East Jerusalem Arabs and Golan Heights Druze. But even here their protests are directed not at toppling the State, but rather at turning back the clock so that they can once again be under the rule of a different state (Jordan and Syria, respectively).

    It would also be incorrect to leave the impression that all Israeli Arab protest was directed at the central government. True, over the entire period such protest constituted 73.7% of all Arab protest (compared to 59.0% of Jewish protest), but 22.9% was leveled at the local authorities (in almost all cases Arab), and 3.4% against foreign powers. Here too, then, rough similarities exist between the two population sectors.

37. Given the fact that a significant part of the duration category has a "not available" component, a separate index was established comprising just intensity and size. There were no significant differences found, and so the more comprehensive "magnitude index" will be reported upon here.

38. Samuel H. Barnes, Max Kaase, et al., *Political Action: Mass Participation in Five Western Democracies* (Beverly Hills, Calif.: Sage, 1979). There are very minor differences between the populations sampled by them and by me. Minimum age in their poll was sixteen, in mine eighteen. Austria also had a maximum age limit of seventy in their poll; there was no age limit in mine.

39. Not all the items from the Barnes and Kaase tables are included here. Only those group public protest activities which are included in my study are compared. Petitions, boycotts, rent strikes, and painting slogans (on walls) are not included in my study, and so were deleted from their totals for proper comparative purposes.

In addition, while two categories were retained--"damaging property" and "personal violence"--it is unclear whether this included private behavior of this type or not. My respondents answered in the affirmative only if such was done in a group context. Thus, compared to the five nations' totals, Israel's overall percentage may be slightly low (although these two categories at most added only two percentage points to the total in the U.S. and less elsewhere).

40. The fact that these percentages do not rise with age group indicates one of two things. On the one hand, if indeed the younger Israelis have already participated in numbers similar to their elders, we may be seeing here the spearhead of a much larger protest cohort as the years go by in the future. On the other hand, this might be an indication of quite a different--and methodologically more problematic-- matter: people tend to remember their protest participation (or most other political activity) for the last few years, and not over their entire lifetime. This might explain why the oldest age group declared its participation at a slightly lower rate than the others. These senior citizens might indeed have protested less in the sixty-plus age of their lives (a natural "conservative" tendency with age), forgetting the politically "passionate activity" (e.g., public protest) of their younger years. (Then again, there was in actuality far less protest in Israel during this age cohort's younger years, i.e., 1955-1970, as we have seen earlier.) An indication that this might be so is the very low response rate of "participated only once" among the last two age-cohort groups, for if their protest activity had taken place decades earlier (and it was a one-time shot) it would be easy to forget such participation (not the case if there was periodic participation on the part of the individual). If the "amnesia hypothesis" is correct, however, this would only strengthen the contention that public protest in Israel is a widespread phenomenon. It would not, however, make any difference in a comparative context to other nations as one would assume that such a phenomenon (forgetfulness) exists in equal measure all over the world. For further analyses of the socio-demographic data see my "The Israeli Protester," *The Jerusalem Quarterly*, No. 26 (Winter, 1983), pp. 127-138.

41. However, some perceivable differences do begin to appear if this aspect is looked at from the standpoint of ideological affiliation, although there is no straightforward linear relationship: 20.1% of those identifying themselves with the moderate right and 21.8% with the right had participated in Israeli protest, whereas of those on the moderate left and the left the respective participation levels were 27.8% and 25.9%. It is not clear why a gap should appear here and not regarding political affiliation, although there is no absolute overlap between the two categories in the Israeli milieu.

42. Op. cit., p. 183.

43. Compare with the results of Barnes and Kaase, *Political Action*, op. cit., p. 567. They used a more sophisticated and detailed polling technique to determine relative deprivation ("material" and "life"), on a scale of -10 to +10. If we disregard the range of -3 to +3 (minor deprivation), then the material deprivation felt by the respondents in the five Western countries ranged from 3.2% in the Netherlands to 19.6% in Great Britain--well within the 12.1% Israeli result as outlined above.

    Incidentally, no comparisons with their results could be made regarding the various socio-demographic factors' relationship to extent of protest participation as analyzed here, owing to their using a "protest potential" index in all their statistical analyese, and not the "protest participation" scores which are presented in gross terms (pp. 548-549). This may have been because the level of actual protest participation was so low, but it still renders socio-demographic comparisons impossible.

44. This has been a standard "problem" in Israeli society for quite a long time, but here too conventional wisdom is far from reality. It should be noted that this poll was taken (by coincidence) exactly one-half year after the most vicious and violent election campaign in Israel's history, in which the "ethnic discrimination" issue

came to be paramount. As the numbers here suggest, it turns out to have been a politically artificial one. A mere 13.7% of the Israeli-born children of these Asian/African immigrants replied "below the average" to our question, and these supposedly were the ones feeling and declaiming "discrimination and deprivation." Even more surprising (from the standpoint of Israeli conventional wisdom on this issue) is the fact that there was not much of a difference between the "below the average" response rate of Likud supporters (13.0%) and Labor Party supporters (10.5%), the former party supposedly standing up for all the discriminated-against (by the Labor Establishment) Edot Ha'mizrakh Israelis, etc. For a discussion of the 1981 campaign and an analysis of what I perceived to be the underlying reason for the turbulence see my "Jihad in the Holy Land," Forum, Nos. 46/47 (Fall/Winter, 1982), pp. 187-200.

45. Nor is there much sense of sexist deprivation in Israel: women chose "below the average" at a 12.6% rate, compared to the men's 11.6% rate.

46. This is true to some extent elsewhere as well. See Barnes and Kaase, op. cit., pp. 137ff.

47. Significantly, when the government began to refuse to bail out large corporations in the mid-eighties, the workers affected (of these bankrupt firms) indulged in intensive and repeated protest events, but failed quite clearly to gather protest support among the public in general, and among their "comrades" (workers belonging to other firms which did not fail) specifically.

Chapter 5

1. When good reason exists, ordinal data may be incorporated into the regression analysis. See the discussion below regarding our "period" variable.

2. For a description of these, see Appendix E.

3. Some thought was given to first including the nominal independent variables preelection year (E-1), election year (E), and postelection year (E+1), plus war year (W) and postwar year (W+1). However, independent variables should ideally be as uncorrelated as possible in order to have significant individual predictive capability. Unfortunately, E-1, E, and E+1 (W and W+1, too) are absolutely correlated, and therefore cannot be concurrently incorporated into the regression. Consequently, a different approach was taken--Analysis of Variance.

4. Actually, a preliminary attempt was published awhile back. See Sam Lehman-Wilzig and Meyer Unger, "The Economic and Political Determinants of Public Protest Frequency and Magnitude: The Israeli Experience," *International Review of Modern Sociology*, vol. 15 (Spring/Autumn, 1985), pp.63-80; and our earlier Hebrew version "*Al Mekha'ah Tziburit Ve'gormehah Ha'kalkaliyyim: Yisrael 1951-1979,*" *Riv'on Le'kalkalah*, No. 114 (September 1982), pp. 275-283. Owing in part to the fewer observations included therein (29 instead of the present 38), more variables succeeded in entering those regression models. As we shall shortly see, the number of ultimately significant variables has been substantially winnowed down.

5. Here again, no previous researcher to my knowledge has taken into account the natural effect of population growth when performing all sorts of highly sophisticated statistical analyses on their data. For the sake of comparison, I did undertake additionally five similar regression runs without the per capita element included, and found some differences although not enough to significantly change the essence of my findings. Thus, the results reported here can be viewed as relevant as well to protest frequency understood in its simple numerical form.

6. Of course, there are examples of interrelationships of this kind. In the latter case, occasionally one will find underprivileged neighborhood demonstrators protesting against settlement policy in the territories as a drain on housing and other social resources.

7. This is not to say that no refinement of the dependent variables has been attempted in the past. It has been, but only regarding level of protest as outlined in

chapter 1, e.g., protest, turmoil, and revolution. See, for example, Douglas Bwy, "Dimensions of Social Conflict in Latin America," in *When Men Revolt and Why*, ed. James C. Davies (New York: The Free Press, 1971), pp.274-291. Bwy also reviews the efforts of others along these lines (p. 279).

8. Whether it is the income tax variable which explains why the upper classes protest more than the lower classes cannot be determined. The guess here is that this constitutes only a part of the explanation, with the rest being the former's high level of political knowledge and protest resources (time, organization, etc.).

9. One important exception to this which proves the rule is the 1987 cancellation of the Lavi jet fighter for primarily economic reasons. Almost half of the government and a sizable part of the public felt very strongly about continuing the project despite the fact that the economic considerations for cancellation were overwhelming (even the army itself supported cancellation for reasons of limited economic resources). On another front, the Labor Party election propaganda in 1988 did try to connect the cost of settling the territories to the continued plight of the inner-city slums and to the development towns' difficulties, with little apparent success.

10. The exact timing of such automatic payments has varied over the years, in accordance with the rate of inflation. When inflation is very high the increases are more frequent, and vice versa. Sometimes the payments are pegged to a cumulative inflation increase (e.g., 8%, whenever that cumulative level is reached), and not a preordained number of months.

11. In addition, the term "unemployment" is a non sequitur among the ultra-Orthodox community, as any and all "free time" must be taken up with the study of *Torah*. Those who are "unemployed" (economically) by normal standards are actually able to participate in a more "constructive" activity by their standards! My thanks to Prof. Menachem Friedman for clarifying this point.

12. This general argument contradicts another theory usually put forward regarding Israeli religious-issue protest: such protest is geared to raising money among supporters overseas (the ultra-Orthodox have even published a very professional booklet with high-quality photos showing themselves being beaten by the Israeli police; the more blood, the more contributions!). If this were the case, we would expect GNPPC to be negatively correlated with RELPROT, as the less money is available from the Israeli authorities, the more need there would be to turn overseas.

13. One additional type of statistical analysis was performed--Canonical Analysis (CA)--which is a further extension of Regression Analysis (RA). Whereas in RA one attempts to form a linear combination of a group of independent variables in order to achieve the highest possible linear correlation with the dependent variable, in CA one has a group of dependent variables (plural) with which the highest canonical correlation is sought. In short, CA attempts to define pairs of new variables, each constituting a linear combination of each group. The correlations are thus "internal" (between the dependent variables and themselves; likewise for the independent variables) and "external" (between the respective canonical variates, i.e., independent and dependent canonical pairs).
As the canonical variates are statistically orthogonal (independent), each successive pair of canonical variates accounts for the residual variation unaccounted for by previously generated pairs (similar to the step-wise RA). Thus, CA helps us study independent aspects hidden in an intricate relationship between two groups of related variables. The prime indicator of such separateness is the relative magnitude of the variables' coefficients in the canonical variates.
Table 5.2 shows the chief canonical variates (in italics). POLPROT and SOCPROT are most highly correlated canonically, and as a variate are correlated chiefly with PER. The next set is SOCPROT and RELPROT, correlated to UNMP and INTX. Finally, ECOPROT residually stands alone in its correlation to INTX.

Table 5.2
Canonical Correlations of Issue-Protests
and Four Major Indicators

Ind. Variable	1st Variate*	2d Variate	3d Variate
POLPROT	*0.705692*	-0.49723	0.00710
ECOPROT	-0.36871	0.08654	*-1.00494*
SOCPROT	*0.52912*	*0.78939*	-0.07601
RELPROT	0.04326	*-0.67447*	0.08120
Dep. Variable			
INF	-0.19682	-0.15480	-0.47836
UNMP	-0.42643	*-0.72888*	-0.26415
PER	*1.25149*	-0.11381	-0.25217
INTX	0.43460	*0.84639*	*-0.78563*
Significance	.0000	.0000	.0011

* Figures listed are the coefficients

14. An alternative explanation can be advanced as well. The stronger is the dominant party within the government, the smaller is the size of the cabinet (as that party has less coalitional need to hand out ministerial goodies). Such a government, led by a self-confident central party, may feel itself impervious to parliamentary (or even coalitional) pressure or attack. As a result, political pressure would tend to find greater outlet in the "street" than within parliament.

15. Expectedly, the number of variables which did enter the models was smaller than in the previous regressions which had 38 observations. Briefly, the results were: PROT-POP (R^2 = .60); POLPROT-POP (R^2 = .43); ECOPROT-INF (R^2 = .74); SOCPROT-CABSZ (R^2 = .15; negative coefficient); RELPROT-PER (R^2 = .45). In other words, these are the factors found to be significant in Israeli protest over the past two decades.

16. Were this the only evidence we had, then any attempted conclusion would have been guilty of the "ecological fallacy"--trying to show how aggregate factors can explain individual behavior. However, by adding attitudinal data (chapter 4), the problem is bypassed to a large extent.

17. In this statistical technique, two independent variables are entered to test for correlation with the dependent variable. This caused a slight problem as the factors to be tested were election year and postelection year (independently), plus war year and postwar year (also independently). The solution was to run the AV a number of times, each with a different twin combination of the four variables.

18. See my "Thunder before the Storm: Pre-election Agitation and Post-election Turmoil," in *The Elections in Israel--1981*, ed. Asher Arian (Tel Aviv: Ramot Press, 1983), pp. 191-212, for a broad discussion not only of these elements, but also of the theoretical literature underpinning the hypothesis.

19. Again, the literature regarding this hypothesis is very rich. A good start is the two review essays in Gurr's *Handbook* by Michael Stohl, "The Nexus of Civil and International Conflict" (chap.7), and Arthur A. Stein and Bruce M. Russett, "Evaluating War: Outcomes and Consequences" (chap. 10). In the Israeli context, a parallel study regarding the effect of war on strike activity is Amira Galin and Barukh Mevorakh, *"Al Politikah Ve'sikhsukhai Avodah,"* Riv'on Le'kalkalah, No. 108 (March, 1981), pp. 35-42.

20. This latter is especially true in the Israeli context where wars have mostly been of relatively short duration: the actual battles last no longer than a few weeks, while (aside from the 1982 war) large-scale troop mobilization lasts a few months at most.

21. The War of Independence was not included because it occurred during 1948, for which protest data were not scored as the country itself came into existence only

mid-year. Another "war"--1968-1970 War of Attrition (with Egypt over the Suez Canal)--was not included because it had no focal point and stretched over three years.

22. It is understood that the first model PROT incorporates all the other four models, so that strictly speaking we do not have five models but rather four specific ones and a single general one.

23. This split is even more marked for the overall PROT category; PER (a socio-political variable) accounts for 35% of the explained variance, while INTX (an economic one) accounts for only an additional 22%.

Chapter 6

1. S.N. Eisenstadt, *"He'arot Le'bayyat Ha'hemshekhiut Shel Ha'defusim Ha'historiyyim Ha'Yehudiyyim Ba'khevrah Ha'Yisraelit," Kivvunim*, No. 6 (February, 1980), p. 79.

2. The entire subject of a Jewish "oppositionist" cultural tradition is a vast one, the adequate discussion of which would carry us very far afield. The presentation in the next few pages, therefore, will be highly schematic, merely delineating the outline of such a *weltanschauung*. Surprisingly, very little has actually been written on the subject. For a seminal introduction see Cecil Roth, *Personalities and Events in Jewish History* (Philadelphia: The Jewish Publication Society of America, 1953), pp.69-77. His conclusion is that the Jew may be considered the "Eternal Protestant .... who always refuses to be satisfied with the present condition of affairs, and will never surrender himself entirely to the prevailing current in ideas, in ideals, in political theory .... Jews are still protestants--protestants against the modern deification of the State as they were against the deification of the Church four centuries ago, and against the juggernaut of Hellenism before the Christian era began .... (p. 77).

3. Some students of the matter are willing to go out on the limb of "comparative civilizations": "Among Jewish teachings is one which is ... virtually unique among world religions ... a recognizable stream of Jewish thought not confined to any period or school but is to be found in biblical, talmudic, kabbalistic, hasidic, and modern sources .... The idea that God has something to answer for, not only prayer to respond *to* ...." Abraham Kaplan, "The Jewish Argument with God," *Commentary*, vol. 70, #4 (October, 1980), pp. 43-44. It would seem that for the biblical period, at least, one would be hard pressed to find contemporaneously another civilization with as many examples of "oppositionism" (see Appendix A). Agreement or disagreement with this contention, however, in no way affects the argument contained in these pages.

4. This is not to negate the converse, which of course was also an integral part of the Jewish heritage: the idea of "duly constituted authority which must be obeyed."

5. For a few examples of officially sanctioned argumentativeness in the Babylonia Talmud, see *Bava Metziah* 59b; *Avodah Zarah* 19a; *Eruvin* 13b; *Sanhedrin* 11b. For a modern legalistic discussion see Joel Roth, *The Halakhic Process: A Systematic Analysis* (New York: The Jewish Theological Seminary of America,1986), chapter 4.

6. See *Shabbat* 54b and 119a; *Tamid* 28a.

7. For instance: "On many occasions German kings and later on Polish governments tried to appoint rabbis, but without success. ... These were direct acts of defiance based on the premise that the government had no jurisdiction in such matters and that any interference by the government was not lawful. ... The principle demonstrated ... the free spirit of the Jews who refused to capitulate to the capricious power of the state when that power acted unethically, illegally, or against their conscience." Leo Landman, "A Further Note on 'The Law of the Kingdom is Law,'" *Jewish Journal of Sociology*, vol. 17, #1 (June, 1975), p. 40.

8. Daniel J. Elazar, *The Covenant Idea in Politics* (Jerusalem: Working Paper No. 22, Workshop in the Covenant Idea and the Jewish Political Tradition, 1983), p. V-21.

Such a historical-cultural link can be drawn to modern Jewry outside of Israel as well. See, for example, Michael Walzer, *Exodus and Revolution* (New York: Basic Books, 1985), where he argues that "it is possible to trace a continuous history from the Exodus to the radical politics of our own time" (p. 25).

9. To be sure, there were some attempts to divorce the renascent people of Israel from their Jewish religious and cultural past. Chief among such movements was "Canaanism," which constituted a recognizable cultural stream during the first years of the State's existence (mostly among certain segments of the intelligentsia and the artistic community), but which found little popular support and soon vanished from the scene.

10. Simon N. Herman, *Jewish Identity: A Social Psychological Perspective* (Beverly Hills: Sage Publications, 1977), p. 177 (table 9.3). When asked to rank themselves on a scale of exclusive Israeliness (= 1) to exclusive Jewishness (= 7), the mean position of the entire sample was 4.2--just beyond the mid-point, slightly towards the *Jewish* side of the spectrum (p. 188). In addition, a 75% majority of the students "recognized the interrelatedness between their feeling Jewish and their feeling Israeli" (pp. 188-189).

11. Charles Liebman and Eliezer Don-Yehiya, "What a Jewish State Means to Israeli Jews," in *Comparative Jewish Politics: Public Life in Israel and the Diaspora*, ed. Sam Lehman-Wilzig and Bernard Susser (Ramat Gan: Bar-Ilan University Press, 1981), pp.101-109.

12. Eliyahu Chasin, *"Panim Be'mar'eh,"* *Politikah*, No. 17 (October, 1987), p. 45. Almost the entire October issue was devoted to the question of Israeliness/Jewishness-- from as "pro-Israeli/anti-Jewish" a perspective as is to be found in Israel today. However, this is not "Canaanism" redux, but rather the emergence of a few relatively small political parties (of the New Left variety) ardently pushing a democratic, secular humanistic program.

13. To be fair, there is one indication that at least regarding the existence of a connection between Israeli protest and Jewish oppositionism throughout history, the average Israeli has strong doubts. In the poll conducted for our study, one of the reasons offered to the respondent to explain the large amount of protest in Israel was: "While in exile the Jews always protested versus the authorities, and continue this tradition also today in Israel." It placed last among the six factors offered (see Appendix B, question #9). However, there are a number of possible reasons for this poor showing. First, the language of the question was flawed as I now realize. The use of the word "always" was quite out of place, and the limitation to "while in exile" removed half of Jewish history from the respondents' consideration! Beyond that, culture/mentality is not something obvious to the average person given its amorphous nature. Third, and finally, Israelis are not noted for their historical knowledge--especially regarding the entire Diaspora experience. Given the overwhelmingly negative picture painted in the schools of that whole period (for understandable Zionist ideological reasons), it is small wonder that Israelis know so little of the Jews' "oppositionism" through the ages. In any case, certainly more exact questions are called for in future polls on the entire subject of "Israeli protest and the Jewish heritage" as perceived by the Israeli public.

14. Harry Eckstein,"Theoretical Approaches to Explaining Collective Violence," in *Handbook of Political Conflict*, ed. Ted R.Gurr et al. (New York: The Free Press, 1980), pp. 135-166. One might add here as well that this socialization process not only functions on a macro-social level but on the micro-personal plane too, as individuals "learn" violence in the family, school, and peer group environments while growing up. For a review of this aspect see Albert Bandura, *Aggression: A Social Learning Analysis* (Englewood Cliffs: Prentice-Hall, 1973).

15. Douglas A. Hibbs, Jr., *Mass Political Violence: A Cross-National Causal Analysis* (New York: John Wiley and Sons, 1973), p. 163. Once again it should be noted that his

study, along with most of the other (few) studies taking "cultural" influences into account, is based on the same (or similarly) flawed data bases as that of Taylor and Hudson, etc.--the *New York Times* plus one regional source. It is for that reason that this chapter takes a more "qualitative" approach to the question of the "culture of protest" within Israeli society, although some indirect quantitative indices will be brought forth as well.

16. There is, of course, one exception to this generalization, and that is the amount of *external* war which Israel suffers. Its possible effects on Israeli extraparliamentarism were already discussed in chapter 4.

17. See for example Hanoch Bartov, *"Anakhnu Nos'im Et Heh'avar Ve'et Ha'masoret Lo Be'aronot Maytim,"* in *Ha'Yisraeli Ke'Yehudi: Yahadut Ve'tzionut Ve'khinukh*, vol. 2 (Tel Aviv: Am Oved, 1977), pp. 35-38. Virtually the whole book is devoted to the question of the relationship of Israeli identity to the Jewish past.

18. Lewis A. Coser, *The Functions of Social Conflict* (New York: The Free Press, 1956), p. 61.

19. There is much controversy as to whether the *ma'abara* protests, as well as the Black Panther demonstrations, were really "spontaneous" or indigenously led phenomena. Some evidence exists in both cases of interested parties who helped these groups initiate and/or organize the extraparliamentary events. See Shlomo Hasson, *Mekha'at Ha'dor Ha'sheni: Tenuot Ironiyyot-Khevratiyyot Bi'Yerushalayyim* (Jerusalem: Institute for Israeli Studies, 1987), pp. 43-44. On the other hand, there is no doubt that such events were a true reflection of deep-rooted frustration, and in many instances of such protest it was the protesters who took matters into their own hands.

20. As we have already seen in chapter 4, by 1981 there was no difference in protest-participation rates between these two central Jewish ethnic groups.

21. In actuality, this really constitutes about 90% of the Israeli resident public. The problem lies in the fact that according to Israeli law there is no overseas voting--only those physically present in Israel on the day of the election may vote. But an estimated 300,000-500,000 Israelis who permanently reside overseas are usually not stricken from the voter rolls, so that about 10% of the officially registered population cannot vote in any case (other than returning to Israel for the elections). And this does not take into account those Israelis (depending on the season in which elections are held, the numbers can range from 50,000 in the winter to a few hundred thousand during the summer vacation) who also cannot vote while overseas even if only temporarily. For an earlier analysis of this problem see Uri Avner, "Voter Participation in the 1973 Elections," in *The Elections in Israel --1973*, ed. Alan Arian (Jerusalem: Jerusalem Academic Press, 1975), pp. 203-218. By his estimation, "real" participation is about 8% higher than announced.

22. Shlomit Levy, *Political Involvement and Attitude* (Jerusalem: The Israel Institute of Applied Social Research, Publication #SL/530/E, 1969), p. 22 (table 3).

23. As reported in Eva Etzioni-Halevy with Rina Shapira, *Political Culture in Israel* (New York: Praeger Publishers, 1977), pp.73-75 (table 4.2).

24. Michal Shamir and John Sullivan, "The Political Context of Tolerance: The United States and Israel," *American Political Science Review*, vol. 77, #4 (December, 1983), p. 915. The poll was conducted in Israel during 1980 (with only the Jewish, and not Arab, responses reported on), and in the U.S. during 1978.

25. Ibid., pp. 917-918. Among their other interesting findings which are germane to our discussion here was the .39 epistemic correlation between "right to criticize" and intolerance (p. 921). In other words, paradoxically (or even contradictorily), the general norm of verbal oppositionism actually influences (in some measure) the Israeli to be intolerant! In addition, of all the general factors tested for as influencing intolerance in both countries, they found that "the general norms factor differs most between the two nations" (p. 922). In other words, more than social status, feelings of psychological security, etc., it is a *political culture* factor which leads Israelis to be more intolerant than their American counterparts.

26. Yochanan Peres and Mira Freund, "Tolerance Israeli Style," *Israeli Democracy*, vol. 1, #3 (Fall, 1987), p.37. On a scale of 1 (totally tolerant) to 5 (totally intolerant), the mean scores were 2.91 and 2.73 against the "most hated" and "second most hated" group (as chosen by each respondent) respectively, regarding limitation of their political and social rights (e.g., prohibited from being elected to the Knesset), and 3.21 and 3.08 respectively regarding the emotional attitudes (e.g., "this group is a threat to the social order") of the respondents vis-a-vis such groups. The small but significant gap between the two types of questions shows that Israelis may have strong *feelings* of intolerance toward other groups, but they are less willing to *actually* legally or politically restrict such groups. In other words, the cognitive norm of democracy is sufficiently strong to mitigate some of the attitudinal intolerance.

27. D'vorah Ben Shaul, "Fight for tolerance," *The Jerusalem Post*, Friday, December 8, 1983, p. 6. This contention is supported in part by the annual polls on democracy published in *Monitin*. For example, in the 1983 poll fully 58% of the representative sample answered that they oppose public criticism of the government's policies regarding foreign affairs and national security (34% legitimated such criticism): Eliyahu Chasin, *"Ha'demokratiah Ha'Yisraelit '83--Geshem Kavaid Omed La'redet,"* *Monitin* (March, 1983), pp. 149, 151. One can well imagine the type of antipathy engendered by such protest demonstrations as occurred during and after the Lebanon War--and indeed as we saw in chapter 3, they led to massive counter-demonstrations supporting the government.

28. Merely one of numerous examples which can be brought to bear illustrating the phenomenon of "satanizing" one's opponent in Israel is the following newspaper report: "[Minister of the Interior] Burg also said that when demonstrators twice in one month used the word 'Nazis' against their opponents, something had gone rotten in Israeli society." Aryeh Rubinstein, "Peace Now demonstrators 'endanger society'," *The Jerusalem Post*, Thursday, January 20, 1983, p. 2. Indeed, this has become quite a "popular" demonizing word of late, used especially by ethnic radicals among the *Edot Ha'mizrakh* through their naming the other side "Ashkenazis."

29. While this does not, of course, explain all Israeli protest, it does suggest the reason that a good part of the protest is directed against other societal groups, directly or indirectly.

30. In our December 1981 poll, the following reason offered for high Israeli protest came in fifth place out of six: "When the ministers and members of Knesset wish for their opinion to be accepted they shout and do protest activities, and this influences the man in the street." Public protest in Israel, then, is probably not a function of copying the political elite's behavior patterns.

31. Shevach Weiss, *Shamranut Mivnit Ve'gemishut Tif'ulit--Nusakh Yisrael* (Tel Aviv: Sifriat Minhal, 1974), p. 14. My translation and emphasis.

32. Brenda Danet, *"Emdat Ha'tzibur Le'gabay Ha'shimush Be'proteksia Ba'minhal Ha'Yisraeli,"* *Medinah U'memshal*, vol. 1, #3 (Spring, 1972), pp. 57-80.

33. The Ombudsman, *Do'kh Shnati 1* (Jerusalem, October 1972), p. 19 (my translation and emphasis). There has been a gradual decline in the number of complaints received annually over the ensuing years, perhaps a result of better bureaucratic treatment. The following are the official numbers as published in the annual Ombudsman Reports:

1972--7,490	1976--6,063	1980--7,857	1984--5,741
1973--6,762	1977--5,542	1981--7,326	1985--5,162
1974--4,937	1978--5,917	1982--6,172	1986--5,612
1975--5,561	1979--6,832	1983--5,761	1987--4,908

34. Avraham Michael and Refael Bar-El, *Shvitot Be'Yisrael: Gishah Kamutit* (Ramat Gan: Bar-Ilan University, 1977), pp. 369 and 386 (tables 12 and 29). Of course, the psycho-cultural factor does not explain the high level of strike activity by itself.

Other objective factors exist as well, as the authors themselves illustrate (pp. 19-31). Of special interest to us is the factor which they call "lack of communication" (between workers and their employers)--an element which we will explore at length in the Israeli political realm over the next two chapters. For an analysis of the connection between strictly political factors and strike activity see Amira Galin and Baruch Mevorakh, *"Al Politikah Ve'sikhsukhai Avodah,"* *Riv'on Le'kalkalah*, No. 108 (March, 1981), pp.35-42.

35. As defined by work days lost as a result of the strike. Ibid., p. 386, column 5.

36. Ehud Sprinzak, *Eesh Ha'yashar Be'aynav: Ee-legalism Ba'khevrah Ha'Yisraelit* (Tel Aviv: Sifriat Poalim, 1986), p. 22 (my translation). This is a seminal, thought-provoking work, which is seriously flawed in one respect: there is almost no statistical evidence brought forth to back up the contentions. Nevertheless, it is my feeling that the general idea is correct, and certainly there is no arguing with the examples described (although these in and of themselves don't "prove" anything from a comparative standpoint, either in Israel over time or between Israel and other nations).

37. For an excellent example of such a reasoned approach to the conflict between Israeli positive law and *halakhic* religious law, see Rabbi Yaakov Ariel, *"Hafarat Pekudah Mishum Mitzvah O Shikulim Musariyyim,"* in *Tekhumin*, vol. 4 (1983), pp. 173-179. Four questions are dealt with pertaining to a soldier's duty in the face of religiously and/or morally problematic orders from a military superior.

38. Simha F. Landau, "Trends in Violence and Aggression: A Cross-Cultural Analysis," *International Journal of Comparative Sociology*, vol. 25, #3-4 (Sept.-Dec., 1984), pp. 133-158. Israel ranks between the middle and the bottom for most indicators of criminal behavior--far better than the U.S., to some extent better than Great Britain (e.g., robbery), but not as well as Japan, to take but three examples of the world's leading democracies. For an in-depth statistical analysis of Israel's criminal trend-line over the years, see Simha F. Landau and Benjamin Beit-Hallahmi, "Israel: Aggression in Psychohistorical Perspective," in *Aggression in Global Perspective*, ed. Arnold P. Goldstein and Marshall H. Segall (New York: Pergamon Press, 1983), pp. 261-286. Most interesting is the graph to be found on p. 276: "Annual rates of robberies and attempted robberies (per 100,000 population)." There is a great deal of similarity between that trend and the public-protest evolution as described in our chapter 3--high rates in the early fifties, a low plateau over the next decade and a half, and a sharp rise from the early seventies onwards. There is almost surely no direct connection between the two phenomena, but it is possible that certain socio-economic variables influenced these two areas of activity in like fashion. This, however, does not contradict the above point regarding the dissimilarity between the public and private domain, for there we were referring to the extent of such activity--still far less (comparatively speaking) in the private sphere than in the public.

39. Vito Tanzi, *"Ha'sibot Ve'hatotzaot Shel Ha'tofa'ah Ba'olam,"* *Riv'on Le'kalkalah*, No. 122 (October, 1984), p. 328.

40. Ben-Zion Zilberfarb, *"Omdanay Ha'kalkalah Ha'shekhorah Be'Yisrael U'bekhul,"* ibid., pp. 320-322.

41. Institute for Applied Social Research, *Seker Da'at Kahal Al Hafganot Shel Me'khusray Avodah* (Jerusalem: March, 1950). Additional findings were that those answering in the negative held their opinion more strongly than those supporting the phenomenon. Also, the only groups exhibiting majority support for these protests were members of the kibbutz collectives (ideologically the most Socialist-oriented Israelis)--59%, and the new immigrants themselves (who suffered most from unemployment)--52%.

42. Etzioni-Halevy with Shapira, *Political Culture*, op. cit., p. 70 (table 4.1). Once again, this was after the Black Panthers but before the Yom Kippur War.

43. Samuel H. Barnes and Max Kaase, et al., *Political Action: Mass Participation in Five*

Western Democracies (Beverly Hills: Sage Publications, 1979), pp. 544-546 (Table TA.2). The words "justified" (my poll) and "approve" (theirs) are not exactly synonymous, but are probably close enough not to have affected the answer rates to any significant degree.

Chapter 7

1. Nathan Yanai, *Party Leadership in Israel: Maintenance and Change* (Ramat Gan: Turtledove Publishing, 1981), p. 39. A good example (among many) of the nonaccountability of Israeli politicians is the following, taken from a relatively recent newspaper article: "Although 13 of the 32 Knesset members from Gush Dan [the central region] have agreed to lobby for action on social problems in the greater Tel Aviv area, only two . . . attended a meeting held by the Association of Poor Neighborhoods on Sunday evening to acquaint them with the issues." Lea Levavi, "Only 2 MKs hear complaints from poor neighborhoods," *The Jerusalem Post*, July 12, 1983, p. 3.

2. Harry Eckstein, "Theoretical Approaches to Explaining Collective Violence," in *Handbook of Political Conflict*, ed. Ted R. Gurr et al. (New York: The Free Press, 1980), p. 150. This is no less true for many of those studies whose declared subject of investigation is the interconnection between communications and politics. Some examples: (1) Richard R. Fagen, *Politics as Communication* (Boston: Little, Brown and Company, 1966), mentions protest only in passing, and even then without reference to blocked systemic channels (p. 48). (2) Robert G. Meadow, *Politics as Communication* (Norwood, N.J.: Albex Publishing Corp., 1980), devotes only three pages (plus a few indirect references here and there) to the subject, in which the following line is most interesting for its concluding two words: "The reasons for demonstrations and protest are many, but most important is the fact that they often are the only channels of communication available for demands . . . to be articulated in totalitarian systems" (p.79). He does concede, though, that in democracies as well "protest is a mode of communication to those without access." (3) Claus Mueller, *The Politics of Communication* (New York: Oxford University Press, 1973), who discusses three forms of "distorted communication"--*directed* (government policy structuring the agenda and the language); *arrested* (limited personal capacity of individuals to engage in political communication); and *constrained* (self-interested structuring and limitation of public communication by private and governmental groups, e.g., business and the media). While of interest, none are close to our concept of systemic decay, and he makes virtually no mention of protest as a relevant element.

3. There is a body of literature which does try to quantify the level of communication development and relate it to political development. In such studies, the number of newspapers, newsprint consumption, telephones, domestic mail, etc., is scored and then correlated to other indices of economic and political development. See, for example, Phillips Cutright, "National Political Development: Measurement and Analysis," *American Sociological Review*, vol.28, #2 (April, 1983), pp. 253-264. However, this is not at all what we are talking about here, as his (and similar) data relate to communications *external* to the political system, whereas our study is referring to *internal* political communication, i.e., passing through the formal channels established by the parliamentary and executive branches of government especially.

4. Samuel P. Huntington, *Political Order in Changing Societies* (New Haven: Yale University Press, 1968).

5. Ibid., pp. 79; 55.

6. Dennis C. Pirages, "Political Stability and Conflict Management," in *Handbook of Political Conflict: Theory and Research,* ed. Ted Robert Gurr (New York: The Free Press, 1980), p. 438.

7. In a later work, Huntington does touch on this type of political decay--specifically regarding the decline of political-party power in the United States. However, as he himself makes clear, there it is not something which must necessarily adversely affect political participation and communication. Not only do many other routes remain open to the citizen (personal contact with elected district representatives, etc.), but the party reforms of the seventies even had the (at least intended) effect of opening the political parties to far greater amounts of citizen input. Michel J. Crozier et al., *The Crisis of Democracy* (New York: New York University Press, 1975), pp. 85-91.

8. S.N. Eisenstadt, "The Effect of Elitism and Petrification in Israel," *The Center Magazine* (July/August, 1985), pp. 25-30; Yonathan Shapira, *Ilit Le'lo Mam'shikhim: Dorot Manhigim Ba'khevra Ha'Yisraelit* (Tel Aviv: Sifriat Poalim, 1984); Peter Y. Medding, *Mapai in Israel: Political Organisation and Government in a New Society* (Cambridge: Cambridge University Press, 1972).

9. Shevach Weiss, *Shamranut Mivnit Ve'gemishut Tif'ulit--Nusakh Yisrael* (Tel Aviv: Sifriat Minhal, 1974), pp. 8-9.

10. There exists quite a large body of literature on the development of Israeli political processes and institutions in the pre-State *yishuv* period. The best treatment can be found in Dan Horowitz and Moshe Lissak, *Mi'yishuv Le'medinah: Yehudei Eretz Yisrael Bitkufat Ha'mandat Ha'Briti Ke'kehiliyya Politit* (Tel Aviv: Am Oved, 1977); a condensed and revised edition in English is *Origins of the Israeli Polity* (Chicago: University of Chicago Press, 1978). In both versions, see especially chapter 4 entitled "Political Mobilization and Institution Building in the Yishuv" for a description of the polity's early development and maturation along the lines of "participation" and "institutionalization," as well as chapter 8 entitled "The State of Israel and the Political Heritage of the Yishuv" for an analysis of the remarkable continuity which marked the changeover from "autonomous political community" to "sovereign State."

11. William Kornhauser, *The Politics of Mass Society* (Glencoe, Ill.: The Free Press, 1959).

12. Gabriel A. Almond and Sidney Verba, *The Civic Culture* (Boston: Little, Brown and Company, 1965).

13. Speaking specifically of the irony of India's case, where a relatively cumbersome and blocked governmental system exists, Bayley noted: "A system that was more responsive to political pressure might be paralyzed by frequent protests and violence." David H. Bayley, "Public Protest and the Political Process in India," in *Issues in Comparative Politics*, ed. Robert J. Jackson and Michael B. Stein (New York: St. Martin's Press, 1971), p. 331.

14. For a discussion of "overload" as a significant problem among many Western democracies today, see Crozier et al., *The Crisis of Democracy*, op. cit., pp. 12-16. He argues: "While it has been traditionally believed that the power of the state depended on the number of decisions it could take, the more decisions the modern state has to handle, the more helpless it becomes" (p. 13).

15. In an unrelated poll conducted for a seminar class of mine in 1987, 252 opinion leaders (i.e., Israel's social, economic, cultural,and political elite) were queried on a host of subjects. In one, they were asked a question regarding possible political reforms if need be. A mere 4% of the respondents were of the opinion that the Israeli political system did not need significant political reform! Of the other 96%, over 20% mentioned expanding the channels of political communication from the public to the government as of high priority.

16. Max Kaase, "The Crisis of Authority: Myth and Reality," in *Challenge to Governance: Studies in Overloaded Politics*, ed. Richard Rose (Beverly Hills: Sage, 1980), p. 176.

17. Benjamin Akzin, "The Role of Parties in Israeli Democracy," *The Journal of Politics*, vol. 17, #4 (November, 1955), p. 509. The author correctly argued that "no

one who wants to understand political life in Israel can afford to ignore that country's parties, representing as they do the single most influential political institution" (ibid.).

18. Actually, one could argue that even before the pioneers ever arrived in Palestine the political parties were already the dominant factor in the Diaspora, especially after the First Zionist Congress in 1897. Many of the pioneers arrived in Palestine with a full load of party ideology and commitment (in some cases, even prior training for the mostly agricultural tasks at hand) already in place--courtesy of the Zionist parties outside of Palestine.

19. Medding, *Mapai in Israel*, op. cit., p. 68. To these may be added athletic teams, publishing houses, newspapers, banks, etc., the majority of whom were *owned* by the political parties.

20. Horowitz and Lissak, *Mi'yishuv*, op. cit., p. 114.

21. Horowitz and Lissak, *Origins*, op. cit., p. 107.

22. Medding, *Mapai*, op.cit., p. 136.

23. S.N. Eisenstadt, *Ha'khevrah Ha'Yisraelit: Rekah, Hitpatkhut U'ba'ayyot* (Jerusalem: Magnes Press, 1967), p. 303. Translation mine.

24. Horowitz and Lissak, *Mi'yishuv*, op. cit., pp. 153ff., point out that some signs of party "oligarchization" could already be found as early as the 1930s, but the dominant elements were still diffusion, representativeness, openness, and flexibility.

25. In the space of a mere three years between 1949 and 1952 the proportion of government workers rose from 12.1 per 1,000 to 20.8, and has stayed at that relatively high level ever since (hitting 22.6 in 1970). Yonathan Shapira, *Ha'demokratiah Be'Yisrael* (Ramat Gan: Masada, 1977), p. 207.

26. Daniel J. Elazar, *The Covenant Idea in Politics* (Jerusalem: Working Paper No. 22, Workshop in the Covenant Idea and the Jewish Political Tradition, 1983), p. V-20.

27. "A *Mapai* member could, if he so desired, live his life in a completely party-circumscribed environment . . . . Much of this was broken down by the . . . development of the state [and] party-neutral activity in many spheres." Medding, *Mapai*, op. cit., p.88. Interestingly, *Mapai*'s own leaders encouraged this, mostly because they also ran the government which constituted a bigger "pie" than their (very large) party (p. 118). In short, *Mapai* underwent a transformation from representing the public *to* the central government to dominance over that same government (Horowitz and Lissak, *Mi'yishuv*, op.cit., p. 16).

    While I do not want to overexaggerate the similarities, there seem to be some interesting parallelisms between on the one hand the Israeli Jews' very strongly held identification with the party (at least within the *yishuv*) as well as the overall social functions which the parties served, and on the other hand the tribal environment from which the Jewish people initially emerged. At the least, Jews seem to be most comfortable within a relatively small socio-political unit, and the Israeli party certainly fit the bill, especially as a contemporary substitute for the Diaspora *kehilla* (local community).

28. Actually, here too one can go even further back in time to see how from the beginning of the Zionist enterprise it was the central "governing" body--the World Zionist Organization and later the Jewish Agency--which controlled and directed settlement of the land. This still holds true in the contemporary period, as a result of the fact that the Israeli government owns over 90% of the land in the country!

29. Gabriel Sheffer, "Elite Cartel, Vertical Domination and Grassroots Discontent in Israel," in *Territorial Politics in Industrialized Nations*, ed. Sidney Tarrow et al. (New York: Praeger Publishers, 1978), p. 77. This also explains why significant expressions of protest from these underprivileged peripheral areas took so long to emerge: "the territorial dispersion of many of the new immigrants into peripheral communities retarded the genesis of a sense of common grievance and of peripheral solidarity" (p. 79).

30. Ibid., p. 80.

31. Thus, there was much talk among the Socialists of changing the Jews' "economic profile," i.e., turning the citizenry away from bourgeois and intellectual professions to more "useful" work. The Revisionists stressed other psychological aspects such as rebuilding the Jewish character along more heroic lines, etc.

32. For a discussion of the reasons for this decline, see my "The End of Ideology?" *Midstream*, vol. 31, #2 (February, 1985), pp. 29-33. In brief, they are: the mass immigration of *Edot Ha'mizrakh* who had no experience, inclination, or understanding of Western ideology; the natural demographic "nativization" of Israeli society which meant that increasing numbers of Israelis saw their State as something quite normal and not as some vast socio-national experimental enterprise; the increasing materialism and Americanization of Israeli society; and the growing gap between the socio-economic ideology of the Labor and *Likud* (*Herut*/Liberal) blocs, and their respective constituencies' material interests (i.e., Labor supporters became middle class; *Likud* supporters became lower class). For clear indications that such a decline has occurred, see my "Hollow at the Core: Manifestations of Israeli Ideological Decay," *Forum*, Nos. 54-55 (Spring, 1985), pp. 25-32. Not all Israeli students agree on the degree of ideological centrality. Horowitz and Lissak (op. cit.) tend to somewhat downplay it as a critical factor in the *yishuv*, whereas Yosef Gorni, *Akhdut Ha'avodah, 1919-1930* (Hakibbutz Hameukhad, 1973), considers it to be a central element underlying the development of the Labor camp specifically, and ultimately Israeli democracy in general.

33. Medding, *Mapai*, op.cit., pp. 86-87.

34. And this despite the fact that the problem was recognized by the party itself: "Dissatisfaction with the role of the individual member in the regular activities of the party branches was constant. Party journals and reports registered continued criticism of apathy, the lack of opportunity for participation," etc. (ibid., p. 92). This was especially true of those distanced geographically from the "center" of the party, as we mentioned earlier. Here too an internal factor came into play: the "lack of specific procedures or constitutional provisions for bringing issues to the branches and their views back to the Central Committee or Secretariat . . . . This resulted in feelings of political inefficacy on the part of potential activists who doubted whether their views expressed in the branches would carry any influence at the centre, even if passed on" (pp. 92-93). It should be noted that some constitutional changes along decentralization lines were instituted in the early 1950s, but these could not stem the centripetal tide soon thereafter (p. 99).

35. Even today, after several internal party reforms, the internal electoral and organizational layers of the larger parties are "impressive" in number. See Asher Arian, *Politics in Israel: The Second Generation* (Chatham, N.J.: Chatham House Publishers, Inc., 1985), p. 112, where the author describes the organizational layers of the various parties. To take but one representative example (in ascending order), *Mapam* has the party convention (itself elected from the local and institutional branches), the council, the center, the executive, the executive committee, and the select committee.

36. Ibid., p. 152. Emphasis mine.

37. Yanai, *Party Leadership*, op. cit., pp. 81; 91. Under great pressure, several parties instituted secret balloting to ensure some sort of "democracy." This too was undermined: "Most parties that adopted the secret ballot as a nominating method introduced inhibiting and corrective arrangements designed to provide some protection to party leaders to limit the likelihood of a surprise outcome . . . . Seven different methods [!] were adopted in an effort to structure the nominating procedure by secret ballot in party bodies" (p.30). To take but one example, Medding points out that "*Mapai*'s internal methods of leadership selection at the parliamentary and ministerial levels were not highly democratic in any sense of

rank and file participation . . . . [There were] limits imposed by the list system demanding the ranking of candidates by a committee, thereby denying possibilities of public or rank and file expressions of confidence or otherwise in their representatives" (op. cit., p. 188).

38. Once again, this is not to say that no one among the party elite understood the problem. Speaking of Moshe Dayan, Medding asserts: "In his view the real problem was one of participation in decisions and elections; that the party 'had not found a way to allow the public entering it, if not to influence, at least to elect or to refuse to elect individuals, to vote for and against.' Under the system of appointments committees he could see no reason why anyone should join the party" (*Mapai*, op.cit., p. 257).

39. Yanai, *Party Leadership*, op. cit., pp. 196-197.

40. Medding, *Mapai*, op. cit., p. 153. The one major attempt on the part of the party's bureaucracy to move toward the younger generation, ultimately only reinforced its antagonistic approach. In 1955 the *Mapai* Secretariat granted organizational permanence to the Young Generation Secretariat in order to reduce the latter's criticism. The gap between the two was too great, however: "For the younger generation's leaders it meant freedom of ideological discussion, freedom to criticise basic values and accepted formulae, freedom to suggest reforms, and freedom to suggest new methods of coping with new challenges and new problems. Consequently, conflict was imminent and almost unavoidable" (p. 80). Soon thereafter, the new body was disbanded. Compare this with the openness of that same party in the 1920s when large numbers of immigrants were actively pursued, even at the expense of transforming the founders into a small minority (Gorni, *Akhdut Ha'avodah*, op. cit., pp. 34-39).

41. As of 1989 the leader of the *Likud* continues to be the septagenarian Yitzchak Shamir who is grooming an ideological protege--Moshe Arens--instead of the younger, more moderate, and *Edot Hamizrakh*, David Levy, who represents the immigrants arriving after the War of Independence in which Begin and Shamir were key players.

42. Eisenstadt, *Ha'khevrah*, op. cit., p. 250. Translation mine.

43. Medding, *Mapai*, op. cit., p.15.

44. See Sarah Honig, "Labour's Young Kibbutzniks Say Membership 'Inflated,'" *The Jerusalem Post*, Wednesday, November 5, 1980, p. 3, where it was reported that "[s]ources close to the present leadership do not deny the basic facts of the kibbutzniks' charge . . . ."

45. *Mapai*, op.cit., p. 30.

46. Emanuel Guttmann, "Citizen Participation in Political Life: Israel," *International Social Science Journal*, vol. 12 (1960), p. 55.

47. Emanuel Guttmann, "Israel," *The Journal of Politics*, vol. 25, #4 (November, 1963), p. 704.

48. Arian, *Politics in Israel*, op. cit., p. 106. His 1981 figure of 10% is slightly lower than mine, and he concludes with 8% for 1984.

49. There are a number of variables of interest here. When this question is cross-tabulated with the question of which protest activities are justified, fully 35% of the party activists answered that no activities whatsoever are justified, as compared with only 8.3% and 10.6% of interest-group activists and independent activists respectively--a political norm of quite different (and understandable) dimensions. Second, an indirect indication of the low status of party work can be found in the fact that as education rises, party activism declines. Finally, a further proof of petrification within the two largest (and oldest) parties can be found in the fact that of *Likud* and Labor voters only 4.1% and 2.8% respectively are active members, as compared to 6.5% and 6.3% among the supporters of the smaller (and newer) *Ratz/Shinui* and *Tehiya* parties respectively.

50. Eliyahu Chasin, "*Ha'demokratiah Ha'Yisraelit '83--Geshem Kavaid Omed La'redet*,"

Monitin (March, 1983), p. 149. Indeed, 18% were willing to abolish the parties in difficult times, and 8% to cancel them altogether. Earlier polls by the magazine had quite similar results.

51. Ephraim Yuchtman Yaar, "Public Trust in Social Institutions," Israeli Democracy, vol. 1, #3 (Fall, 1987), p. 32 (table 1). This was far behind the government (32.7% combined) and the Knesset (26.8% combined), although they too came in only in sixth and fifth places respectively (behind the army #1, courts #2, universities #3, and police #4). Following the government in order were the Histadrut, rabbinate, big business, and press, with the parties bringing up the rear as noted.

52. For a good survey of these reformed systems, see Giora Goldberg and Steven A. Hoffman, "Nominations in Israel: The Politics of Institutionalization," in The Elections in Israel--1981, ed. Asher Arian (Tel Aviv: Ramot Publishing, 1983), pp. 61-87. They note among other things how the "representativeness" (relative to the general population) of Herut's and Labor's candidates has increased as a result of such reforms (pp. 85-86).

53. Yitzchak Galnoor, "Ha'demokratiah Ha'Yisraelit Ve'hishtatfut Ha'ezrakh," Molad, vol. 9 (new series), issue 41 (1982), p. 77 (my translation). He goes on to note that "the process of strengthening the independence of these various groups is slow."

54. Yael Yishai, Kevutzot Interess Be'Yisrael (Tel Aviv: Am Oved, 1987), pp. 128-129 (translation mine). In general, this is a pathbreaking book on the subject in the Israeli context. However, it must be added that its entire perspective is from "above", i.e., it is the groups' leadership responses (actually one questionnaire response per organization) which form the basis of the findings, and not the attitudes or behavior patterns of the members themselves. Second, and very important to note in light of some of the findings which "contradict" the present analysis, this is a study of the most institutionalized interest groups in Israeli society, i.e., those who have the resources (financial or personal) to get their messages across in a relatively orderly or "parliamentary" fashion. As the author herself admits, it does not account for many quasi-institutionalized groups whose access to the authorities is far more circumscribed. It also does not account for many groups which disappeared from the scene by the mid-eighties as a result of failure and frustration at not being able to get their message across and/or influence the decision-makers (p. 187).

55. Ibid., p. 190. For an in-depth discussion of the ties between such groups and the political party system, see her chapter 6: "The Goals of Activity: Groups in a Parteienstaat" (pp. 114-127).

56. The complex web of interconnections with the Establishment explains some of Yishai's findings which seemingly belie the analysis presented in this chapter. For example, only 17%, 17% and 7% of such interest groups "cannot/do not" ever meet with members of Knesset, cabinet ministers, or high-level government officials, respectively, to present their demands (ibid., p. 169), while over three-quarters appear before parliamentary committees when need be (p. 165). Not one group (!) would admit to no successful influence as a result of its activity, and over half felt that they were greatly successful (p. 179). However, an indication of their self-inflation can be see in the fact that when the question is put to those within the system, the results are quite different. When Yishai queried the legal counselors of fifteen ministries as to the contribution of such interest groups in the legislative process, only one answered that they are an important factor in initiating draft laws (eleven said that they were no factor at all), and only two felt that these groups were very influential (seven felt "not at all") in changing existing statutes (p. 171). We shall return at length to the entire subject of "success" in chapter 9.

57. To be sure, many groups combine parliamentary and extraparliamentary activity. Yishai discusses the case of Gush Emunim as one such example (ibid., p. 164). In fact, of the relatively established and staid interest groups which she surveyed, fully 31.5% (p. 165) admitted to going the public protest route on occasion as well (more than those who used the weapons of strike or petition).

Chapter 8

1. For a more extensive discussion of the points to be made here, see my "Public Protests against Central and Local Government in Israel, 1950-1979," *The Jewish Journal of Sociology*, vol. 24, #2 (December, 1982), pp. 99-115. The present analysis, however, does add the years 1949 and 1980-1986 to that study.

2. See, for example, Daniel J. Elazar, *Israel: From Ideological to Territorial Democracy* (Jerusalem; Jerusalem Institute for Federal Studies, 1978).

3. Ibid., p. 20

4. Ibid.

5. Shevach Weiss, *Shamranut Mivnit Ve'gemishut Tifulit--Nusakh Yisrael* (Tel Aviv: Sifriat Minhal, 1974), p. 41 (my translation. The author goes on to lament that this is all well and good in theory, but in practice it does not seem to work. However, despite the fact that his book is full of statistics, here he brings none to buttress this latter lament. In any case, the later seventies and eighties did see the fuller use of such committees in many municipalities.

6. "3 Jerusalem quarters get 'citizen panels,'" *The Jerusalem Post*, Friday, February 5, 1982, p. 2. For a comprehensive examination of the local institutions and processes developed through this national experiment, see Paul King et al., *Project Renewal in Israel: Urban Revitalization through Partnership* (Lanham, Md.: University Press of America; The Jerusalem Center for Public Affairs/Center for Jewish Community Studies, 1987), especially chapters 4-6.

7. See the following two articles especially: Alan Arian and Shevach Weiss, "The Changing Pattern of Split-Ticket Voting," in *The Elections in Israel--1969*, ed. Alan Arian (Jerusalem: Jerusalem Academic Press, 1972), pp. 81-95; and Daniel J. Elazar, "The Local Elections: Sharpening the Trend toward Territorial Democracy," in *The Elections in Israel--1973*, ed. Alan Arian (Jerusalem: Jerusalem Academic Press, 1975), pp. 226-227. Technically, 1973 was the last campaign in which ticket-splitting was possible, for the new elections law placed the municipal vote on a five-year cycle, whereas the Knesset term of office is four years.

8. The very names of these lists aptly illustrate their novel (for Israel) approach to decentralized politics. Some examples: Nahariah--"We Care"; Rishon Le-Zion-- "For Rishon"; and Kiryat Ono--"Our City."

9. The extent of such a local takeover was even bigger than the pure numbers indicate, for many additional truly independent candidates ran under the official aegis of central parties which had little choice but to swallow the bitter pill of such independence for the sake of party electoral glory. See Elazar, *from Ideological*, op. cit., p. 9. A notorious example of this was Tel Aviv mayor Shlomo Lahat's declaration in early 1988--during the endemic disturbances in the "administered territories"--that as far as he was concerned the government should give back almost all of those areas in return for peace. This was nothing short of "traitorous" for a member of the Liberal/*Likud* Party to say, but he was not banished (Moshe Amirav, a minor party functionary, *was* thrown out at the same time for similar utterances), but merely requested to tone down his voice on non-local matters!

10. For a trenchant analysis of the appalling situation of Israeli local politics in the fifties see Marver H. Bernstein, *The Politics of Israel* (Princeton: Princeton University Press, 1957), chapter 12. More specifically, from 1953 to 1978 the town of Tirat Hacarmel, for example, suffered the resignations of four local mayors while an additional five were fired by the local council. The direct election of the mayor since then has ended such instability. for an in-depth analysis of the effects of the local election reform, as seen thrugh the eyes of the elected local representatives themselves, see Avraham Brichte and Avraham Levi, *"Ha'arakhat Shinui Shitat He'bekhirot Le'rashay Ha'reshuyyot Ba'shilton Ha'mekomi Be'Yisrael"* (Haifa: Department of Political Science, University of haifa, April 1985--Research Report). The authors also found that almost two-thirds of the respondents wanted their own (councilmanic) elections to be direct as well (p. 16).

11. Without getting unduly bogged down in some complicated statistical manipulations, much the same argument can be made *within* the local government network in Israel by comparing the relative increase or decrease of protest addressed to the various local authorities based on their size and age. When controlled for population increase, a comparison between the older three major cities as one group and the (mostly) newer towns as another group clearly shows that the latter have done far better protest-wise than the former. This is most probably a result in part of the greater opportunities for the post-1948 immigrants to enter local politics in the nonestablished towns, as well as the greater ease with which "new" local institutions could be developed as compared to the major urban systems which had the institutional pattern already in place for quite some time. Nevertheless, even the latter have done better from a protest perspective than the central government. For a detailed discussion of such a statistical analysis, see my article "Public Protests against Central and Local," op. cit., pp. 103-104 and 108-110, which includes some data as well on the relative success of the *Edot Ha'mizrakh* in penetrating and ultimately dominating local politics (as compared to a continued minority position in the Knesset). For an interesting study which illustrates the importance of the type of local government structure regarding protest see Harlan Hahn, "Civil Responses to Riots: A Reappraisal of Kerner Commission Data," *Public Opinion Quarterly*, vol. 34, #1 (Spring, 1970), pp. 101-107.

12. In my article upon which this analysis is based, I added another table which took into account the period of *six* months before the election date, and four periods of six months each after the formation of the government. The results were virtually identical and only strengthened the impression that there is a significant difference between the actual campaign period and all other postelection (i.e., "normal") periods. See my "Thunder before the Storm: pre-election Agitation and Post-election Turmoil," in *The Elections in Israel--1981*, ed. Asher Arian (Tel Aviv: Ramot Press, 1983), p. 195 (table 2).

13. The 1949 January election campaign was not included because of the very unstable external situation (the war had not yet formally ended), plus the fact that no protest data were scored in our study for late 1948 (the preelection period). Second, the 1981 preelection total of 29 events both understates and overstates the amount of public agitation during the 1981 campaign period. There were several reports of "incidents" involving a single person or a few people; these individual incidents were not included, as they fell beneath the "10" threshold used throughout our study. But on those days when the papers reported that there were "a number" of such incidents, they were combined so that an event score could be given.

14. Once again, my six-month postelection periodicization (up to two years after the elections) is definitely to be explained in good part by the economic cycle argument.

15. Murray Edelman, *The Symbolic Uses of Politics* (Urbana, Ill.: University of Illinois Press, 1964), p. 30.

16. As early as the 1969 election campaign it was noted that "the terminology of the style issue is somewhat vague, making it difficult to assign to it any one meaning .... [T]he closer a party was to power ... the more generalized was the style of its platform." Efraim Torgovnik, "Party Factions and Election Issues," in *The Elections in Israel--1969*, ed. Alan Arian (Jerusalem: Jerusalem Academic Press, 1972), pp. 23; 34.

17. Edelman, *Symbolic Uses*, op. cit., pp. 30; 190.

18. It is not complete self-delusion in the Israeli context: "During elections votes become such a valued commodity that, at least for a while, the power structure is altered and becomes less centralized. It is fascinating to observe how at such times, when the individual is being consulted about the future of the state, he feels at one with it. . . ." Emmanuel Marx, "Anthropological Studies in a Centralized State:

Max Gluckman and the Bernstein Israel Research Project," *Jewish Journal of Sociology*, vol.17, #2 (December, 1975), p. 144.

19. As noted in chapter 3, television may indirectly reinforce some of these noncommunication factors. For example, by visually and most palpably illustrating how the rich live, television has the effect of heightening feelings of relative deprivation on the part of the poorer segments of the population who might otherwise never come into contact with such a lifestyle.

20. Amitai Etzioni, *Demonstration Democracy* (New York: Gordon and Breach, 1979), pp. 12-13.

21. Benjamin D. Singer, "Mass Media and Communication Processes in the Detroit Riot of 1967," *Public Opinion Quarterly*, vol. 34, #2 (Summer, 1970), pp. 244-245. For a more wide-ranging (albeit non-empirical) analysis of the sundry connections between the media and violent protest, see Gladys Engel Lang and Kurt Lang, "Some Pertinent Questions on Collective Violence and the News Media," *Journal of Social Issues*, vol. 28, #1 (Winter, 1972), pp. 93-110. Their overall conclusion is that the media certainly do influence such events, but not always in the direction of increased violence.

22. For an elaboration of this point see Gadi Wolfsfeld, "Symbiosis of Press and Protest: An Exchange Analysis," *Journalism Quarterly*, vol. 61, #3 (Autumn, 1984), pp. 550-555; 742.

23. Nor does there seem to be a decline in this medium's power to transmit such messages, despite the novelty having worn off now for some time. Writing at the height of the daily anti-Vietnam War demonstrations, Etzioni correctly argued: "Even today, a demonstration, despite its daily 'routine' nature, gains more attention from the mass media (i.e., communicates more effectively) than any other legitimate political act by an equal number of citizens." *Demonstration Democracy*, op. cit., p. 14.

24. There is at least one other possible explanation for such a drop. The Israeli media are regularly accused of highlighting the negative aspects of Israeli society, thereby contributing to the public's high level of tension and ill temper. Indeed, throughout the strike, the newspapers were full of reports about politicians and citizens alike who "loved the strike; it gives us a chance to take it easy for a while, and get away from being faced daily with graphic portrayals of our problems." As a result of this theory, traffic accidents were also compared during these three periods (from official police data), and it was found that this variable (which theoretically should be connected to the public state of mind) was not affected by the strike. My thanks to Gavriel Yehuda who (for a Master's seminar) researched all the data pertaining to the TV strike.

25. There was an extremely small further increase in the number of overall items during the third period.
    All of the above data do not take into account the veritable explosion of turmoil in the administered territories which occurred in early December 1987, subsequent to the end of the television strike. In light of our analysis here, the timing of these "disturbances" would seem to be not entirely coincidental.

26. Not all agree with this contention. Shlomo Hasson, in his interesting monograph *Mekha'at Ha'dor Ha'sheni: Tenuot Ironiyyot-Khevratiyyot Bi'Yerushalayyim* (Jerusalem: Institute for Israeli Studies, 1987), p. 50, argues that their problem was precisely the reverse--their neighborhood already had a few "local bosses" who were so plugged into the Establishment that they would not rock the boat by transmitting "problematic" messages from their constituents to the authorities. Such a situation (if indeed the case) does not contradict our thesis but rather provides an interesting variation on the theme of blocked political communication, in this case the fault of the "nerve endings" and not the actual neuron.

27. For an analysis of this "cooptation" process, see Ehud Sprinzak, *Nitzanei Politikah Shel De'legitimiut Be'Yisrael, 1967-1972* (Jerusalem: Levi Eshkol Institute, 1973). By the 1980s, however, that leadership no longer really represented the poorer

neighborhoods (Charlie Biton had by now joined the Communist Party--anathema to virtually all the *Edot Ha'mizrakh*, even the poorest among them, because of that party's pro-Arab stance). As a result, protest reemerged in several of these neighborhoods.

28. The case of *Maki* was different. In short order, this Communist party began to shift its focus to (and gather increasing support from) the Arab sector, ultimately in 1965 resulting in a split-up into two different parties. The "Jewish Communists" (retaining the name *Maki*) renounced anti-Zionism and, while not exactly becoming part of the Establishment, slowly moved toward the Zionist left (especially after the 1967 war), which was represented in the government (e.g., *Mapam*). The anti-Zionist Communist residue (*Rakah*), now representing mainly (parts of) the Arab sector, had problems of a different sort because of this pro-Arab stance (though much of its leadership remained Jewish)--the military government until 1965 and other forms of "control" later on. As we have already discussed Israeli Arab protest in chapter 4, we shall not do so here, but it does constitute an exception of sorts to the "outgroup" analysis presented above--at least insofar as the pre-1976 years are concerned.

29. Interestingly, during 1984-1986 party-initiated protest rose, passing the 10% mark each year. This may have been a result of the closing off of the system (by the National Unity Government) to the smaller opposition parties who had difficulty getting their own messages through to the bloated government which could easily disregard any parliamentary criticism or input on their part.

30. For an interesting presentation of this group's history and ideology, see I. Domb, *The Transformation* (London: privately published, 1958). See too Emile Marmorstein, *Heaven at Bay: The Jewish Kulturkampf in the Holy Land* (London: Oxford University Press, 1969), who surveys the "internal" struggle between all the ultra-religious sects in Israel.

31. For the period 1950-1979 such an attempt was made, although some error was probably involved in the scoring. Beyond the problems mentioned above, another was the fact that occasionally a protest event would be attended by at least two of these three groups. My basic criterion was either who initiated the protest and/or who preponderantly attended. The *Neturei Karta* were found to account for about 47% of all religious-issue protest, while the "Establishment" religious-party supporters/identifiers of *Agudath Yisrael* and *Mizrachi/Hapoel Hamizrachi* (constituting a population at least a few dozen times the size) initiated only about 40% of such protest. (The rest was apportioned among antireligious secularists, non-Jews and non-Orthodox "traditionalists".) See my article (coauthored with Giora Goldberg) "Religious Protest and Police Reaction in a Theo-democracy: Israel, 1950-1979," *Journal of Church and State*, vol. 25, #3 (Autumn, 1983), pp. 495ff.

32. This would include those who recently joined the new *SHAS* party (ultra-religious *Edot Ha'mizrakh*).

33. To be sure, there are other possible factors at work here as well. The more frequent protesters are those who disagree the most with the State's religious policy. In addition, there are some "internal" elements: protest against the "wicked" secular policy-makers is a weapon for mobilizing support within each sect in Israel and overseas at the expense of rival sects or for large donations. On occasion, the actual protest is addressed not against the Israeli authorities but against some fellow sect "straying" too far from the accepted line.

34. Answer "d" is a conventional wisdom of sorts in Israeli society: the public is ostensibly influenced by the uncivil behavior of its representatives. To take but one example of this belief, it was reported that Jerusalem Mayor Teddy Kollek "deplores the violent language being used at cabinet meetings, Knesset meetings and the Histadrut Executive, but because of it, he understands the violence in the streets of the capital." Robert Rosenberg, "Kollek blasts violence as political expression," *The Jerusalem Post*, Tuesday, November 27, 1979, p. 3.

35. The relatively low score of this answer is not altogether surprising. The Barnes and Kaase, et al. study found quite low correlations between policy dissatisfaction and protest potential (ranging from r = .13 to r = .28). See Samuel Barnes and Max Kaase, et al., *Political Action: Mass Participation in Five Western Democracies* (Beverly Hills: Sage, 1979), p. 438.

36. Nor is merely the public aware of this problem. In a project undertaken by a seminar class of mine at Bar-Ilan University in the winter of 1987, an opinion poll was conducted among Israel's opinion leaders regarding a host of issues regarding the present and future (among the respondents were ministers, MKs, chief rabbis, school principals, media personalities, professors, judges, public officials, corporate managers, etc.). One of the questions was: "In order to fix and improve the Israeli political system it would be best to": (the respondents could choose up to two preferences among seven answers). In third place for top preference (after "changing the election system" and "changing to a presidential system") was the following: "to develop more ways of enabling the public to participate in decision-making"--another indication of the "political communication" problem, even among those who probably have far less difficulty in making their own wishes known to the powers-that-be.

37. An even stronger tendency toward extraparliamentary activity, albeit not at all surprising, can be found among "active independents' (48.9% participated in protest) and members of pressure groups (66.7%). Even inactive members of political parties tended to protest twice as much (34.3%) as the huge inactive-unaffiliated public (17.1%).

38. Robert A. Dahl, "Political Man," in *Modern Political Analysis* (Englewood Cliffs, N.J.: Prentice-Hall, Inc., 2d ed., 1970), pp. 77-99.

39. As noted, this is not the whole, or only answer. A usually apathetic or publicly lazy citizen may not find formally joining a public-interest group (party or otherwise) to be worth the effort, if the intent is merely to protest against one specific law or policy. On the other hand, almost all active party members will at one time or another find themselves in opposition to the governing coalition (of which their party is not at that time a member)--and thus might wish to vociferously through protest deliver a message to the government (which could still be done through the proper parliamentary channels if the activist wished to do so).

40. Alan Marsh, *Protest and Political Consciousness* (London: Sage, 1977), p. 27. Regarding American protest specifically, Etzioni found that: "They [demonstrations] are not to replace existing democratic instruments but to complement them." *Demonstration Democracy*, op. cit., p. 45.

41. Eva Etzioni-Halevy with Rina Shapira, *Political Culture in Israel* (New York: Praeger Publishers, 1977), pp. 68-77 ("Political Involvement"); pp. 77-79 ("Political Efficacy"). This general introduction to the issue includes all the previous Israeli survey results on the matter. For a more recent illustration of the gap, see Rina Shapira et al., "Ha'shita Ha'politit Be'Yisrael--Hemshekhiyyut O Shinui: Do'kh Mekhkar," in *Ha'maarekhet Ha'politit Ha'Yisraelit: Hatzaot Le'shinui*, ed. Baruch Susser (Tel Aviv, 1987), pp. 153-162. They found that on a scale of 1 ("not at all") to 6 ("very much"), Israelis scored 3.6 regarding their "wish to influence," and only 2.6 on "ability to influence."

42. Etzioni-Halevy and Shapira (ibid., p. 79), for example, wrote: "Perhaps many Israelis sense themselves to be politically impotent not on election day but in interelectoral periods . . . . Possibly they may feel that there are no adequate extraelectoral channels through which they can express their demands." No proof was brought to buttress these assumptions.

43. *Demonstration Democracy*, op. cit., p. 17.

44. Peter M. Hall and John P. Hewitt, "The Quasi-theory of Communication and the Management of Dissent," *Social Problems*, vol. 18, #1 (Summer, 1970), p. 19.

45. Ibid., p. 24.

Chapter 9

1. Gideon Aran, *Eretz Yisrael Bain Dat U'politikah: Ha'tnuah Le'atzirat Ha'nesigah Be'Sinai U'lekakhehah* (Jerusalem; The Jerusalem Institute for Israel Studies, 1985).
2. William A. Gamson, *The Strategy of Social Protest* (Homewood, Ill.: The Dorsey Press, 1975), p. 28. Gamson further complicates the issue (not unnecessarily) by dividing success into two parts: *acceptance* of the protest group as a valid spokesman for a legitimate set of interests, and *new advantages* gained by the group's beneficiaries. This is close to my second question as raised above. "Acceptance" is further defined by four indicators: consultation, negotiations, formal recognition, inclusion. For a schematic but suggestive analysis of such "cooptation" in the Israeli context, see Ehus Sprinzak, *Nitzanei Politikah Shel De'legitimiut Be'Yisrael, 1967-1972* (Jerusalem: Levi Eshkol Institute, 1973).
3. See Ted R. Gurr, ed., *Handbook of Political Conflict: Theory and Research* (New York: The Free Press, 1980), p. 245. For a fascinating (and rather bitter) scholarly dispute on the relevance of "long-term success" (among other points at issue) see Jack A. Goldstone, "The Weakness of Organization; A New Look at Gamson's *The Strategy of Social Protest*," *American Journal of Sociology*, vol. 85, #5 (March, 1980), pp. 1017-1042; and Gamson's rejoinder, "Understanding the Careers of Challenging Groups: A Commentary on Goldstone," ibid., pp. 1043-1060. Goldstone criticizes Gamson's not going further than an upper limit of fifteen years(!) beyond the lifespan of a protest group in order to measure its success. He found that 31% of the 53 American protest groups surveyed (between 1800 and 1945) achieved their success more than *thirty years* after the protest campaign, and in one case (American Baseball Players' Association) success was achieved about *one hundred years* after the initial protest. Gamson's not unreasonable reply is to question the utility of such protest-success measurement given the huge time gap between protest "cause" and ultimate successful "effect."
4. Gamson, *Strategy*, ibid., p. 36; Goldstone, "Weakness of Organization," ibid., p. 1026, table 4.
5. Susan Welch, "The Impact of Urban Riots on Urban Expenditures," *American Journal of Political Science*, vol. 19, #4 (1975), p. 757. Another study on these urban riots was undertaken by Harlan Hahn, "Civic Responses to Riots: A Reappraisal of Kerner Commission Data," *Public Opinion Quarterly*, vol. 34, #1 (Spring, 1970), pp. 101-107. His findings regarding "success" are in line with Gamson's percentages, albeit somewhat lower.
6. Mark Iris, "Systems in Crisis: American and Israeli Response to Urban Ethnic Protest" (Chicago: Doctoral Dissertation submitted to the Department of Political Science, Northwestern University, 1978), chapter 4.
7. Gadi Wolfsfeld, *The Politics of Provocation: Participation and Protest in Israel* (Albany, N.Y.: SUNY Press, 1988), chapter 7.
8. If perceived success is defined only by the first two answers ("always" or "usually"), then the results are 23.3% for the non-protesters and 30.8% for the protesters.
9. Ehud Sprinzak, *Eesh Ha'yashar Be'aynav: Ee-legalism Be'khevrah Ha'Yisraelit* (Tel Aviv: Sifriat Poalim, 1986). We discussed at some length Sprinzak's thesis in chapter 6.
10. Op. cit., table 7-2.
11. See Gadi Wolfsfeld, "*Pe'ilut Politit Be'Yisrael--Ha'mikreh Shel Yamit*," *Medinah, Memshal, Ve'yakhasim Bain-Le'umiyyim*, No. 22 (Winter, 1984), pp. 39-50. The author shows how all sides seemed to tacitly understand what the outer limits of "acceptable" protest behavior were, with little stepping over that line except at the very bitter end (and even then, with very minimal personal injury). See too Appendix B (question #1) for the demarcation points of protest legitimacy among the Israeli public.
12. *The Politics of Provocation*, op. cit., table 7-6.

13. For a detailed listing of the twenty-eight campaigns and breakdown of their respective average scores see Appendix C. My thanks to the following political-science colleagues for their help in answering this particularly difficult"test": Prof. Stuart Cohen, Prof. Eliezer Don-Yehiya, Prof. Daniel Elazar, Prof. Yitzchak Galnoor, Dr. Giora Goldberg, Prof. Yaakov Landau, Dr. Yoav Peled, Dr. Yaakov Reuveni, Dr. Michal Shamir, and Prof. Bernard Susser. This list is in no way exhaustive, and is not meant to suggest that these are the only authorities on Israeli politics.

14. After completing his "test," Prof. Cohen suggested that a modified equation be used to score the success/failure of each protest: the overall accomplishment or achievement of the protesters' intended goal, minus the likelihood that such an achievement would have come to pass even without the protest, equals the "net success" of the protest campaign. Such a formula was tried on students in my seminar on "Israeli Extraparliamentary Politics" (toward the end of their coursework) and the thirteen respondents here came up with an overall average of 2.5--identical to that of the experts, and certainly no lower (as one might have expected) than the experts' straightforward calculation.

    For whatever it is worth, I took the "test" myself and my own straightforward overall score was 2.3. In short, there seems to be litle doubt that at least for the fourth protest period under consideration here, the chances of protest "success" were less than 50% (a score of 2.5 on a scale from 1 to 5 translates into a 37.5% success ratio).

15. This finding is supported by Gamson's study, if "success" is defined as "gaining acceptance" (and not by "new advantages"): of those groups with 10,000 members or fewer, only 30% succeeded, whereas for those with over 10,000 members fully two-thirds were successful (*Strategy of Protest*, op. cit., p. 49).

16. In the case of the connection between violence and success, Gamson's study comes to the opposite conclusion: 62% of violence users gained acceptance and 75% gained new advantages, versus only 50% and 53% respectively for the peaceful protesters (ibid., p. 79). However, here a further distinguishing characterstic may be necessary--the receiver of violence. For example, Carol McClurg Miller, in her "Riot Violence and Protest Outcomes," *Journal of Political and Military Sociology*, vol. 6, #1 (Spring, 1978), pp. 49-63, found that assaulting police lowered the chances of gaining concessions from the political authorities, whereas assaults on civilians increased the chances of gaining such concessions.

17. For some statistically sophsticated attempts to uncover the relative weights of some of these factors, see Paul D. Schumaker, "Policy Responsiveness to Protest-Group Demands," *The Journal of Politics*, vol. 37, #2 (May, 1975), especially pp. 510-512 where he finds that "protester-controlled variables" are less important ($R^2 = .18$ for the case studies he scored) than external "social-support variables" ($R^2 = .34$). On the other hand, using Gamson's data, quite different conclusions are arrived at by Homer R. Steedly and John W. Foley in "The Success of Protest Groups: Multivariate Analyses," *Social Science Research*, vol. 8, #1 (March, 1979), pp. 1-15. Their summation: "We found that the forces that lead to protest group success are, in order of relative importance, a desire on the part of the protest group not to replace an established member of the polity, the number of alliances a group has with other groups, the absence of factional disputes, quite specific and limited goals, and a willingness to use sanctions against other groups."

    Goldstone's conclusions are altogether different, and quite suggestive for the Israeli context. He found "a near-perfect match between periods of protest group success and periods of broad crises" (op. cit., p. 1040). Indeed, in what amounts to a credo for patience, he offers this intriguing conclusion: "Any group capable of expressing its aims in some fashion . . . , and adopting nondisplacement goals, has excellent chances of eventually attaining its aims, provided it maintains its challenge until a crisis arises that makes success likely" (p. 1041). As noted above, such crises may take over thirty years in arriving in America, but are far more frequent in Israel. But here again Israeli protesters are faced with a double possibility. On the one hand, such frequent crises may increase their chances of "quick" success; on the other, the "normality of crisis" in Israel may entirely negate this element as a factor of success, owing to the authorities becoming inured to crisis.

18. Gurr, *Handbook*, op. cit., p. 264.
19. As one who has followed Israeli protest and its relationship to the government over the years, Ari Rath (managing editor of the *Jerusalem Post*) also perceives the systemic factor as critical, but from a somewhat different perspective. Asked to score the general success/failure of Israeli protest on our scale of 1 to 5 he gave it a 3. The reason for protest not succeeding all that much? "The political Establishment is just too strong." Here the emphasis is not so much on the ability to get around individual political responsibility on the part of specific politicians, but rather on the overall unity of the Establishment despite its many ideological and political internal differences. Calling the Israeli leadership an "inbred political class," Rath sees the monolithic nature of the government as the determining systemic factor rather than its lack of accountability.

Chapter 10

1. A useful start would be to conduct an opinion survey among several national publics in which the respondents could be queried on the question of "government responsibility" regarding each of these several economic factors.
2. These three elements--history, theology/philosophy (or ideology), and law/institutions--constitute a starting point for similar investigations in other countries. For example, what are some of the possibilities regarding a similar study of the United States? One might well look at the religious contentiousness of the early Puritans, the obvious oppositionism (regarding their native countries) of many later immigrants (of which the Vietnamese "boat people" are but the latest example), the War of Independence and Civil War, the centrality of the First Amendment (free speech, etc.), the political institutionalization of checks and balances, American capitalism as a form of economic dialectical intercourse, sporadic eruptions of populism and antielitism, States' Rights, muckraking (of which Woodward and Bernstein are but the most famous example), the cycle of popular uprisings, riots, and protest movements (from Shays' Rebellion to the "antinuclear" movement), etc., etc.
   To be sure, these three categories do not exhaust the possibilities. We can perceive the existence (or nonexistence) of a culture of oppositionism through an investigation of the arts as well, especially literature and drama. On the purely political-constitutional front, one could perhaps statistically measure the historical frequency of government and/or constitutional change (democratic or otherwise). In short, the lack of substantial purely quantitative data regarding a nation's past need not be a deterrent to studying the roots of the political culture from a "protest" standpoint.
3. To return to the American example for a moment, it might well be found that "illegalism" and "circumvention" are not very acceptable in that culture, but the high utilization rate of formal channels of protest (e.g., letter writing to elected officials) still indicates a fairly deep cultural acceptance and pattern of protest activity. All these were found in the Israeli case to support the findings of the more traditional attitudinal data brought to bear as well. Similar studies in other countries could perhaps even expand the investigation to other areas of social behavior more relevant to their specific case study.
4. David Sanders, *Patterns of Political Instability* (London: The Macmillan Press, Ltd., 1981), p. xiv.
5. That Israel's ineffectual election system is severely flawed has been recognized by a good part of its leadership from the inception of the State. Already in the 1950s

Prime Minister Ben-Gurion attempted to push through the Knesset a law changing the system (he lost by five votes), and subsequent periodic efforts have not been any more successful--despite the fact that almost every significant political party (except for the National Religious Party) has promised in its platform at one time or another to carry out such reform (Labor, *Likud*, Democratic Movement for Change, *Shinui*, etc.). The reasons for their failure (in many cases, of nerve) are known to all--fear of losing the support of their small party coalition partners upon whom governments in Israel rise or fall, as well as the party leadership's worry that party candidates and representatives might become too "independent" of the party apparatus.

6. Baruch Susser, ed., *Ha'maarekhet Ha'politit Ha'Yisraelit: Hatzaot Le'shinui* (Tel Aviv: 1987). For a more wide-ranging discussion of my personal thoughts on the matter, see my article therein: *"Reformah Politit Be'Yisrael--Le'kakhim Min Ha'nisayon Ha'Amerikani,"* pp. 62-79.

7. Although this follows classical representation theory, such a proposed system may not be as completely effective as many think. In a highly suggestive cross-national study, surveying all the significant types of Western election systems, Bogdanor comes to the conclusion that it is not the element of *number* of district representatives which causes or reinforces the ties between parliamentarian and constituent, but rather three other aspects related to the system in general: the existence of local primaries, the weakness of the parties, and the degree of subcultural segmentation. See Vernon Bogdanor, *Representatives of the People? Parliamentarians and Constituents in Western Democracies* (Hants, England: Gower Publishing Co., Ltd., 1985), pp. 293-301. At present, two of these three core elements in Israel (local primaries and across-the-board subcultural segmentation) are absent or not all that significant.

8. See Peter Y. Medding, *Mapai in Israel: Political Organization and Government in a New Society* (England: Cambridge University Press, 1972), chapters 7 and 8; Myron Aronoff, "Party Center and Local Branch Relationships: The Israel Labor Party," in *The Elections in Israel--1969*, ed. Alan Arian (Jerusalem: Jerusalem Academic Press, 1972), pp. 150-183; Moshe M. Czudnowski, "Legislative Recruitment under Proportional Representation in Israel: A Model and a Case Study," *Midwest Journal of Political Science*, vol. 14, #2 (May, 1970), pp. 216-248; Yonathan Shapira, *Illit Le'lo Mam'shikhim* (Tel Aviv: Sifriat Poalim, 1984); Giora Goldberg and Steven A. Hoffman, "Nominations in Israel: The Politics of Institutionalization," in *The Elections in Israel--1981*, ed. Asher Arian (Tel Aviv: Ramot Publishing, 1983), pp. 61-87. A somewhat less oligarchical picture is drawn by Dan Horowitz and Moshe Lissak in *Mi'yishuv Le'medinah: Yehudei Eretz Yisrael Bitkufat Ha'mandat Ha'Briti Ke'kehiliyya Politit* (Tel Aviv: Am Oved Publishers Ltd., 1977), especially chapter 5. They distinguish between the Socialist-Labor parties and the "civic" parties where elite turnover was greater.

9. In the *Likud*, for example, the party's Central Committee members now determine the party-list placement of candidates through secret ballot, thereby at least reflecting each candidate's strength and popularity among the party's full complement of delegates. In Labor, at present, of the "realistic" places on the party list twenty-nine candidates are elected by the (over 1,000-strong) Central Committee, while twenty-three others are elected by the various local branches and other Labor institutions (e.g., the United Kibbutz Movement).

10. One could theoretically argue that since the Central Committee delegates were elected by the party rank and file, the eventual Knesset list candidates which they elect are an indirect expression of broad party member preferences. In reality, though, many of these delegates--when on the hustings within their local branches as candidates for Central Committee membership--do not declare (or do not know) for whom they will vote in the party's nominating convention. There is little chance, then, for the party rank and file to influence the ultimate list through their delegate-selection vote.

11. Daniel Elazar and Chaim Kalchheim, ed., *Local Government in Israel* (Lanham, Md.: University Press of America; The Jerusalem Center for Public Affairs/Center for Jewish Community Studies, 1988), p. 283 (table 7.6).

12. For an extended discussion of the possibilities along these lines, see Giora Goldberg, *Ha'yemin Hakhadash: Khairut Ha'prat Ve'seder Khevrati* (Tel Aviv: Kivunim, 1987), chapters 2-4).

13. Indeed, against all professional prognostications the stringent 1985-86 New Economic Policy (causing relatively high levels of unemployment and severe reductions in real wages) did not engender social turmoil as was direly predicted. Perhaps the government's public-relations campaign (which extended beyond television chats by a popular industriaist, Buma Shavit, to newspaper ad exhortations/explanations, radio spots, etc.) did have a significant effect. Of course, the drastic reduction in inflation as a result of the new policies also was a factor in limiting a further rise in protest during that difficult period.

14. To be sure, there is at least one danger here, and that involves the increased difficulty of collective decision-making on the part of the government whenever the number of ministers increases. Yet here too the Israeli government has been moving in the right direction as it copies (with some remaining significant differences) the British model. Israel's larger government now constitutes more of a forum for airing the sundry sides of the issue at hand, while the ministers' real work lies in supervising their respective ministries. A smaller inner cabinet for making the tougher (and usually more important) government decisions has evolved, with the added effect of turning the "junior" ministers' attention more in the direction of their own specific office, and less toward the national issues-- usually to the benefit of all concerned, especially the public.

15. The poll was carried out by my students in a research seminar entitled "Toward the Future: Politics and Society in the Postindustrial Age," (Dept. of Political Studies, Bar-Ilan University). Each questionnaire was filled out in the presence of a respective student (in a small number of cases the interview was conducted over the phone). The sample encompassed 252 "opinion leaders": cabinet ministers, members of Knesset, mayors and municipal council heads, rabbis, school principals, high-level government bureaucrats, upper-echelon corporate executives, mass media editors and reporters, classical (and popular) culture personalities, army officers, judges and leading lawyers, etc. Since the poll was not intended to sample a "normal" cross-section of society, the socio-demographic variables of the respondents were skewed--but in all cases in a direction which should be considered "natural"' given the characteristics of opinion leaders in Israeli society: 85.7% were between the ages of 35 and 64; 85.3% completed their college education (or higher); 74.6% defined themselves as working in a "high-level position" (37.7%) or at "the top of their profession" (36.9%); and unfortunately, but realistically unavoidable, what with the low state of feminism in Israel today) 88.5% were males, only 11.5% females.

16. Susser, op. cit., p. 191. However, when directly asked their opinion on devolution of authority to the localities, 50% responded "absolutely agree" or "agree." When queried regarding changing the election system to direct district representation, 68% responded likewise; 66% also answered in the affirmative regarding the referendum option (Ibid., p. 190).

17. Some, but by no means all, of the questions and problems relating to this specific rubric have been most recently addressed in Gadi Wolfsfeld's book *The Politics of Provocation: Participation and Protest in Israel* (Albany, N.Y.: SUNY Press, 1988), in chapters 5 and 6.

18. The question can be asked more broadly: Is there any connection between the extent of parliamentary activism in general and extraparliamentarism? One could compare cross-nationally the levels of protest, etc., of certain countries with the levels of "political participation." For a good example of the latter, see Sidney Verba et al., *The Modes of Democratic Participation: A Cross-National Comparison*

(Beverly Hills: Sage Professional Papers in Comparative Politics, 01-013, 1971), and their later "The Modes of Participation: Continuities in Research," *Comparative Political Studies*, vol. 6, #2 (July, 1973), pp. 235-250.

19. While on the topic of protest "success," it need hardly be restated that our treatment-albeit original in its own way--was far from complete or definitive. First, this sort of questionnaire (scoring protest campaigns) could be extended in two different directions: asking the general public (thereby fleshing out our poll's single question response on the matter), and the politicians, to score the success of such protest drives. Second, more extensive quantitative work could be done along the lines of the Iris and Etzioni-Halevy studies which tested for the government's budgetary changes resulting from protest campaigns calling for increased resource allocation in selected areas. To be sure, such further work should focus its attention no less on the *reasons* for such success (or lack of)--an aspect of the question which our attempt only partly addressed, with none-too-definitive answers.

20. Increased use of other data sources as mentioned throughout our study is also called for. While the reporting (and licensing) practices of the police regarding protest differ from country to country, in many cases police records are a treasure trove of additional data which supplement (both quantitatively and especially qualitatively) the more public information presented in the mass media. To be sure, there are several methodological problems involved here, not least of which is access as well as objectivity. Nevertheless, with the proper scientifically skeptical approach to such archival material, further advances can surely be made along the road to data accuracy and comprehensiveness.

21. Indeed, for the researcher interested in investigating the demographic protest phenomenon in greater depth, this approach might be of great utility as the protest population sample (with names) would already in large part be in hand. One might go on to query these petitioners about their other extraparliamentary activities, i.e., whether petition signing is viewed as a complementary (or exclusive), primary (or secondary), and effective (or purely declaratory) mode of extraparliamentary activity.

Appendix E

1. All of the data (with the exception of cabinet size) were "obtained" from the annual statistical yearbooks put out by the Bureau of Labor Statistics from 1949 onwards. However, because of the relatively primitive state of the data in the earlier years, various mathematical manipulations had to be performed in order to render the data consistent over all thirty-eight years. Cabinet size was obtained from the annual government yearbooks.

2. These tax brackets significantly understate the burden on the average Israeli, as social security payments are very high (16% most recently), a value-added tax of 15% has been in effect (through most of the eighties), purchase taxes are high too, and import tariffs for certain big-ticket items (cars, refrigerators, carpets) reach into the hundreds of percent! And all this does not include municipal property taxes and other public service payments mandated by law.

3. See Mancur Olson, Jr., "Rapid Growth as a Destabilizing Force," *Journal of Economic History*, vol. 23, #4 (December, 1963), pp. 529-552.

4. The Multiple Range Analysis showed no homogeneity between any contiguous periods: only periods 1 and 3 or periods 1 and 4 fell into the same parameter range, but given the gap of at least sixteen years between them, there is no historical justification for viewing either set as one distinct period.

Bibliography

Akzin, Benjamin. "The Role of Parties in Israeli Democracy," *The Journal of Politics*, vol. 17, #4 (November, 1955), pp. 507-545.

Almond, Gabriel A., and Verba, Sidney. *The Civic Culture* (Boston: Little, Brown and Company, 1965).

Aran, Gideon. *Eretz Yisrael Bain Dat U'politikah: Ha'tnuah   Le'atzirat   Ha'nesigah Be'Sinai U'lekakhehah* [The Land of Israel between Politics and Religion: The Movement to Stop the Withdrawal from Sinai and the Lessons to Be Learned] (Jerusalem: The Jerusalem Institute for Israel Studies, 1985).

Arian, Alan (Asher). *The Choosing People* (Cleveland: Case Western Reserve University Press, 1973).

-----. *Politics in Israel: The Second Generation* (Chatham, N.J.: Chatham House Publishers, Inc., 1985).

Arian, Asher, and Shamir, Michal. "The Primarily Political Functions of the Left-Right Continuum," in *The Elections in Israel--1981*, ed. Asher Arian (Tel Aviv: Ramot Publishing, 1983), pp. 259-279.

Arian, Alan, and Weiss, Shevach. "The Changing Pattern of Split-Ticket Voting," in *The Elections in Israel--1969*, ed. A. Arian (Jerusalem: Jerusalem Academic Press, 1972), pp. 81-95.

Ariel, Yaakov. "*Hafarat Pekudah Mishum Mitzvah O Shikulim Musariyyim*" [Disobeying an Order Because of a Religious Commandment or Moral Considerations], in *Tekhumin*, vol. 4 (1983), pp. 173-179.

Aronoff, Myron J. "Party Center and Local Branch Relationships: The Israel Labor Party," in *The Elections in Israel--1969*, ed. Alan Arian (Jerusalem: Jerusalem Academic Press, 1972), pp. 150-183.

Avineri, Shlomo. "Israel: Two Nations?" in *Israel: Social Structure and Change*, ed. M. Curtis and M. Chertoff (New Brunswick: Transaction Books, 1973), pp. 281-305.

Avner, Uri. "Voter Participation in the 1973 Elections," in *The Elections in Israel--1973*, ed. Alan Arian (Jerusalem: Jerusalem Academic Press, 1975), pp. 203-218.

Azar, Edward E., et al. "A Quantitative Comparison of Source Coverage for Event Data," *International Studies Quarterly*, vol. 16, #3 (September, 1972), pp. 373-388.

Bagdikian, Ben H. "The Politics of American Newspapers," *Columbia Journalism Review*, vol. 10, #6 (March-April, 1972), pp. 8-13.

Bandura, Albert. *Aggression: A Social Learning Analysis* (Englewood Cliffs: Prentice-Hall, 1973).

Barnes, Samuel H., and Kaase, Max, et al. *Political Action: Mass Participation in Five Western Democracies* (Beverly Hills, Calif.: Sage, 1979).

Bar-On, Mordechai. *Shalom Akhshav: Le'diyuknah Shel Tenuah* [Peace Now: Portrait of a Movement] (Tel Aviv: Hakibbutz Hameukhad, 1985).

Bartov, Hanoch. "*Anakhnu Nos'im Et Heh'avar Ve'et Ha'masoret Lo Be'aronot Maytim*" [We Carry the Past and Tradition Not in Coffins], in *Ha'Yisraeli Ke'Yehudi: Yahadut Ve'tzionut Ve'khinukh* [The Israeli as Jew: Judaism, Zionism, and Education], vol. 2 (Tel Aviv: Am Oved, 1977), pp. 35-38.

Bayley, David H. "Public Protest and the Political Process in India," in *Issues in Comparative Politics*, ed. Robert J. Jackson and Michael B. Stein (New York: St. Martin's Press, 1971), pp. 324-332.

Ben Shaul, D'vorah. "Fight for tolerance," *The Jerusalem Post*, Friday, December 8, 1983, p. 6.

Berdugo, Daniel. *"Teguvat Ha'mishtarah Le'hafganot Be'Yisrael Ve'hadeevuakh Ha'itoni"* [The Police Reaction to Demonstrations in Israel and Subsequent Press Coverage] (Ramat Gan: Master's Thesis presented to the Department of Political Studies, Bar-Ilan University, 1988; unpublished).

Bernstein, Marver H. *The Politics of Israel* (Princeton: Princeton University Press, 1957).

Bogdanor, Vernon. *Representatives of the People? Parliamentarians and Constituents in Western Democracies* (Hants, England: Gower Publishing Co. Ltd., 1985).

Bowen, Ezra. "The Posse Stops a 'Softie': Scientists blackball a political theorist," *Time Magazine*, May 11, 1987, p. 36.

Breed, Warren. "Social Control in the Newsroom: A Functional Analysis," *Social Forces*, vol. 33, #4 (May, 1955), pp. 326-335.

Brichte, Avraham, and Levi, Avraham. *"Ha'arakhat Shinui Shitat Ha'bekhirot Le'rashay Ha'reshuyyot Ba'shilton Ha'mekomi Be'Yisrael"* [Implementation of Electoral Reform for Local Government Mayoral Elections in Israel] (Haifa: Department of Political Science, University of Haifa, April, 1985--Research Report).

Bueno de Mesquita, Bruce. "Theories of International Conflict: An Analysis and Appraisal," in *Handbook of Political Conflict: Theory and Research*, ed. Ted R. Gurr (New York: The Free Press, 1980), pp. 361-398.

Burrowes, Robert. "Theory Si, Data No! A Decade of Cross-National Political Research," *World Politics*, vol. 25, #1 (October, 1972), pp. 120-144.

Bwy, Douglas. "Political Instability in Latin America: The Cross-Cultural Test of a Causal Model," *Latin American Research Review*, vol. 3 (Spring, 1968), pp. 17-66.

-----. "Dimensions of Social Conflict in Latin America," in *When Men Revolt and Why*, ed. James C. Davies (New York: The Free Press, 1971), pp. 274-291.

Campbell, Donald T. "'Degrees of Freedom' and the Case Study," *Comparative Political Studies*, vol. 8, #2 (July, 1975), pp. 178-193.

Cantor, Norman. *The Age of Protest* (London: George Allen and Unwin, Ltd., 1970).

Chasin, Eliyahu. *"Ha'demokratiah Ha'Yisraelit '83--Geshem Kavaid Omed La'redet"* [Israeli Democracy '83--A Heavy Rain Is About to Fall], Monitin (March, 1983), pp. 149-151.

-----. *"Panim Ba'mar'eh"* [Faces in the Mirror], *Politikah*, No. 17 (October, 1987), pp. 44-47.

Cohen, Erik. "The Black Panthers in Israeli Society," *Jewish Journal of Sociology*, vol. 14, #1 (June, 1972), pp. 93-110.

Cooper, M. N. "A Reinterpretation of the Causes of Turmoil: The Effects of Culture and Modernity," *Comparative Political Studies*, vol. 7, #3 (October, 1974), pp. 267-291.

Coser, Lewis A. *The Functions of Social Conflict* (New York: The Free Press, 1956).

-----. *Continuities in the Study of Social Conflict* (New York: The Free Press, 1967).

Cromer, Gerald. "The Israeli Black Panthers: Fighting for Credibility and a Cause," *Victimology: An International Journal*, vol. 1, #3 (Fall, 1976), pp. 403-413.

Crozier, Michel J., et al. *The Crisis of Democracy* (New York: New York University Press, 1975).

Cutright, Phillips. "National Political Development: Measurement and Analysis," *American Sociological Review*, vol. 28, #2 (April, 1963), pp. 253-264.

Czudnowski, Moshe M. "Legislative Recruitment under Proportional Representation in Israel: A Model and a Case Study," *Midwest Journal of Political Science*, vol. 14, #2 (May, 1970), pp. 216-248.

Dahl, Robert A. "Political Man," in *Modern Political Analysis* (Englewood Cliffs, N.J.: Prentice-Hall, Inc., 2d ed., 1970), pp. 77-99.

Danet, Brenda. *"Emdat Ha'tzibur Le'gabay Ha'shimush Be'proteksia Ba'minhal Ha'Yisraeli"* [The Public's Stand regarding the Use of Personal Connections in the Israeli Public Administration], *Medinah U'memshal*, vol. 1, #3 (Spring, 1972), pp. 57-80.

Danzger, M. Herbert. "Validating Conflict Data," *American Sociological Review*, vol. 40, #5 (October, 1975), pp. 570-584.

Dean, Macabee. "The Numbers Game," *The Jerusalem Post* (October 1, 1982), p. 18.

Domb, I. *The Transformation* (London: privately published, 1958).

Don-Yehiya, Eliezer. *Shituf Ve'konflikt Bain Makhanot Politiyyim: Ha'makhaneh Ha'dati U'tnuat Ha'avodah U'mashbair Ha'khinukh Be'Yisrael* [Cooperation and Conflict between Political Camps: The Religious Camp and the Labor Movement and the Education Crisis in Israel] (Jerusalem: Doctoral Dissertation presented to the Department of Political Science, Hebrew University, 1977).

Doran, Charles F., et al. "A Test of Cross-National Event Reliability: Global versus Regional Data Sources," *International Studies Quarterly*, vol. 17, #2 (June, 1973), pp. 175-203.

Eckstein, Harry. "Theoretical Approaches to Explaining Collective Political Violence," in *Handbook of Political Conflict*, ed. Ted R. Gurr et al. (New York: The Free Press, 1980), pp. 135-166.

Edelman, Murray. *The Symbolic Uses of Politics* (Urbana, Ill.: University of Illinois Press, 1964), p. 30.

Eisenstadt, S. N. *Modernization: Protest and Change* (Englewood Cliffs, N.J.: Prentice-Hall, 1966).

-----. *Ha'khevrah Ha'Yisraelit: Rekah, Hitpatkhut U'ba'ayyot* [Israeli Society: Background, Development, and Problems] (Jerusalem: Magnes Press, 1967).

-----. *"He'arot Le'bayyat Ha'hemshekhiut Shel Ha'defusim Ha'historiyyim Ha'Yehudiyyim Ba'khevrah Ha'Yisraelit"* [Remarks on the Problem of the Continuity of Historical Jewish Patterns in Israeli Society], *Kivvunim*, No. 6 (February, 1980), pp. 69-83.

-----. "The Effect of Elitism and Petrification in Israel," *The Center Magazine* (July/August, 1985), pp. 25-30.

Elazar, Daniel J. "The Local Elections: Sharpening the Trend toward Territorial Democracy," in *The Elections in Israel--1973*, ed. Alan Arian (Jerusalem: Jerusalem Academic Press, 1975), pp. 219-237.

-----. *Israel: From Ideological to Territorial Democracy* (Jerusalem: Jerusalem Institute for Federal Studies, 1978).

-----. *The Covenant Idea in Politics* (Jerusalem: Working Paper No. 22, Workshop in the Covenant Idea and the Jewish Political Tradition, 1983).

Elazar, Daniel, and Kalchheim, Chaim, ed. *Local Government in Israel* (Lanham, Md.: University Press of America; The Jerusalem Center for Public Affairs/Center for Jewish Community Studies, 1988).

Etzioni, Amitai. *Demonstration Democracy* (New York: Gordon and Breach, 1979.

Etzioni-Halevy, Eva. "Protest Politics in the Israeli Democracy," *Political Science Quarterly*, vol. 90, #3 (Fall, 1975), pp. 497-520.

Etzioni-Halevy, Eva, with Shapira, Rina. *Political Culture in Israel* (New York: Praeger Publishers, 1977).

Eulau, Heinz. "Comparative Political Analysis: A Methodological Note," *Midwest Journal of Political Science*, vol. 6, #4 (November, 1962), pp. 397-407.

Fagen, Richard R. *Politics as Communication* (Boston: Little, Brown and Company, 1966).

Feierabend, Ivo K. and Rosalind L. "Aggressive Behaviors within Polities, 1948-1962: A Cross National Study," *Journal of Conflict Resolution*, vol. 10, #3 (September, 1966), pp. 249-271.

Friedrich, Carl J. "Some Methodological Reflections on the Problems of Political Data in Cross-National Research," in *Comparing Nations: The Use of Quantitative Data in Cross-National Research*, ed. Richard L. Merritt and Stein Rokkan (New Haven: Yale University Press, 1966), pp. 57-72.

Galin, Amira, and Mevorakh, Baruch. *"Al Politikah Ve'sikhsukhei Avodah"* [On Politics and Labor Conflict], *Riv'on Le'kalkalah*, No. 108 (March, 1981), pp. 35-42.

Galnoor, Yitzchak. *"Ha'demokratiah Ha'Yisraelit Ve'hishtatfut Ha'ezrakh"* [Israeli Democracy and Citizen Participation], *Molad*, vol. 9 (new series), issue 41 (1982), pp. 71-82.

-----. *Steering the Polity: Communication and Politics in Israel* (Beverly Hills: Sage Publications, 1982).

Gamson, William A. *The Strategy of Social Protest* (Homewood, Ill.:Dorsey, 1975).

-----. "Understanding the Careers of Challenging Groups: A Commentary on Goldstone," *American Journal of Sociology*, vol. 85, #5 (March, 1980), pp. 1043-1060.

Gamson, William A., and Yuchtman, Ephraim. "Police and Society in Israel," in *Police and Society*, ed. David H. Bayley (Beverly Hills: Sage Publications, 1977), pp. 195-218.

Gillespie, John V., and Nesvold, Betty A., eds. *Macro-quantitative Analysis: Conflict, Development, and Democratization* (Beverly Hills: Sage Publications, 1971).

Galin, Amira, and Mevorach, Baruch. *"Al Politikah Ve'sikhsukhai Avodah"* [On Politics and Labor Conflict], *Riv'on Le'kalkalah*, No. 108 (March, 1981), pp. 35-42.

Goldberg, Giora. *Ha'yemin Ha'khadash: Khairut Ha'prat Ve'seder Khevrati* [The New Right: Personal Freedom and Social Order] (Tel Aviv: Kivunim, 1987).

Goldberg, Giora, and Hoffman, Stephen A. "Nominations in Israel: The Politics of Institutionalization," in *The Elections in Israel--1981*, ed. Asher Arian (Tel Aviv: Ramot Publishing, 1983), pp. 61-87.

Goldberg, Giora, and Lehman-Wilzig, Sam. *"Teguvat Ha'mishtarah Al Mekha'ah Tziburit Be'Yisrael"* [Police Reaction to Public Protest in Israel], *Megamot*, vol. 29, #2 (August, 1985), pp. 223-229.

Goldstone, Jack A. "The Weakness of Organization: A New Look at Gamson's *The Strategy of Protest*," *American Journal of Sociology*, vol. 85, #5 (March, 1980), pp. 1017-1042.

Gorni, Yosef. *Achdut Ha'avodah*, 1919-1930 (n.p.: Hakibbutz Hameukhad, 1973).

Graham, Hugh D., and Gurr, Ted R. *Violence in America: Historical and Comparative Perspectives* (Washington, D.C.: U.S. Government Printing Office, 1969).

Gunders, Shulamith M. "Head Hunting," *The Jerusalem Post*, June 28, 1985, p. 18.

Gurevitch, Michael. "Television in the Election Campaign: Its Audience and Functions," in *The Elections in Israel--1969*, ed. Alan Arian et al. (Jerusalem: Jerusalem Academic Press, 1972), pp. 220-236.

Gurr, Ted R. "A Causal Model of Civil Strife: A Comparative Analysis Using New Indices," *American Political Science Review*, vol. 62, #4 (December, 1968), pp. 1104-1124.

-----. ed. *Handbook of Political Conflict: Theory and Research* (New York: The Free Press, 1980).

Gurr, Ted Robert, and Duvall, Raymond. "Civil Conflict in the 1960s: A Reciprocal Theoretical System with Parameter Estimates," *Comparative Political Studies*, vol. 6, #2 (July, 1973), pp. 135-170.

-----. "Introduction to a Formal Theory of Political Conflict," in *The Uses of Controversy in Sociology*, ed. Lewis A. Coser and Otto N. Larsen (New York: The Free Press, 1976), pp. 139-154.

Guttmann, Emanuel. "Citizen Participation in Political Life: Israel," *International Social Science Journal*, vol. 12, #1 (1960), pp. 53-62.

-----. "Israel," *The Journal of Politics*, vol. 25, #4 (November, 1963), pp. 703-717.

Hacohen, Dvorah. "Mass Immigration and the Israeli Political System, 1948-1953," *Studies in Zionism*, vol. 8, #1 (Spring 1987), pp. 99-113.

Hahn, Harlan. "Civic Responses to Riots: A Reappraisal of Kerner Commission Data," *Public Opinion Quarterly*, vol. 34, #1 (Spring, 1970), pp. 101-107.

Hall, Peter M., and Hewitt, John P. "The Quasi-theory of Communication and the Management of Dissent," *Social Problems*, vol. 18, #1 (Summer, 1970), pp. 17-27.

Hasson, Shlomo. *Mekha'at Ha'dor Ha'sheni: Tenuot Ironiyyot-Khevratiyyot Bi'Yerushalayyim* [The Protest of the Second Generation: Urban Social Movements in Jerusalem] (Jerusalem: Institute for Israeli Studies, 1987).

Hazlewood, Leo A., and West, Gerald. "Bivariate Associations, Factor Structures, and Substantive Impact: The Source Coverage Problem Revisited," *International Studies Quarterly*, vol. 18, #3 (September, 1974), pp. 317-337.

Herman, Simon N. *Jewish Identity: A Social Psychological Perspective* (Beverly Hills: Sage Publications, 1977).

Hibbs, Jr., Douglas A. *Mass Political Violence: A Cross-National Causal Analysis* (New York: John Wiley, 1973).

Honig, Sarah. "Labour's Young Kibbutzniks Say Membership 'Inflated,'" *The Jerusalem Post*, Wednesday, November 5, 1980, p. 3.

Horowitz, Dan, and Lissak, Moshe. *Mi'yishuv Le'medinah: Yehudei Eretz Yisrael Bitkufat Ha'mandat Ha'Briti Ke'kehiliyya Politit* [The Origins of the Israeli Polity: The Political System of the Jewish Community in Palestine under the Mandate] (Tel Aviv: Am Oved, 1977).

-----. *Origins of the Israeli Polity* (Chicago: University of Chicago Press, 1978).

Hudson, Michael C. *Conditions of Political Violence and Instability: A Preliminary Test of Three Hypotheses* (Beverly Hills: Sage Comparative Politics Series--#01-005, 1970).

Huntington, Samuel P. *Political Order in Changing Societies* (New Haven: Yale University Press, 1968).

Iglitzin, Lynne B. "Violence and American Democracy," *Journal of Social Issues*, vol. 26, #1 (Winter, 1970), pp. 165-186.

Institute for Applied Social Research. *Seker Da'at Kahal Al Hafganot Shel Me'khusray Avodah* [Public Opinion Poll on Protests of Unemployed Workers] (Jerusalem, March, 1950).

Iris, Mark. "Systems in Crisis: American and Israeli Response to Urban Ethnic Protest" (Chicago: Doctoral Dissertation presented to the Department of Political Science, Northwestern University, 1978).

Israel Government Statistical Yearbook (Jerusalem: Government Printing Office, 1956).

Jackman, Robert W., and Boyd, William A. "Multiple Sources in the Collection of Data on Political Conflict," *American Journal of Political Science*, vol. 23, #2 (May, 1979), pp. 434-458.

Jackson, Robert J., and Stein, Michael. "The Issue of Political Protest," in *Issues in Comparative Politics*, ed. Robert J. Jackson and Michael Stein (New York: St. Martin's Press, 1971), pp. 265-284.

Jacobs, Herbert A. "To count a crowd," *Columbia Journalism Review*, vol. 6, #1 (Spring, 1967), pp. 37-40.

Kaase, Max. "The Crisis of Authority: Myth and Reality," in *Challenge to Governance: Studies in Overloaded Politics*, ed. Richard Rose (Beverly Hills: Sage, 1980), pp. 175-198.

Kaplan, Abraham. "The Jewish Argument with God," *Commentary*, vol. 70, #4 (October, 1980), pp. 43-47.

King, Paul, et al. *Project Renewal in Israel: Urban Revitalization through Partnership* (Lanham, Md.: University Press of America; The Jerusalem Center for Public Affairs/Center for Jewish Community Studies, 1987).

Kornhauser, William. *The Politics of Mass Society* (Glencoe, Ill.: The Free Press, 1959).

Kritzer, Herbert M. "Political Protest and Political Violence: A Nonrecursive Causal Model," *Social Forces*, vol. 55, #3 (March, 1977), pp. 630-640.

Landau, Jacob M. *The Arabs in Israel: A Political Study* (London: Oxford University Press, 1969).

Landau, Simha F. *"Ha'eem Ha'khevra Ha'Yisraelit Alimah Yoter May'akherot"* [Is Israeli Society More Violent Than Others?], in *Ha'omnam Kasheh Le'hiyyot Yisraeli?* [Is It Really Harder to Be an Israeli?], ed. Alouph Hareven (Jerusalem: Van Leer Foundation, 1983), pp. 171-200.

-----. "Trends in Violence and Aggression: A Cross-Cultural Analysis," *International Journal of Comparative Sociology*, vol. 25, #3-4 (Sept.-Dec., 1984), pp. 133-158.

Landau, Simha F., and Beit-Hallahmi, Benjamin. "Israel: Aggression in Psychohistorical Perspective," in *Aggression in Global Perspective*, ed. Arnold P. Goldstein and Marshall H. Segall (New York: Pergamon Press, 1983), pp. 261-286.

Landman, Leo. "A Further Note on 'The Law of the Kingdom Is Law,'" *Jewish Journal of Sociology*, vol. 17, #1 (June, 1975), pp. 37-41.

Lang, Gladys Engel and Kurt. "Some Pertinent Questions on Collective Violence and the News Media," *Journal of Social Issues*, vol. 28, #1 (Winter, 1972), pp. 93-110.

Lehman-Wilzig, Sam. "Public Protest and Systemic Stability in Israel: 1960-1979," in *Comparative Jewish Politics: Public Life in Israel and the Diaspora*, ed. Sam Lehman-Wilzig and Bernard Susser (Ramat Gan: Bar-Ilan University Press, 1981), pp. 171-210.

-----. "Public Protests against Central and Local Government in Israel, 1950-1979," *The Jewish Journal of Sociology*, vol. 24, #2 (December, 1982), pp. 99-115.

-----. "Jihad in the Holy Land," *Forum*, Nos. 46/47 (Fall/Winter, 1982), pp. 187-200.

-----. "The Israeli Protester," *The Jerusalem Quarterly*, No. 26 (Winter, 1983), pp. 127-138.

-----. "Thunder before the Storm: Pre-election Agitation and Post-election Turmoil," in *The Elections in Israel--1981*, ed. A. Arian (Tel Aviv: Ramot Press, 1983), pp. 191-212.

-----. "Public Demonstrators and the Israeli Police: The Policy and Practice of Successful Protest Control," *Police Studies*, vol. 6, #2 (Summer, 1983), pp. 44-52.

-----. "The End of Ideology?" *Midstream*, vol. 31, #2 (February, 1985), pp. 29-33.

-----. "Hollow at the Core: Manifestations of Israeli Ideological Decay," *Forum*, Nos. 54-55 (Spring, 1985), pp. 25-32).

-----. *"Reformah Politit Be'Yisrael: Le'kakhim Min Ha'nisayon Ha'Amerikani"* [Political Reform in Israel: Lessons from the American Experience], in *Ha'maarekhet Ha'politit Be'Yisrael: Hatzaot Le'shinui* [The Israeli Political System: Suggestions for Change], ed. Baruch Susser (Tel Aviv, 1987), pp. 62-79.

Lehman-Wilzig, Sam, and Goldberg, Giora. "Religious Protest and Police Reaction in a Theo-democracy: Israel, 1950-1979," *Journal of Church and State*, vol. 25, #3 (Autumn, 1983), pp. 491-505. Reprinted in Hebrew as *"Mekha'ah Datit Ut'guva Be'taiyo-Demokratiah,"* in *Avaryanut Ve'stiyyah Khevratit*, vol. 12 (1984), pp. 23-31.

Lehman-Wilzig, Sam, and Unger, Meyer. "The Economic and Political Determinants of Public Protest Frequency and Magnitude: The Israeli Experience," *International Review of Modern Sociology*, vol. 15 (Spring/Autumn, 1985), pp. 63-80.

Levavi, Lea. "Only 2 MKs hear complaints from poor neighborhoods," *The Jerusalem Post*, July 12, 1983, p. 3.

Levitan, Dov. *"Aliyat Marvad Ha'kesamim Ke'hemshaikh Histori Le'aliyot Mi'Taiman May'az TRM"B: Nituakh Socio-Politi Shel Aliyatam U'Klitatam Shel Yehudai Taiman Be'Yisrael Be'ait Ha'khadasha"* [Operation Magic Carpet as a Historical Continuation of Jewish Emigration from Yemen since 1882: A Socio-political Analysis of the Immigration and Absorption of the Yemenite Jews in Israel in Modern Times] (Ramat Gan: Master's Thesis presented to the Department of Political Studies, Bar-Ilan University, 1983).

Levy, S. G. "A 150-Year Study of Political Violence in the United States," in *Violence in America: Historical and Comparative Perspectives*, ed. Hugh D. Graham and Ted R. Gurr (New York: Signet, 1969), pp. 81-91.

Levy, Shlomit. *Political Involvement and Attitude* (Jerusalem: The Israel Institute of Applied Social Research, Publication #SL/530/E, 1969).

Liebman, Charles, and Don-Yehiya, Eliezer. "What a Jewish State Means to Israeli Jews," in *Comparative Jewish Politics: Public Life in Israel and the Diaspora*, ed. Sam Lehman-Wilzig and Bernard Susser (Ramat Gan: Bar-Ilan University Press, 1981), pp. 101-109.

Lijphart, Arend. "The Comparable-Cases Strategy in Comparative Research," *Comparative Political Studies*, vol. 8, #2 (July, 1975), pp. 158-177.

Lissak, Moshe. "Continuity and Change in the Voting Patterns of Oriental Jews," in *The Elections in Israel--1973*, ed. Asher Arian (Jerusalem: Jerusalem Academic Press, 1975), pp. 264-277.

Lustick, Ian. *Arabs in the Jewish State: Israel's Control of a National Minority* (Austin: University of Texas Press, 1980).

Mack, Andrew. "Numbers Are Not Enough: A Critique of Internal/External Conflict Behavior Research," *Comparative Politics*, vol. 7, #4 (July, 1975), pp. 597-618.

Marmorstein, Emile. *Heaven at Bay: The Jewish Kulturkampf in the Holy Land* (London: Oxford University Press, 1969).

Marsh, Alan. *Protest and Political Consciousness* (London: Sage, 1977).

Marx, Emanuel. "Anthropological Studies in a Centralized State: Max Gluckman and the Bernstein Israel Research Project," *Jewish Journal of Sociology*, vol. 17, #2 (December, 1975), pp. 131-150.

McPhail, Clark. "Civil Disorder Participation: A Critical Examination of Recent Research," *American Sociological Review*, vol. 36, #6 (December, 1971), pp. 1058-1073.

Meadow, Robert G. *Politics as Communication* (Norwood. N.J.: Ablex Publishing Corp., 1980).

Medding, Peter Y. *Mapai in Israel: Political Organization and Government in a New Society* (England: Cambridge University Press, 1972).

Merritt, Richard L., and Rokkan, Stein. *Comparing Nations: The Use of Quantitative Data in Cross-National Research* (New Haven: Yale University Press, 1966).

Meyer, Ernie. "Parents Can be Unreasonable at Times," *The Jerusalem Post*, Sept. 10, 1975, p. 2.

Michael, Avraham, and Bar-El, Refael. *Shvitot Be'Yisrael: Gishah Kamutit* [Strikes in Israel: Quantitative Approach] (Ramat Gan: Bar-Ilan University Press, 1977).

Miller, Carol McClurg. "Riot Violence and Protest Outcomes," *Journal of Political and Military Sociology*, vol. 6, #1 (Spring, 1978), pp. 49-63.

Mueller, Claus. *The Politics of Communication* (New York: Oxford University Press, 1973).

Muller, Edward N. "The Psychology of Political Protest and Violence," in *Handbook of Political Conflict: Theory and Research*, ed. Ted R. Gurr (New York: The Free Press, 1980), pp. 69-99.

Naroll, Raoul. *Data Quality Control: A New Research Technique* (Glencoe, Ill.: The Free Press, 1962).

Oberschall, Anthony. "Theories of Social Conflict," *Annual Review of Sociology*, vol. 4 (1978), pp. 291-315.

Olson, Jr., Mancur. "Rapid Growth as a Destabilizing Force," *Journal of Economic History*, vol. 23, #4 (December, 1963), pp. 529-552.

Ombudsman. *Do'kh Shnati 1* [First Annual Report] (Jerusalem, October, 1972).

Parvin, Manoucher. "Economic Determinants of Political Unrest: An Econometric Approach," *Journal of Conflict Resolution*, vol. 17, #2 (June, 1973), pp. 271-296.

Peres, Yochanan. *Politikah Ve'adatiut Be'shalosh Sh'khunot Oni* [Politics and Ethnicity in Three Poor Neighborhoods] (n.p.: Modi'in Ezrakhi Ltd.--Ha'mercaz Le'mekhkarim Shimushiyyim, October, 1972).

-----. *Yakhassay Edot Be'Yisrael* [Ethnic Group Relations in Israel] (Tel Aviv: Sifriat Poalim, 1976).

Peres, Yochanan, and Freund, Mira. "Tolerance Israeli Style," *Israeli Democracy*, vol. 1, #3 (Fall, 1987), pp. 35-39.

Pirages, Dennis C. "Political Stability and Conflict Management," in *Handbook of Political Conflict: Theory and Research*, ed. Ted R. Gurr (New York: The Free Press, 1980), pp. 425-460.

Ra'anan, Zvi. *Gush Emunim* [The Bloc of the Faithful] (Tel Aviv: Sifriat Poalim, 1981).

Reches, Eli. *"Arvi'yei Yisrael Ve'hagadah Ha'maaravit"* [The Arabs of Israel and the West Bank], in *Bain Milkhamah Le'hesderim* [Between War and Temporary Arrangements], ed. Alouph Hareven (Tel Aviv: Makhon Shiloach Le'kheker Hamizrakh Ha'tikhon Ve'Afrikah, 1977), pp. 107-126.

Report of the Committee on Income Distribution and Social Inequality (Tel Aviv, 1971).

Rosenberg, Robert. "Kollek blasts violence as political expression," *The Jerusalem Post*, Tuesday, Nov. 27, 1979, p. 3.

Roth, Cecil. *Personalities and Events in Jewish History* (Philadelphia: The Jewish Publication Society of America, 1953).

Roth, Joel. *The Halakhic Process: A Systemic Analysis* (New York: The Jewish Theological Seminary of America, 1986).

Rubinstein, Aryeh. "Peace Now demonstrators 'endanger society,'" *The Jerusalem Post*, Thursday, January 20, 1983, p. 2.

Sanders, David. *Patterns of Political Instability* (London: The Macmillan Press Ltd., 1981).

Scarrow, Howard A. *Comparative Political Analysis: An Introduction* (New York: Harper and Row, 1969).

Schiff, Ze'ev, and Ya'ari, Ehud. *Israel's Lebanon War*, ed. and trans. Ina Friedman (New York: Simon and Schuster, 1984).

Schumaker, Paul D. "Policy Responsiveness to Protest-Group Demands," *The Journal of Politics*, vol. 37, #2 (May, 1975), pp. 488-521.

Scolnick, Jr., Joseph M. "An Appraisal of Studies of the Linkage between Domestic and International Conflict," *Comparative Political Studies*, vol. 6, #4 (January, 1974), pp. 485-509.

Segev, Tom. 1949: *Ha'Yisraelim Ha'rishonim* [1949: The First Israelis] (Jerusalem: The Domino Press, 1984).

Shama, Avraham, and Iris, Mark. *Immigration without Integration: Third World Jews in Israel* (Cambridge, Mass.: Schenkman Publishing Co., 1977).

Shamir, Michal, and Sullivan, John. "The Political Context of Tolerance: The United States and Israel," *The American Political Science Review*, vol. 77, #4 (December, 1983), pp. 911-928.

Shapira, Rina, et al. *"Ha'shita Ha'politit Be'Yisrael--Hemshekhiyyut O Shinui: Do'kh Mekhkar"* [The Political System in Israel--Continuity or Change: Research Report], in *Ha'maarekhet Ha'politit Ha'Yisraelit: Hatzaot Le'shinui* [The Israeli Political System: Suggestions for Change], ed. Baruch Susser (Tel Aviv, 1987), pp. 139-209.

Shapira, Yonathan. *Ha'demokratiah Be'Yisrael* (Ramat Gan: Masada, 1977).

-----. *Ilit Le'lo Mam'shikhim: Dorot Manhigim Ba'khevra Ha'Yisraelit* [An Elite without Successors: Generations of Leaders in Israeli Society] (Tel Aviv: Sifriat Poalim, 1984).

Sheffer, Gabriel. "Elite Cartel, Vertical Domination, and Grassroots Discontent in Israel," in *Territorial Politics in Industrialized Nations*, ed. Sidney Tarrow et al (New York: Praeger Publishers, 1978), pp. 64-96.

-----. *"Alimut U'politikah,"* *Ha'aretz*, May 8, 1981, p. 14.

Sigelman, Lee. "Reporting the News: An Organizational Analysis," *American Journal of Sociology*, vol. 79, #1 (July, 1973), pp. 132-151.

Singer, Benjamin D. "Mass Media and Communication Processes in the Detroit Riot of 1967," *Public Opinion Quarterly*, vol. 34, #2 (Summer, 1970), pp. 236-245.

Snyder, David. "Theoretical and Methodological Problems in the Analysis of Government Coercion and Collective Violence," *Journal of Political and Military Sociology*, vol. 4, #2 (Fall, 1976), pp. 277-293.

-----. "Collective Violence: Research Agenda and Some Strategic Considerations," *Journal of Conflict Resolution*, vol. 22, #3 (September, 1978), pp. 499-534.

Snyder, David, and Kelly, William R. "Conflict Intensity, Media Sensitivity, and the Validity of Newspaper Data," *American Sociological Review*, vol. 42, #1 (February, 1977), pp. 105-123.

Snyder, David, and Tilly, Charles. "Hardship and Collective Violence in France, 1830 to 1960," *American Sociological Review*, vol. 37, #5 (October, 1972), pp. 520-532.

Sprinzak, Ehud. *Nitzanei Politikah Shel De'legitimiut Be'Yisrael, 1967-1972* [Sparks of Political Delegitimacy in Israel] (Jerusalem: Levi Eshkol Institute, 1973).

--------. *"Gush Emunim: Model Ha'karkhon Shel Ha'kitzoniyyut Ha'politit"* [Gush Emunim: The Iceberg Model of Political Extremism], *Medinah, Memshal, Ve'yakhasim Bain-Le'umiyyim*, No. 17 (Spring, 1981), pp. 22-49.

-----. *"Politikah Khutz-Parlamentarit Be'Yisrael"* [Extraparliamentary Politics in Israel], *Skirah Khodshit* (August-September, 1984), pp. 35-45.

-----. *Eesh Ha'yashar Be'aynav: Ee-legalism Ba'khevrah Ha'Yisraelit* [Every Man Whatsoever Is Right in His Own Eyes--Illegalism In Israeli Society] (Tel Aviv: Sifriat Poalim, 1986).

Steedly, Homer R., and Foley, John W. "The Success of Protest Groups: Multivariate Analyses," *Social Science Research*, vol. 8, #1 (March, 1979), pp. 1-15.

Stein, Arthur A., and Russett, Bruce M. "Evaluating War: Outcomes and Consequences," in *Handbook of Political Conflict: Theory and Research*, ed. Ted R. Gurr (New York: The Free Press, 1980), pp. 399-424.

Stohl, Michael. "The Nexus of Civil and International Conflict," in *Handbook of Political Conflict: Theory and Research*, ed. Ted R. Gurr (New York: The Free Press, 1980), pp. 297-330.

Susser, Baruch, ed. *Ha'maarekhet Ha'politit Ha'Yisraelit: Hatzaot Le'shinui* [The Israeli Political System: Suggestions for Change] (Tel Aviv, 1987).

Tanter, Raymond. "Dimensions of Conflict Behavior within and between Nations, 1958-1960," *Journal of Conflict Resolution*, vol. 10, #1 (March, 1966), pp. 41-64.

Tanzi, Vito. *"Ha'sibot Ve'hatotzaot Shel Ha'tofa'ah Ba'olam"* [The Reasons and the Consequences for the Phenomenon in the World], *Riv'on Le'kalkalah*, No. 122 (October, 1984), pp. 323-328.

Taylor, Charles L., and Jodice, David A. *World Handbook of Political and Social Indicators*, vol. 2 (New Haven: Yale University Press, 1983, 3d edition).

"3 Jerusalem quarters get 'citizen panels,'" *The Jerusalem Post*, Friday, February 5, 1982, p. 2.

Tilly, Charles, Louise, and Richard. *The Rebellious Century*, 1830-1930 (Cambridge, Mass.: Harvard University Press, 1975).

Torgovnik, Efraim. "Party Factions and Election Issues," in *The Elections in Israel--1969*, ed. Alan Arian (Jerusalem: Jerusalem Academic Press, 1972), pp. 21-40.

Tuchman, Gaye. "Objectivity as a Strategic Ritual: An Examination of a Newsman's Notion of Objectivity," *American Journal of Sociology*, vol. 77, #4 (January, 1972), pp. 660-670.

-----. "Making News by Doing Work: Routinizing the Unexpected," *American Journal of Sociology*, vol. 79, #1 (July, 1973), pp. 110-131.

Unger, Meyer, and Lehman-Wilzig, Sam. *"Al Mekha'ah Tziburit Ve'gormehah Ha'kalkaliyyim: Yisrael, 1951-1979"* [The Economic Background of Public Protest: Israel, 1951-1979], *Riv'on Le'kalkalah*, No. 114 (September, 1982), pp. 275-283.

Verba, Sidney, et al. *The Modes of Democratic Participation: A Cross-National Comparison* (Beverly Hills: Sage Professional Papers in Comparative Politics, 01-013, 1971).

-----. "The Modes of Participation: Continuities in Research," *Comparative Political Studies*, vol. 6, #2 (July, 1973), pp. 235-250.

Walzer, Michael. *Exodus and Revolution* (New York: Basic Books, 1985).

Weisbrod, Lilly. "Protest and Dissidence in Israel," in *Cross-Currents in Israeli Culture and Politics*, ed. Myron J. Aronoff (New Brunswick, N.J.: Transaction Books, 1984), pp. 51-68.

Weiss, Shevach. *Shamranut Mivnit Ve'gemishut Tif'ulit--Nusakh Yisrael* [Structural Conservatism and Functional Flexibility--The Israeli Version] (Tel Aviv: Sifriat Minhal, 1974).

Welch, Susan. "The Impact of Urban Riots on Urban Expenditures," *American Journal of Political Science*, vol. 19, #4 (November, 1975), pp. 741-760.

White, David M. "The 'Gatekeeper': A Case Study in the Selection of News," *Journalism Quarterly*, vol. 27, #4 (Fall, 1950), pp. 383-390.

Wilkenfeld, Jonathan, et al. "Conflict Interactions in the Middle East, 1949-1967," *The Journal of Conflict Resolution*, vol. 16, #2 (June, 1972), pp. 135-154.

Wolfensohn, Avraham. *May'ha'tenakh Le'tnuat Ha'avodah* [From the Bible to Israel's Labor Movement] (Tel Aviv: Am Oved, 1975).

Wolfsfeld, Gadi. *"Pe'ilut Politit Be'Yisrael--Ha'mikreh Shel Yamit"* [Political Action in Israel: The Case of Yamit], *Medinah, Memshal, Ve'yakhasim Bain-Le'umiyyim*, No. 22 (Winter, 1984), pp. 39-50.

-----. "Collective Action and Media Strategy: The Case of Yamit," *The Journal of Conflict Resolution*, vol. 28, #3 (Autumn, 1984), pp. 550-555; 742.

-----. "Symbiosis of Press and Protest: An Exchange Analysis," *Journalism Quarterly*, vol. 61, #3 (Autumn, 1984), pp. 363-381.

-----. *The Politics of Provocation: Participation and Protest in Israel* (Albany, N.Y.: SUNY Press, 1988).

Yanai, Nathan. *Party Leadership in Israel: Maintenance and Change* (Ramat Gan: Turtledove Publishing, 1981).

Yishai, Yael. *Kevutzot Interess Be'Yisrael: Miv'khanah Shel Demokratiah* [Interest Groups in Israel: The Test of Democracy] (Tel Aviv: Am Oved, 1987).

Yuchtman Yaar, Ephraim. "Public Trust in Social Institutions," *Israeli Democracy*, vol. 1, #3 (Fall, 1987), pp. 31-34.

Yudelman, Michael. "'Special' police treatment for ultra-orthodox," *The Jerusalem Post*, Friday, May 6, 1983, p. 3.

Zilberfarb, Ben-Zion. *"Omdanay Ha'kalkalah Ha'shekhorah Be'Yisrael U'bekhul"* [Estimates of the Black Economy in Israel and Overseas], *Riv'on Le'kalkalah*, No. 122 (October, 1984), pp. 319-322.

Zimmerman, Ekkart. "Macro-comparative Research on Political Protest," in *Handbook of Political Conflict: Theory and Research*, ed. Ted R. Gurr (New York: The Free Press, 1980), pp. 167-237.

INDEX

African Digest, 13.
Agranat Commission, 37.
Almog, Yeshai, 81.
Almond, Gabriel, 91.
America, United States of, 12, 50-51, 59-60, 73, 83, 85, 93, 114, 127-128, 134.
Arab: Israeli, 11, 55-58; Palestinian, 54, 57, 83; world, 60, 79. *See also* Protest.
Arab-Israeli Conflict, 37, 56-57, 129-130.
Argov, Shlomo, 41.
Argumentativeness, 77, 122.
Arian, Asher, 98.
Army, Israeli, 46, 129.
Ashkenazi, Motti, 37, 40.
Ashkenazim, 39.
Asian Recorder, 13.
Austria, 12, 59-60, 62, 85.

Barnes, Samuel H., 10, 59, 62, 85, 122.
Begin, Menachem, 30, 52, 97.
Beirut, 41.
Belgium, 83.
Ben-Gurion, David, 33-34, 93, 95, 97, 107.
Black: economy, 83; market, 29, 83; medicine, 83.
Black Panthers, 2, 36-40, 45, 50, 55-56, 63, 85, 94, 105-107, 114, 122.
Bnei Brak, 48.
Border Patrol, 46.
Britain, 12, 59-60, 62, 83, 85, 129.
British Mandate, 32, 34, 48, 80.
Bueno de Mesquita, Bruce, 8.
Bureaucracy: government, 82, 89, 128-129; party, 94-97, 123.
Burg, Yosef, 48.

Cabinet Size, 67, 73, 129.
Campbell, Donald T., 7-8.
Cantor, Norman, 38.
Catholics, 133.
China, 134.
Christians, 55, 133.
Civil War, 79.
Coercion, 10.
Communication: blocked, 11, 22, 89, 91-93, 99, 109-110, 123-125, 130-131, 133; efficacy, 105; political, 3, 10, 35, 50, 57, 62,
73-74, 89, 92, 95-110, 113-114, 118-119, 122-126, 128-129, 133.
Comptroller, State, 82, 89, 122, 129.
Conflict: internal, 79, 89; tradition of, 79. *See also* Protest.
Constitution, 91.
Cooptation, 1, 37.
Corruption, 83, 128.
Coser, Lewis, 79.
Courts, 91.
Covenant, 77.
Culture: anti-authoritarian, 84; arts, 134; authoritarian, 79; Central and Eastern Europe, 79; civic, 91; continuity of, 78; economic, 128; general Israeli, 81, 125; Levantine, 79; political, 10-12, 22, 45, 55, 57, 65, 78-79, 81, 85, 89, 91, 104, 108-109, 122, 132; protest, 3, 72, 78-80, 82, 84-85, 89, 123-124; secular, 71; of violence, 79.

Danet, Brenda, 82.
Dash, 37.
Data: aggregate, 12; attitudinal, 12; Israeli, 15, 17-19; sources, 5, 13-21, 120-121, 133-134.
Dayan, Moshe, 37.
De Tocqueville, Alexis, 38.
Deadline Data, 13.
Decay, Political, 90, 133.
Demonstrations. *See also* Protest.
Detroit Riots, 105.
Disobedience, 77, 83, 122.
Doran, Charles F., 15.
Druze, 55, 133.
Duvall, Raymond, 12.

Eckstein, Harry, 79, 89.
Economy: distortion, 129; governmental, control, 128; psychology, 128.
Edelman, Murray, 103-104.
Edot Ha'mizrakh, 34, 38, 63, 93.
Egypt: non-combatancy, 75; peace negotiations, 40-41; protest against, 53, 113.
Eisenstadt, S.N. 90, 92, 97.
Elazar, Daniel, 101.
Elections: campaigns, 38, 102-104; direct, 101-102, 126-127; local,

127; periods, 22, 67, 71, 74-76,102-104; primaries, 126-127; system, 89, 99, 108, 118, 123, 126-127, 131; voting percentage, 80, 127. *See also* Local; Reform.
Elites, 90-92, 94-96, 98, 113, 115-116, 123-125, 129-131.
Etzioni, Amitai, 105, 110.
Etzioni-Halevy, Eva, 1.
Eulau, Heinz, 8.
Extraparliamentarism. *See also* Protest.

Feierabend, Ivo & Rosalind, 14.
Facts on File, 15.
France: arms embargo, 35; Fourth Republic, 90; ministries, 129; Moslems in, 133; poll, 12.
Friedrich, Carl, 9.

Galnoor, Yitzchak, 98.
Gamson, William, 48, 114.
Germany: Weimar, 90; West, 12, 59-60, 85, 126, 133.
GNP, 29, 33, 68, 71, 83, 121.
Golan Heights, 54.
Goldstone, Jack, 114.
Government, National Unity, 35, 37, 42, 105, 107.
Gurr, Ted R., 8, 12, 118.
Gush Emunim, 2, 40, 50, 54-55, 94.

Ha'aretz, 106.
Haifa, 33, 61.
Hall, Peter, 110.
Hamula, 56.
Hewitt, John, 110.
Histadrut, 50-51.
Housing, 29-30, 32, 34, 38-39, 42, 52-53, 114.
Huntington, Samuel, 89-90.

Ideology, 94, 102-103.
Illegalism, 82-83, 116.
Immigrants, 29-32, 36, 38-39, 44-45.
Immigration: acceptance of, 73; and party membership, 97; mass, 56, 69, 72-73, 79, 92-93, 121; post-1948, 27, 106; Russian, 39.
Income, 38, 62-63.
Inflation, 42, 67-70, 103-104, 113-114, 120-121, 129.
Institutionalization, Political, 90.
Interest, Political, 80, 89, 9, 104, 125.
Intifada, 57.

Intolerance. *See also* Tolerance.
Iris, Mark, 114-115.
Israel, State of, 8, 29, 31-32, 57, 77-78, 80, 91-93, 107.
Italy, 12, 90.
Ivtzan, Arye, 48.

Jackson, Robert J., & Stein, Michael B., 11.
Jarring, Gunnar, 51.
Jerusalem, 18, 36, 38, 43, 48, 51-53, 61, 63, 101.
Jerusalem Post, 15-21.
Jodice, David A., 13-16, 121.
Jordan, 75.
Judaism, and Israel, 78.

Kaase, Max, 2, 59, 62, 85, 92, 122.
Kach, 51.
Keesing's Contemporary Archives, 15.
Kibbutz, 53, 93, 97, 101.
Kiryat Shmona, 53.
Knesset, 31, 53, 55, 71, 81-82, 89, 91, 96, 101, 107-108, 118, 125-126, 130-131, 134.
Kollek, Teddy, 101.
Kornhauser, William, 91.
Kulturkampf, 43.

Land Day, 55, 57.
Land Settlement, 93.
Lavon Affair, 33, 35.
Leadership. *See also* Elites.
Levine, Nachum, 29.
Levy, David, 97.
Lijphart, Arend, 7.
Local: committees, 101-102; elections, 101; government, 100-102, 127, 131; party lists, 101-102, 127; politics, 90; reform, 126-127.

Ma'abarot, 29-30, 36, 40, 63.
Ma'ariv, 17, 106.
Marsh, Alan, 109.
Marx, Karl, 38.
Me'a She'arim, 48.
Medding, Peter, 91-92, 97.
Meir, Golda, 37.
Methodology: Analysis of Variance, 74; cross-national studies, 8, 11-12, 83, 89, 120; general 2-3, 124; Gini Index, 67, 73; hypotheses, 9; Index of Reaction, 46, 48-49; problems, 43, 89, 113-

114, 116-118, 120, 131; regression
     analysis, 3, 22, 65, 67-73, 76, 120;
     single nation case study, 7-9, 11-12,
     16, 120.
Middle East Journal, 13, 15.
Modernization, 29-31, 36, 60.
Moslems, 133.

Netherlands, 12, 59-60, 85.
Neturei Karta, 60, 71, 107.
New York Times, 13, 15.

Ombudsman. *See also* Comptroller,
     State.
Oppositionism, 77-80, 84, 122, 124, 133.

Palestine. *See also Yishuv*.
Participation: unconventional
     political, 10; political, 80, 90-92, 104.
Parties: *Agudat Yisrael*, 71, 107; all, 81;
     atrophy/ossification, 92-97, 99, 118;
     Communist, 30, 32, 35, 51, 58, 107;
     control, 50, 92, 126; *Herut*, 30, 107;
     Labor (*Mapai*), 30-31, 33, 35, 37, 48,
     50, 72, 92, 95, 97, 101, 128;
     leadership, 89, 126; Liberals, 107;
     Likud, 37, 48, 63, 97, 101-102, 128;
     list, 89, 101-102, 125-126;
     membership decline, 92-94, 97-98,
     118, 123; *Mizrachi*, 107;
     mobilization, 94; nominations
     process, 89, 96, 98, 126; oligarchy,
     95-96, 126; *Rafi*, 97; religious, 31-
     32, 48; size, 94-95, 123; trust in, 98.
Peace Now, 2, 40, 50, 55.
Periphery, 93, 97, 123.
Petach Tikva, 43, 52.
Petition, 134.
PLO, 41.
Police: and crime, 83; archival material,
     48; political orientation, 48; protest
     licensing, 17; reaction to protest, 21,
     32-33, 46-49, 51, 114, 132-133.
Poll, 21, 59, 63, 78, 82, 84-85, 98, 108,
     115, 130.
Population Growth, 67.
Presidency, 91, 130.
Prime Minister, 91, 130-131, 134.
Project Renewal, 101.
Proteksiah, 62, 82-83.
Protest: age of participants, 60-61;
     aggregate data, 2, 59; alliances, 117;
     Arab, 55-58, 129; campaigns, 20, 43,
     113-117, 119, 122-124, 132, 134;
     collective, 79; demographics, 3,

59-64; development of Israeli, 27-
     45; dimensions, 9; duration, 21, 43,
     52; economic-issue, 29, 33, 42-44,
     47-50, 57-58, 67-70, 72, 74, 121;
     education of participants, 61-62;
     elections, 102-104, 123,
     133; ethnicity of participants,
     60-61; frequency, 3, 7, 17, 27-43,
     49, 67, 72, 74, 99, 105-107, 120-
     121, 124, 133; gender of
     participants, 60-61; general, 77, 79;
     goals, 57, 113, 118-119, 124, 132;
     group, 1-2, 50, 131-133; income of
     participants, 61-63; innovative, 20,
     53; intensity, 20-21, 27, 32, 46, 49,
     52, 77, 116-117, 122, 133; internal
     party, 96; issue, 21, 27, 29-30, 47-
     49, 67-68, 117, 121; Jewish, 32, 46,
     57-58, 63; journalism, 134;
     legal/illegal, 115-116; level of
     authority, 21, 48, 51-52, 55,
     58, 100-102, 133; license, 18, 85;
     location, 21, 54-55, 58; magnitude,
     20, 58-59; nationality, 21, 55-
     58; organization, 21, 37, 50-51, 57-
     58, 107, 117, 131-132; outgroup,
     106; participation, 59-64, 85, 98,
     116, 124, 133; party affiliation
     of participants, 60-61; periods,
     27, 46, 58, 67, 70, 72, 121-122;
     political-issue, 30, 33, 35, 37, 40-
     42, 44, 47-50, 52, 57-58, 67-70,
     72-75, 129; poster, 134; religious-
     issue, 30-31, 37, 43-44, 47-52, 57-
     58, 67-68, 70-72; religiosity
     of participants, 60-61; reporting,
     18-20; residence of participants,
     60-61; size, 20-21, 49-50, 57-58,
     117, 133; social-issue, 29, 33-34,
     36-37, 39, 42-44, 47-50, 52, 57-
     58, 67-73, 84, 121, 129; strategy,
     117, 132-133; success, 4, 113-119,
     123-124, 133; timing, 117; type,
     21, 53-54, 60; violence, 20, 32, 34,
     39, 43-44, 49, 51, 57, 79, 81, 83,
     105, 110, 116, 118-119, 124, 132;
     war, 34-35, 41, 45, 59, 60, 75;
     waves, 84, 105.
Protestants, 133.

Rath, Ari, 20.
Rationing, 29.
Rebellion, 77-78, 122.
Referendum, 131.
Reform: economic, 128, 131; electoral,

125, 130-131; political, 108, 125,
130-131, 133.
Relative Deprivation, 10, 38-39, 56, 62,
71, 73, 120-121.
Religion and State, 78, 80.
Reparations, 30.
Representation, Proportional, 89, 125.
Revolution, 9, 78-79, 90.
Rogers Plan, 35, 51.

Sabra and Shatilla, 41.
Sadat, Anwar, 51.
Sanders, David, 8-9.
Scarrow, Howard A., 7-8.
Shapira, Yonathan, 90.
Sharon, Ariel, 41.
Sheffer, Gabriel, 93.
Shinui, 37, 94.
Siakh, 35.
Sinai, 40.
Singer, Benjamin, 105.
Socialism, 69, 84, 128.
Socialization, Political, 36.
Soviet Union: emigration policy, 35;
Jewish concern, 51.
Sovlanut. See also Tolerance.
Sprinzak, Ehud, 1-2, 82-83.
Snyder, David, 9, 12.
Statism (*Mamlakhtiut*), 93.
Status Quo Agreement, 31, 43.
Strike: political, 53, 57, 82; television,
106.
Sweden, 83.

Taxation, 29, 67-71, 83, 120-121, 127-
129.
Taylor, Charles L., 13-16, 125.
Tel Aviv, 41, 52, 61.
Television, 38-39, 54, 83, 104-106, 110,
123, 125, 127-128, 134.
Territories, 35, 37, 42, 53-54, 57, 73,
84, 113, 129.
Terrorism, 83.
Ticket-splitting, 101-102, 127.
Tolerance: American political, 80;
Israeli political, 80-81.

Treason, 81.
Turmoil, 9-11, 120.
Tzena, 29, 63.
Underground, Jewish, 83.
Unemployment, 29, 68-71, 84, 103-
104, 113, 120-121.
United Nations, 51, 57.
Variables: cultural, 72; economic, 68-
72, 75-76; political, 74-76;
population, 72-73; social, 72-73,
76; war, 74.
Verba, Sidney, 91.
Voluntarism, 50, 93-94, 123.

Wadi Salib, 33, 40, 63.
War: of Attrition, 34, 37, 105; of
Independence, 27, 29, 57; Lebanon
(Operation Peace for Galilee), 41-
42, 45, 52-53, 75, 134; Six Day, 35,
51, 54, 57; Vietnam, 134; World
War II, 34; Yom Kippur, 32, 37,
41, 45, 57, 75, 84, 134.
War Periods, 22, 67, 117.
Weiss, Shevach, 91, 101.
Welch, Susan, 114, 116.
West Bank and Gaza. *See also*
Territories.
White House, 110, 134.
Wilde, Oscar, 113.
Wolfsfeld, Gadi, 1-2, 114-117, 122,
124.

Yamit, 40, 113.
Yanai, Nathan, 96.
*Yearbook of the Encyclopedia
Britannica*, 13.
Yemenites, 29, 34.
Yeshiva, 71.
Yishai, Yael, 98.
Yishuv, 79-80, 92-94, 128.
Yuchtman, Ephraim, 48.

Zemach, Mina, 21.
Zimmerman, Ekkart, 14.
Zionism, 79, 94.

SAM N. LEHMAN-WILZIG is Senior Lecturer in the Department of Political Studies at Bar-Ilan University. He is author of numerous articles on Israeli protest and is coeditor of *Comparative Jewish Politics: Public Life in Israel and the Diaspora*.

OL/JS   031PF

LEHMAN —